Deconstructing Martial Arts

Paul Bowman

Professor of Cultural Studies
Cardiff University, UK

CARDIFF
UNIVERSITY

PRIFYSGOL
CAERDYⱠD

Published by
Cardiff University Press
Cardiff University
PO Box 430
1st Floor, 30-36 Newport Road
Cardiff CF24 0DE
https://cardiffuniversitypress.org

Text © Paul Bowman 2019

First published 2019

Cover design by Hugh Griffiths

Print and digital versions typeset by Siliconchips Services Ltd.

ISBN (Paperback): 978-1-911653-00-4
ISBN (PDF): 978-1-911653-03-5
ISBN (EPUB): 978-1-911653-01-1
ISBN (Kindle): 978-1-911653-02-8

DOI: https://doi.org/10.18573/book1

The full text of this book has been peer-reviewed to ensure high academic standards. For full review policies, see https://www.cardiffuniversitypress.org/site/research-integrity/

Suggested citation:
Bowman, P. 2019. *Deconstructing Martial Arts*. Cardiff: Cardiff University Press. DOI: https://doi.org/10.18573/book1. License: CC-BY-NC-ND 4.0

To read the free, open access version of this book online, visit https://doi.org/10.18573/book1 or scan this QR code with your mobile device:

Contents

Acknowledgements

This work is the result of preoccupations, reflections, theoretical and analytical explorations and research projects that have been developing and coalescing over several years. It represents a contribution to the current elaboration of the new field of martial arts studies and it also seeks to intervene into the emerging field of physical cultural studies. For its existence I am indebted to a range of individuals. Thanks go first to all at Cardiff University Press for considering this book in the first place. Second, thanks go to the editorial board of the Physical Cultural Studies book series: David Aldous, Eva Bischcoff, Eric Burkart, Alex Channon, Broderick Chow, Sara Delamont, T.J. Desch-Obi, Daniel Jaquet, George Jennings, Ben Judkins, Royona Mitra, Janet O'Shea, and Ben Spatz.

Invitations to speak at fascinating conferences, seminars and events produced the germs and core ideas of several of the chapters, so I owe thanks to several of my hosts. First, for their kind invitation to give a keynote at the conference *Martial Arts and Society: On the Societal Relevance of Martial Arts, Combat Sports and Self-Defence* (the 5th Annual Meeting of the Committee for Martial Arts Studies in the German Association for Sports Sciences, German Sport University, Cologne, 6-8 October 2016), I thank Prof Dr Swen Körner, Leo Istas, and the DVS committee. The keynote I gave there has been combined with an editorial written for the journal *Martial Arts Studies* on the same issues and it ultimately became Chapter Two (Judkins and Bowman 2017).

Equally, I would like to thank Dr Haili Ma, formerly of the School of Modern Languages at Cardiff University, for her kind invitation to me to give a public lecture to mark the Chinese New Year celebrations at Cardiff University in 2017. Chapter Five developed from that original presentation. Similarly, I thank Professor Stéphane Symons for an invitation to speak about the philosophy of Asian martial arts at a public festival of philosophy in Leuven in 2017. The presentation I gave there grew into Chapter Six. Also, I would also like to thank Evelina Kazakevičiūtė for her invitation to present what became Chapter Seven at a conference on film dialogue at Cardiff University in 2017. (A different version of this paper appears in the special themed Issue 13 of *JOMEC Journal* edited by Kazakevičiūtė.)

Others have invited me to write pieces that I have reworked and incorporated here. Olivier Bernard invited me to write a piece on martial arts studies to be translated into French and published in a collection to be published by Université Laval Press. I have adapted and refocused that paper and worked it up as the Introduction to the present book. Similarly, Chapter One was developed from an editorial written for the journal *Martial Arts Studies* (Bowman and Judkins 2017). Thanks also to Tim Trausch, who invited me to write an afterword to his collection, *Chinese Martial Arts and Media Culture*. This became the core of Chapter Three. Finally in this category, Chapter Four developed from a work first written for a collection entitled *Conversations on Embodiment* edited by Jennifer Leigh (Leigh 2018).

All of the presentations and papers that have been incorporated into the various chapters of *Deconstructing Martial Arts* have been modified, adapted, refocused, retooled and developed for the present context. I thank everyone who invited me to contribute to their projects for stimulating me to look into matters that I might otherwise have avoided entirely, whether because of their complexity, my lack of expertise, or both. I would also like to thank Kyle Barrowman, who has always proved to be a tireless and invaluable intellectual sparring partner and whose eagle-eyes have improved many manuscripts over recent years. Final thanks are due to the anonymous peer reviewers whose insightful readings offered some extremely valuable comments, criticisms and suggestions. In reworking the final draft of this manuscript, I have attempted to engage with both the letter and the spirit of their comments. Needless to say, all errors are entirely my own.

Preface

What is the essence of the martial arts? What is their place within or their relationship to culture and society? This book, *Deconstructing Martial Arts*, analyses issues and debates that arise in scholarly, practitioner and popular cultural discussions and treatments of martial arts, and it argues that martial arts are dynamic and variable constructs whose meanings and values shift, mutate and transform depending on the context. Martial arts serve multiple functions and can be valued and devalued in numerous ways. Furthermore, it argues that the act of *deconstructing* martial arts can be a valuable approach both in the scholarly study of martial arts in culture and society and in expanding wider understandings of what and why martial arts are. Placing martial arts in relation to key questions and concerns of media and cultural studies around identity, value, imagination and embodiment, *Deconstructing Martial Arts* seeks to show that the approach known as deconstruction is a uniquely insightful method of cultural analysis. To do so, the book deconstructs key aspects of martial arts to reveal the ways that their construction always involves political, ideological and mythological dimensions.

Using deconstruction as a method of analysis, *Deconstructing Martial Arts* contributes both to academic debates and practitioner understandings of martial arts as cultural practices. The Introduction demonstrates that martial arts are variable social constructs and sets out the key concerns of the emergent field of martial arts studies. The work then interrogates the question of whether martial arts might be regarded as 'trivial', as some perspectives and values might suspect (Chapter One). After deconstructing and recasting this debate, Chapter Two explores the problem of definition. Can we define martial arts? Do we need to? The chapter argues that, contrary to many impulses in the study of martial arts, what is required is rigorous theory and analysis before definition in martial arts studies. This is because, as Chapter Three clarifies, martial arts are constituted via all manner of supplements, including media supplements.

Chapter Four takes this insight into the realm of a key emergent field of study, 'embodiment', in order to problematize certain understandings of embodiment. In a field of practice saturated with – indeed, constituted by – media images, how can embodiment be approached without reference to media, culture, language and signification? But, it asks, once you follow this line of approach, what happens to embodiment? Chapter Five connects the reconfigured notion of embodiment with the idea of martial arts as hybrid, heterogeneous and eclectic discursive constructs, and brings this back into conversation with a well-worn theme, namely the proposition that the Western discourse of Eastern martial arts may be 'orientalist'. The chapter studies the core place of Taoism in such discourses but complicates the charge of orientalism by emphasising the incompletion and fragmentariness of all discourses. This displaces the discussion into the realm of incompletion and the inevitability of invention.

Chapter Six takes this focus further by interrogating 'martial arts mind-sets', which are typically imagined as ranging from supposed Zen-like serenity to something more akin to violent psychosis. This chapter moves from familiar contemporary connections that are made between Eastern martial arts and 'mindfulness' and proposes instead a possible relation to 'madness'. Given a certain 'undecidability' here, the final chapter (Chapter Seven) enquires into the wider cultural and discursive status of martial arts by way of a key deconstructive approach: The exploration of supplementary, minor and marginal spaces. In this case, screen dialogue about martial arts in non-martial arts films is examined, in order to glean unexpected insights into their wider cultural currency. Finally, in the face of such supplementarity, eclecticism, hybridity and undecidability, the Conclusion asks not where martial arts studies *should* draw the line around its object(s) of attention, but *why* line-drawing and boundary-marking is held to be so essential, not only in martial arts studies but also very frequently in all academic work and indeed all discourse.

The book is designed to be read from beginning to end, but its chapters could in fact be approached in any order. Furthermore, readers may wish to know that in its focus and orientation the book also falls into two distinct sections or halves. The Introduction, Chapters One and Two and the Conclusion are heavily invested in academic, theoretical and disciplinary questions of the emergence of the field, its orientations, questions of definition, theory, and so on. Chapters Three to Seven, on the other hand, explore more obviously 'cultural' questions and may therefore feel more accessible, especially to newer readers of either my own work, deconstruction, martial arts studies, or cultural theory more generally. However, the approach and orientation of all chapters is united by one thing: The analytical practice of deconstruction, deployed specifically for deconstructing martial arts.

(De)Constructing Martial Arts (Studies)

Deconstructing What?

First things first. What are martial arts? What do we mean when we say 'martial arts'? These two questions can be regarded as either very similar to each other or very different. Simplifying in the extreme, we might propose that, although there is a spectrum of possible answers, there are two main positions on these matters. On the one hand, there is a kind of strict or rigorously literalist position, which holds that only certain kinds of things can properly be regarded as martial arts, and that to fit the bill they must meet certain criteria, such as having been designed for or used on the battlefield, or being some (implicitly bodily) part of the 'arts of war'. On the other hand, there is an ostensibly more relaxed, 'loose' or open-ended position, which might either be called cultural, 'discursive', or (pejoratively) 'relativist'. This holds that, because all of the terms and concepts that we use are variable conventional constructs, a category like 'martial arts' only ever refers to whatever people think and say are 'martial arts'. Both the category and the practices are heavily cultural and contextual.

There are strong criticisms of both positions. The literalist position tends to exclude a great many practices that are widely recognised as martial arts. Literalist positions may not accept that judo, taijiquan (aka tai chi or taiji), aikido or even MMA, for instance, should be regarded as martial arts, for a range of reasons (all boiling down to the idea that they were not developed specifically with the battlefield in mind). So, they would be excluded from attention, even though many other people, in line with conventional usage, would be happy to apply the term 'martial arts' to them. In other words, strict or rigorous literalist positions impose rigid criteria that exclude practices deemed to be 'too far' away from being martial arts 'proper' – such as practices that may focus on health cultivation, esoteric matters, or even practices with 'too much' of a focus on sport or personal development. In being fixated on war or battle,

How to cite this book chapter:
Bowman, P. 2019. *Deconstructing Martial Arts*. Pp. 1–17. Cardiff: Cardiff University Press. DOI: https://doi.org/10.18573/book1.a. License: CC-BY-NC-ND 4.0

a literalist position might even exclude the range of practices that make up the brutal world of full contact combat sports, such as MMA. Accordingly, one criticism of literalist positions is that in their quest for rigour and precision they can effectively become *self-blinding* or myopic positions which, in their putative insistence on 'reality', somewhat ironically end up refusing to accept what many (or most) others take to be reality – at least the lived reality of what people think of and do 'as' martial arts in a given culture or society at a given time.

Meanwhile, a culturalist or discursive position can be subject to the criticism that it is too 'relativist' or too open or flexible to be meaningful. In his important discussion of the problem of establishing a 'concept' of martial arts, Benjamin N. Judkins examines a range of scholarly approaches to martial arts and proposes that, when it comes to 'discursive' understandings of martial arts, 'self-identification is a poor metric to judge what activities qualify as a martial art, or how we as researchers should structure our comparative case studies'. To his mind, 'this has always been a potential weakness of the sociological approach'; so, he asks, 'lacking a universally agreed upon definition, how should we move forward?' (Judkins 2016a, 9)

Judkins himself moves forward by pointing out that definition is not really the question. The question is really one of *why* we are studying this possible object or field called 'martial arts' in the first place. In his discussion, Judkins deconstructs the ways in which different kinds of attempts to define or even demarcate the category of martial arts tend to fall down or unravel. For instance, he notes that it is not possible to separate off 'military' from 'civilian' combat training or practices, as the likes of Donn Draeger once attempted to do. No cultural or social category is hermetically sealed. Each is always, effectively or potentially, connected to and even infused with elements of others. Military and civilian realms may seem to be poles apart, and, in many respects, they often can be. But, as the history of the development of martial arts in the US shows us, the growth of civilian and police 'martial arts' practice was often indebted to and driven by returning servicemen (Krug 2001). The US is the big example, but other Western countries have similar narratives. The civilian/military distinction is even murkier in Asian countries, where martial arts narratives are replete with tales of civilian pioneers entering military life and vice versa (see for example Gillis 2008 for a fascinating set of stories).

In his next move, following Peter Lorge's influential discussion of martial arts in China, Judkins points out that even prominent Chinese military generals have (in)famously dismissed the martial utility of unarmed combat training (Judkins 2016a, 7–8; cf. Lorge 2012, 3–4). This may seem ironic. However, the real irony is that many of these 'dismissive' generals nonetheless continued to advocate the importance of unarmed combat training for their soldiers despite their conviction that unarmed combat training was not directly useful in war. This is because the importance of such 'useless' training derived from the sense that combat training builds character, resilience and spirit.

All of this complicates things further. Indeed, it could be said to make the whole literalist position fall to pieces – not least because of the possibility that things as 'non-martial' as intense aerobic exercise, on the one hand, or meditation, on the other, might be of more 'combat value' than literal combat training itself.

Many modern martial artists will recognise this idea. In technical (and polite) Chinese terms, this is the distinction between 'gong' and 'fa', or the deep skill, energy, force and sensitivity required (gong) to make what are otherwise merely the external semblance (fa) of techniques 'work' (Nulty 2017). In more general terms, how many times have martial arts practitioners looked at the demonstration of a technique and said or thought something like 'that would *never* work, at least *not if you did it like that*'? The sense is that what is more important in combat is an intensity and single-minded determination of purpose (spirit). How many of us have ever suspected, as I have, that in a dangerous situation it would be preferable to have an ultra-competitive ice-hockey, rugby or American football player on one's side than a serene old tenth dan who can do amazing technical things but has never had a real fight? This is not simply a prejudice based on doubting someone's ability. It is an intuition that someone who is used to intense physical competition will be more able to deal with non-compliant opponents and to handle what Miller calls the 'chemical dump' that explodes in our bodies in situations of extreme stress (Miller 2008; Miller and Eisler 2011).

Certain forms of ('non-martial') intense exercise popular today involve dealing with equivalent if not identical physical and psychological stresses, training with as much 'spirit' as possible and taking the body to the limits of exhaustion in different ways. Because of their physiological and often psychological similarity to what happens to a person in a physical conflict or confrontation, these intense exercise programmes are sometimes wholeheartedly embraced, advocated by, or included in military and/or 'reality-based' martial arts such as krav maga for precisely this 'combat-like' reason. On the flipside, as is more well-known (or more widely believed), ultra-slow movement or static meditation practices emphasize and 'train' qualities like relaxed precision and calm detachment, and they have long been associated with the generation of both budō 'fighting spirit' and – 'paradoxically' – the cultivation of a peaceful outlook (Benesch 2016; see also Reid and Croucher 1984).

As a long-time reader of the work of the deconstructive philosopher Jacques Derrida, what shines out from all of this is the extent to which practices (if not ideas) of 'the martial' or 'martial art' seem constantly to be *supplemented* by non-martial – or not literally martial – elements (Derrida 1976; see also Bowman 2008). In Derrida's work, the notion of the *supplement* is deployed to demonstrate the ways that things we tend to want to consign to the category of the secondary, the add-on, the non-essential, the extra, and so on, are actually in a very real sense 'primary' (Bennington and Derrida 2008). Or else, put differently, there is no 'primary', no 'essence', no 'pure', despite our desire for this to be so. Rather, there are only ever supplementary ingredients, practices or procedures. The idea of the 'essence' is itself an effect – a kind of illusion, or even delusion (Derrida 1998).

Of course, this is not to say that the 'essence effect' is somehow fake. Imagine your ideal martial arts class. Practitioners may think of a martial arts training session which starts or ends with some kind of meditation, then breath training, then physical exercises for strength or flexibility, then maybe forms training, then applications, then ever freer sparring, maybe also weapons, until they may have felt that they were 'really' doing 'real fighting'. We might come away from such sessions feeling that we really have experienced the essence of martial arts training. And maybe we did experience something profound. But the point is that the experience of what we think of as one thing is always a subjective experience of multiple supplementary elements being brought together in a certain way.

This is so even if we think that it is only 'one thing' that we are doing. Whether we are doing standing *qigong* training or some kind of real-world combat scenario training, we are never simply doing 'one thing'. Each of these supposedly unitary activities is made up of myriad supplementary components, each of which could be ever further dissected and divided up into ever more differentiated elements. But, because we have a sense of ourselves as unitary, and because we have to use shared languages, we are always inclined (or required) to simplify things so that heterogeneity and multiplicity are given one name and imagined as having one essence.

This might help explain why practitioners of certain martial arts styles feel most strongly (often negatively, or critically) not about different styles but about practitioners of 'the same' style – what they regard as 'their style' – who practice *differently* and 'therefore', they believe, *wrongly*. Different practitioners with different approaches to training in different schools and clubs of the 'same style' can easily regard each other's approaches as 'wrong' because each will feel that the essence of the style cannot be conveyed other than via the correct practices – *their* practices.

At issue is the inevitable emergence of *difference* within putative or nominal *sameness* (Derrida 1988). Styles and systems cannot but change, from teacher to teacher, and even over time under the same teacher; because styles and systems are not fixed essences but rather constructs. They are constructed through constantly changing practices and combinations of elements. *They are constructs, not essences.* Linguistic terms and imaginations work in many ways to try to persuade us that this or that martial art is always one thing. But, to put it bluntly, it is never one thing.

Hence, it is heartening that more and more scholars today are prepared to move away from making direct ontological or essentialist (what I earlier called 'literalist') statements about what this or that martial art 'is' or indeed what martial arts 'are'. The very category 'martial art' or 'martial arts' is first and foremost a contemporary construct. It has a history. It is only within the last few decades that the notion of 'martial art' has become an intelligible term that is widely understood as the kind of thing we all tend to think it means (Farrer and Whalen-Bridge 2011; Judkins 2014a). What non-specialists tend to think the term 'martial arts' means frequently involves some vague evocation of punching and kicking, coming from Asia, and – surprisingly frequently, still, half a century after their heyday – being exemplified by figures like Bruce Lee or Jackie Chan, whose very names have become shorthand for 'martial arts' (or 'kung fu').

Contemporary martial arts studies scholars have attempted to negotiate the variably and changeably constructed character of the practices, as well as the terms and categories we have available for conceptualising them, in various ways (Tan 2004; Bennett 2015; Judkins and Nielson 2015; Moenig 2015). In an opposite but effectively identical approach (that may be regarded as controversial because of its barefaced straightforwardness), the historian Peter Lorge elected to study the place of unarmed and armed combat training practices via the historical texts about them throughout Chinese history without excessively problematizing the term 'martial arts' at all. Lorge preferred to proceed in terms of a sense of the obviousness of the object to be analysed (Lorge 2012).

Following what is 'obviously' part of the thing under analysis is a valid route – although the question immediately arises: Where do you draw the line? In studying this or that martial art, must we also study strength training, dietary practices, micro- and macro-ideologies, religious beliefs, and so on? What about the kinds of literature or television programmes that practitioners watch, or experienced in their formative years? As Derrida argued, context may be everything, and will always be incredibly important to understanding specific things, but when it comes to a context, how do you draw a line between what is inside and what is outside of a context? (Derrida 1988)

Indeed, a sense of the 'obviousness' of the object is the very thing that opens the door to all of the problems already discussed, and that Judkins has insightfully dissected (Judkins 2016a). For once you scratch the surface of what's 'obviously in' and 'obviously out' of our purview, everything becomes grey – and what Derrida would call 'undecidable'. That is (to recall our earlier discussion of what is most useful), it may for instance be undecidable what is more important in krav maga training – how to handle a knife or how to keep going in the face of all terrors and adversities in a combat situation. The famously experienced author and self-defence instructor Rory Miller takes it even further. He states that, were you to be slapped in the face by a stranger, if you are the kind of person who would instantly feel outrage, anger and aggression, then he has little to nothing to teach you. You have already 'got it' – the key to self-defence – a kind of righteous rage, and a capacity to retaliate ferociously (Miller 2008). If, however, you are someone who would freeze or feel fear, shock, confusion, even embarrassment, then perhaps he may *never* be able to teach you anything worthwhile. You may never 'get it'. You may always be incapacitated by fear, and you may always freeze. If this is true, then the question becomes one of whether therefore *any* pedagogy and hence *any* category akin to 'martial arts' is worthwhile on any 'literal' level.

This line of thinking opens out onto the possibility that there may be a 'myth of pedagogy' (Rancière 1991) that runs far deeper and wider than the familiar stories many martial artists know about instructors teaching absolute rubbish to hapless students who believe they are learning effective techniques or profound truths. If Miller's observation has any value, then perhaps the matters of teaching and learning in martial arts need to be rethought (Bowman 2016b). For the implication would seem to be that many people could never effectively 'learn' the most important aspect of self-defence – the aspect that might be called the ability to become a kind of *berserker*.

This is to evoke one of the most popular of myths that circulates among competitive fighters: That 'fighters are born, not made'. This is the idea that good fighters have an innate fighting spirit, and that unless you have this you cannot succeed as a fighter. Of course, a wide range of different kinds of evidence contradicts this enduring myth. The importance, and the palpable and measurable effects, of training strongly suggest that fighters are made, not born (Loïc Wacquant 2004, 2005, 2009).

Nonetheless, it is easy to get caught in an oscillation between accepting Miller's statement (and maybe also the myth of the natural born fighter), on the one hand, and believing in the more observable development of novices into experts, on the other. It is not uncommon to see uncoordinated, timid, non-aggressive and incompetent people entering the club on day one and their undergoing a complete physical and psychological transformation over time. (It may have happened to you. I think it may have happened to me, possibly, and more than once, at least partially.) Those who adhere to a 'natural born fighter' myth could argue that the person who entered on day one nonetheless had a 'spark' or 'hidden essence' that was cultivated. Others may retort that one does not need a spark or an essence, that all that is required is the desire, an effective teacher, and 'the means of correct training' (Foucault 1977).

But is this really the be-all and end-all of martial arts? Some readers will have noticed that this discussion has so far been presupposing one specific kind of outcome (effective self-defence skill) and conflating that with another ('being a fighter', either in the sense of fighting 'on the street' or doing competitive combat sports well). There is often a lot of conceptual drift and conflation in these waters. Despite its obviousness and familiarity, the range of meanings of 'martial arts' is not set in stone, and connotations frequently leach and bleed into each other. Certainly, not everyone enters a training hall or club for reasons of 'self-defence', 'competition' or 'fighting'. People may not even know their reasons. They may have more or less than one 'reason'. There may be multiple vague attractions. It may just be 'something to do', perhaps to avoid something else. If there are reasons, these may oscillate between different possible outcomes, or merge and mutate. Reasons may change over time, emerging, receding, moving into and out of existence.

Scott Park Phillips offers an excellent overview of many of the most common reasons why people send their children to martial arts classes:

> The most common reason people give for putting their children in martial arts classes is so that they will learn how to act with moral self-discipline. The list of qualities that the average parent wants their kid to learn in martial arts classes includes leadership, protecting the weak, legal and moral self-defense, overcoming challenges, persistence in the face of adversity, seeing the big picture, self-discipline, self-improvement, self-motivation, cooperation, teamwork, body confidence and awareness, love of exercise, learning from failures, and the ability to concentrate and focus. This is a lot of expectations to have! Why, if the main purpose of martial arts was fighting, would this ever have come about? The answer is simple: martial arts were always about more than fighting. (Phillips 2016, 29)

As he notes at the end of this list of common assumptions, this is a hell of a lot of reasons to train – or, more specifically, a hell of a lot of hopes and expectations (to project) about the outcomes of sending children to martial arts classes. And, as Phillips' final claim makes clear, this is because the term 'martial arts' is in many contemporary ways a misnomer: Martial arts are not about learning how to win a literal war – they are always about other things.

Does this mean that the term 'martial arts' today often functions as a kind of marketing tool to 'sell' exercise and self-development to children? There could certainly be some truth in this. After all, it can sometimes be easier to persuade children to find value in and do something by making cool-sounding associations: Big tough gorillas eat fruit; sharks eat fish and/or eating fish will make you clever; meat will give you big muscles; lions drink water; karate will make you tough; and so on. There is certainly some value in exploring this kind of intentional or accidental 'misrecognition' of one's own activities and investments. The psychoanalyst Jacques Lacan theorised misrecognition as inevitable and fundamental to the formation of identity and the workings of the symbolic order; later thinkers incorporated this idea into various theories of ideology (Althusser 1971; Silverman 1983; Lacan 2001). Indeed, throughout his provocative study, Phillips argues that martial arts – Chinese martial arts in particular – have for an extremely long time been misrecognised as principally or primarily *martial* when they are in fact much more a matter of *art*. Phillips' specific argument is that Chinese martial arts are at root the modern descendants or residues of ancient Chinese *theatrical* traditions (Phillips 2016).

Phillips' overall argument about 'possible origins' may be controversial, but his contention that martial arts are always about more and other than fighting is helpful. Sixt Wetzler has proposed that the most common range of reasons for attending martial arts classes include the following: 'Preparation for violent conflict', 'play', 'competition', 'performance', 'transcendent goals', and 'health care' (Wetzler 2015, 26). To this we might add the parental or vicariously projected categories set out by Phillips; and then the categories applicable to children made to take martial arts classes. These would include 'having been sent to classes as a child by parents' or 'having been made to do it at school until it just became "something that I do"' and on, to the whole range of ex post facto rationalisations that could be invented and sincerely believed at any moment.

The point is that, in addition to the good reasons and good categories proposed by Wetzler, one should also remember the often less than good reasons and often less than good categories that also organise the 'decision' (or obligation, or automatism) to 'do' martial arts. Reasons given for martial art training can either be ex post facto rationalisations with no bearing on whatever true story there might be, or they may arise long into a period of training. In other words, one problem with Wetzler's proposed categories is that they are individualistic, rationalistic and 'Cartesian' – as if we are all Descartes and we wake up one day and say, 'I think [I am interested in transcendent goals and healthcare] therefore I am [going to go to practice kung fu, not krav maga]'. But the world does not work anything like as simply as that. Often, reasons are imposed, or generated, or simulated.

A friend once told me about something that would often happen in the kung fu class she attended. The instructor (or *sifu*) would at points sit the whole class down and proceed to give them a lecture on the philosophy that underpinned the art. When she told me this, I was horrified to hear about such a practice in a martial arts lesson. She said she certainly found it very frustrating and boring. We both agreed that surely not many people take martial arts classes for lectures, and that martial arts philosophy lectures did not really strike us as being an appropriate or valid part of martial arts classes as such.

Of course, the idea that at least some martial arts 'are philosophical' is widespread. Certainly, I am not saying that 'philosophy' is not present in martial arts, or in martial arts classes. Nor is it to say that martial arts – or indeed martial art classes – cannot or should not be philosophized. But all of these are very different things. To say that something 'is' philosophical begs the question of what we think we mean by that. Are we saying we can philosophize it – or about it? Or are we saying that it is itself an example of a philosophical thing? These are very different propositions. We might philosophize (about) anything, maybe everything. But is that the same as saying that everything is philosophical? (I explore this more fully in Chapter Six.)

What does philosophy even mean? Derrida spent a lot of time pondering matters such as this. To his mind, the conundrum of what is inside and what is outside philosophy was the core problem of philosophy itself. Inevitably, lots of philosophers (and non-philosophers) disagreed with him. Indeed, despite any evidence to the contrary, many philosophers still refuse to recognise Derrida as a philosopher.

Interestingly, as with 'martial arts', the questions of what *philosophy* is and what it is to *do philosophy* do not seem to have necessary or ineluctable answers either. People do different things and call it philosophy, and they disagree with what other people do under the title philosophy. This is the same as what happens in and around martial arts. At best, 'philosophy' (or 'martial arts') is one term for many possible activities. But the form and content, start and end, and inside and outside of activities that may or may not be called martial arts are interminably and incessantly up for disagreement and dispute. Some see judo as a martial art; others insist that it is really 'only' a sport. Some see taiji as a martial art; others argue that it is at best a kind of calisthenics, maybe even closer to a religion than to combat.

In and around the academic world, there are long-running battles around defining 'martial arts'. As mentioned, some have built up lists of criteria to be met before they will accept that this or that activity could be dignified with the term 'martial art'. Others have argued quite persuasively (and often using the criteria that the self-appointed gatekeepers of propriety have themselves proposed) that activities as unexpected as *Star Wars*-inspired Lightsaber combat, and indeed even certain forms of computer gaming, fulfil all of the criteria to be regarded as martial arts (Judkins 2016a; Goto-Jones 2016).

But, with no unequivocal definition or delimitation of martial arts, not to mention any agreement on pedagogy, motivations, outcomes or philosophy, where do we go? The obvious place to go in such a situation is the university. Universities are normally regarded as the places where disagreements and the attempt to find answers are welcomed and housed. However, one question has long recurred: Can martial arts ever be taken seriously and studied in the university as a legitimate subject, field or object of attention? (Bowman 2015a)

Constructing Martial Arts Studies

Whether martial arts can become a serious object of academic attention has long been a familiar question, especially to people whose interests straddle the worlds of martial arts and academia. Undoubtedly, for many who asked, it was widely assumed that the answer would always be no. No, martial arts cannot, could not, will not and would not be taken seriously within the university. And yet, research into this question actually returns a different answer. Digging deeper reveals that studies of martial arts have long appeared in all kinds of academic contexts and publications. Indeed, studies of martial arts can and do take place in all kinds of academic fields. Studies of martial arts have long appeared in fields as diverse as anthropology, film studies, law, management, philosophy, psychology, sociology, sports science, history, medicine, and more.

Nonetheless, the question of whether martial arts can become a serious *field* of academic study *in its own right* is a very different matter (Bowman 2015a). The question of establishing a field is a very different thing to choosing a case study within a pre-existing field. It is eminently easy to imagine academic studies of just about anything: Farting, fidgeting, nose-picking, nail-biting – you name it – could all be objects of study in any number of disciplines. Such studies could appear in almost any field, from anthropology to psychology to film to philosophy to history and beyond. However, it is quite another matter to propose that such a topic could or should mutate from being a specific object of study *within* a discipline, and morph into a disciplinary field in its own right.

Is there a call for fart studies, fidgetology, rhinopraxicology, or suchlike? There need to be pressing reasons for the development of a discrete new field – reasons based on answering some demand, filling a lack, redressing some kind of inadequacy or limitation. Answering a demand or responding to a lack has led to the emergence of many 'suffix-studies' subjects in recent decades: Cultural studies, media studies, gender studies, Afro-American and other ethnic identity studies, film studies, sports studies, management studies, postcolonial studies, and so on. The rationale for the development of a new sub-ject always involves answering a need or a demand, by redressing a perceived lack or limitation in the present configuration of the disciplines. Researchers may find that a specific topic that they regard as important has inadequate space to develop within current disciplinary spaces, or that current approaches to it are inadequate or even stifling. Or a topic may simply be entirely absent, unrepresented, overlooked; and the development of ways to study it may not fit into any established disciplinary space.

All of the above-mentioned 'suffix-studies' subjects emerged in recent dec-ades to fill a perceived gap. The driving forces for their development came from both inside and outside the university. Such fields endure, and research proliferates under their umbrellas, for as long as and to the extent that they adequately accommodate the direction of research questions. Taught courses in universities and colleges continue for as long as students turn up to take them and as long as they are deemed legitimate by the powers that be.

So, to what extent is there a demand or a need for an enduring field of martial arts studies? Can it really be something tangible and enduring? Is work that is currently being done under this title actually doing something unique, new or different, or are we really only ever dealing with discrete studies of martial arts organised by established disciplinary concerns? On the one hand, it is certain that there will always be studies of martial arts that can be straightforwardly positioned as fitting comfortably into established academic fields. There will be straightforward 'case studies' of martial arts that are written in film studies, literary studies, anthropology, psychology, area studies, history, sports studies, and so on. But, on the other hand, there are questions whose exploration entails breaking out of and moving beyond conventional disciplinary parameters.

This kind of work can be difficult, particularly for scholars working in isolation. In the academic world, it is always safer and easier to stick to the established questions, methods, points of reference and protocols of discussion within a pre-established disciplinary field than to explore things differently, to explore different things, or to explore different things differently. Fortunately, many academics and scholars from many disciplines are now being drawn together under the umbrella or banner of 'martial arts studies', attending specific conferences and publishing in newly emergent journals and book series. The immediate effect of this is that people researching questions in and around martial arts are coming to feel less isolated and more able to locate or express their interests in terms of an emerging discourse.

The importance of developing a collectivity cannot be overstated. It is absolutely vital for researchers. On the one hand, it produces not just affiliations and supportive conversations, but also informed disagreement and focused criticisms, even rifts, all of which stimulate both circumspect and precise questions, argumentation, analysis and methods. On the other hand, it must be remembered that, in the university, if you cannot demonstrate what your research contributes to, then you cannot easily justify your activities. And if you cannot justify your activities then you will sooner or later encounter innumerable pressures to change them. There are certainly no funding opportunities available for projects that cannot relate their point, purpose and value to existing discourses.

So, the establishment of a discourse is essential to the production of meaningful work. As the psychoanalyst Jacques Lacan put it, the first signifier (the 'unary signifier') is always essentially meaningless or unintelligible. It is only when there is more than one – when there are binaries, iterations, reiterations, responses, differences, positions, and ultimately constellations – that meanings and values can start to be formed. Without a discourse, individual utterances will be taken to be nothing other than odd, eccentric, isolated, unintelligible, and therefore meaningless or irrelevant follies. A context of reception needs to be established.

Fortunately, in recent years, researchers have been attracted to martial arts studies conferences and to publishing in and reading self-consciously martial arts studies publications. This cross-disciplinary attraction to martial arts studies events and publications has enabled many kinds of discussions and interactions to take place across disciplinary divides, where before they would have been unlikely. Inevitably, this cross-fertilization has begun to produce thought and work that exceeds the confines of any one discipline. The net result is that different work is happening, completely new discussions are underway, organised by new questions, in new debates, generating all kinds of new knowledge.

In this sense, martial arts studies is the term for an interdisciplinary research nexus. A shared interest in the organising terms – all that is conjured up by the term 'martial arts' – is what holds the field together. I was about to say that a shared interest in martial arts is the 'glue' that binds it together, but I don't think that this is correct. We may not even agree on what the term designates or evokes. We may not agree on an approach to the object or field. Yet 'martial arts' provides the *magnetism* that draws researchers together. People are *attracted* to the field, because of a shared interest in what is perceived to be a shared object. Whether people stay within the field or not depends on whether they are stimulated by what they find in it (Bowman and Judkins 2017).

This is why martial arts studies has to be a circumspect, open, interested and interesting field of serious research, one that responds and speaks to a range of academic and cultural concerns, rather than being organised by too much certainty (Bowman and Judkins 2017). As Stuart Hall once argued, 'certainty stimulates orthodoxy' (Hall, Morley, and Chen 1996, 44), and orthodoxy is anathema to genuine thinking. I have argued elsewhere that too much certainty is surely one of the key reasons why so many earlier attempts to generate an academic field for the study of martial arts failed (Bowman and Judkins 2017).

In the end, the specific kind of certainty that scuppered earlier attempts to establish what we are today calling martial arts studies boiled down to certainty about what 'martial arts' is (or are). This is why I have always insisted on remaining open to what people think and feel and say 'martial arts' may mean. Hence, the academic study of martial arts should be open to the possibility of examining whatever people refer to as martial arts. However, at the same time as being entirely open to this, I am considerably less hospitable to most efforts to produce 'academic' definitions of martial arts. I do not mind the use of short-hand characterisations of the things we might be referring to when we say 'martial arts'. Nor do I mind the production of frameworks for grouping or distinguishing between practices. But I am resistant to any supposedly academic work that proposes a definition of martial arts and then only looks at things that fall into that definition. At best, this produces self-inflicted myopia, where one only sees what one wants to see. At worst, it produces the invention of theoretical worlds that bear no relation to anyone else's reality. I often encounter a feeling of suspicion in the face of many kinds of academic categories for precisely this reason: I tend to suspect that certain categories and frameworks neither reflect the world nor help us to gain insight into it, but rather invent a theoretical world. Certainly, the best academic categories, schemas, frameworks, and so on, can produce extremely useful ways of conceptualising and grasping reality. But bad categories can actually stop us from seeing reality.

This is why I have so often argued against definition (Bowman 2017d, 2017c, 2017b), and will do so again in Chapter Two. For, first, definition itself often seems more disabling than enabling, at least when it comes to my concerns about the places and functions of martial arts in culture. (Moreover, I often suspect that the drive to define reveals a drive to control, by policing things into categories and hierarchies, which the definer often seems to want to control.) Second, definition often seems 'logically' self-defeating. After all, if you already claim to know in advance what 'martial arts' are, then why would you need to study them academically? If you have already decided what they are, then you have already implicitly decided how to study them. So, the production of knowledge about them will always be the production of the 'same-old, same-old'. This is why Donn Draeger's 'hoplology' project failed. It already claimed to know, in advance, what it was studying. This is why sociobiological and social Darwinist approaches strike me as fairly feeble too. If everything must be as it is for evolutionary advantage, then that can only mean that we can all pack up early and go home – as if everything's been solved and resolved!

No. Quite other than this, martial arts studies does not need a definition of martial arts, nor indeed a strong attachment to a specific orientation of study. In fact, fixation on either of these points will curtail it. Martial arts studies needs to be responsive to the actual practices, discourses, institutions, agents and agencies that operate under the term or using the category 'martial arts'. What we will find under the term will take variable forms, depending on time, place and context. The social, cultural and even political status of each instance or (re)iteration of 'martial arts' will have multiple dimensions, and will be fruitful for multiple types of enquiry.

The kinds of enquiry carried out by a sociologist will differ from that of a psychologist, semiotician or historian. Each form of enquiry produces specific genres and orientations of insight. Indeed, because of this, once again we might say that the kind of object constructed by various different genres of disciplinary attention produces yet another construct, also called 'martial arts'. Different academic discourses produce a different 'disciplinary object' (Bowman 2015a, 2007; see also Mowitt 1992), even if they each have the same name. Even 'the same' martial art becomes something quite different when it is put under the lens of the psychologist to when it is put under the lens of the philosopher or that of the historian or that of the ethnologist, and so on. Each different discourse, each different manifestation, is a result of different combinations of elements, different emphases, different inclusions and exclusions.

In discussing 'martial arts' in different contexts or discourses, then, one is inevitably going to be discussing different things, different constructs. Saying this might reopen the charge of relativism. But context is always everything – universally. Everything is relative, always. But one thing stays the same: For the martial arts practitioner and for the martial arts researcher, martial arts are an 'object of knowledge', not an 'object of consumption' (Spatz 2015). They are not used up in one moment of consumption, the way a matchstick is finished and worthless a few seconds after it has been struck. Rather, they are infinitely and infinitesimally expansive; ever unfolding; ever familiar yet ever mysterious and enigmatic (Mroz 2017). There is always more to work out, always more to be gained, whether in the form of moving into new fields and unexplored terrain, or whether in the form of unearthing the 'internal foreign territories' of that which is supposedly familiar, by deconstructing what is supposedly 'well-known'. As Hegel put it, and as I have felt compelled to repeat on multiple occasions: 'What is "familiarly known" is not properly known, just for the reason that it is "familiar" ... [Familiarity itself] is the commonest form of self-deception' (Hegel 2005, 35; cf. Bowman 2010d, 45, 58).

The Construction of this Book

In what follows, Chapter One engages with the question of whether martial arts and the emergent field of martial arts studies should be regarded as trivial. In doing so, it explores possible rationales and *raisons d'être* of the field in terms of a reflection on the legitimation of academic subjects, especially those closest to martial arts studies and from which martial arts studies can be seen to have emerged. It argues that the designation of martial arts as trivial reflects a specific Western popular cultural history with connections to orientalism (Bowman 2013b; see also Lo 2005). This evinces not only specific cultural values but also the complex economy of forces that structure cultural outlooks and interpretations. Specifically, the chapter considers representations and strategies by which martial arts ideas and images have become trivial in Western popular culture. In so doing, the chapter further illustrates the value of deconstruction as an analytical approach to culture and its practices.

Chapter Two argues against all forms of scientism and the widespread perceived need to define martial arts in order to study martial arts or 'do' martial arts studies. It argues instead for the necessity of theory before definition, including theorisation of the orientation of the field of martial arts studies itself. Accordingly, the chapter criticises certain previous (and current) academic approaches to martial arts, particularly the failed project of hoplology. It then examines the much more promising approaches of current scholarship, such as that of Sixt Wetzler, before critiquing certain aspects of its orientation. Instead of accepting Wetzler's 'polysystem theory' approach uncritically, the chapter argues instead for the values of a poststructuralist 'discourse' approach in martial arts studies.

Chapter Three begins to deconstruct the idea that martial arts are purely physical or embodied practices. It does so by focusing on the contexts, forces and structures outside of embodied practices that influence, inform or even orientate physical culture in myriad complex ways. It approaches these in terms of Jacques Derrida's notion of the supplement. This notion has already been touched upon earlier in the Introduction (above), but Chapter Three is the first chapter in which its full deconstructive potential will be explored.

Chapter Four presents embodiment as a uniquely challenging problem for certain traditions and approaches to scholarship, particularly those that are implicitly or explicitly organised by the aim of establishing meanings. Such an orientation is exemplified by semiotics, of course, but the chapter argues that even approaches designed to critique semiotics and other forms of 'logocentrism' (i.e., approaches that focus on words and meanings) ultimately struggle in the face of dealing with aspects of embodiment. Even Derridean deconstruction – which was developed as a strident critique of logocentrism – struggles to move beyond the focus on words and meanings. So, the question becomes one of whether scholars interested in embodiment should reject or move beyond approaches like deconstruction.

Drawing on a loosely autobiographical narrative that touches on aspects both of my own academic training and my investment in martial arts and other physical cultural practices, this chapter argues that it is not simply possible to 'reject' or 'move beyond' the logocentrism of traditional 'search for meaning' orientations. It argues that, even though this observation may seem relatively passé to some, 'embodiment' is still very productively conceived of as 'embodiment of' – i.e., as the embodiment of *something else*; specifically, as the performative and interpretive elaboration of something *other* that is received, perceived, felt, constructed, believed, assumed or otherwise lived as being either an aim, ideal, desire, objective, fantasy, or as a norm, or indeed as the warding off of something undesired or feared. The chapter poses questions of how to 'capture', 'convey' or 'communicate' embodiment in words, and it interrogates the necessity of the current hegemony of the written word in academia. However, it seeks to avoid any kind of evangelism about new approaches or understandings of embodiment, and twists around at the end to propose that even certain forms of what we perhaps too quickly regard as 'enlightening' or 'emancipating' practices and techniques of embodiment might be regarded as traps, or indeed prisons.

In a different way, our understanding of culture and history may also amount to a kind of trap. Certainly, embodiment is always supplemented by the semiotic, and the emergence of martial arts discourses and practices in the West has to be assessed against the backdrop of a complex cultural history. Accordingly, Chapter Five explores the mid to late 20th Century explosion in the circulation of ideas connected with Taoism and Zen (Chan) Buddhism in Western popular culture. It argues that the introduction of ostensibly Chinese and Japanese philosophical notions into Western contexts and consciousnesses was never a simple act of transparent cross-cultural communication, from East to West. Rather, it always involved huge imaginative leaps and complex processes of projection, translation and transformation.

With reference to examples such as the hippy counterculture, the films and writings of Bruce Lee, the TV series *Kung Fu* (1972-1975), and others, the chapter argues that Western popular cultural encounters with ideas, ideals and conceptual universes like those of Taoism were always 'in bits'. However, it insists that this is not a negative or bad thing, and that, in fact, thinking about the ways in which ideas and practices travel and how they transform, over time and place, across cultures and within cultures, can teach us a great deal about how culture and communication always 'work' – or don't – and what we might make of such fragmentation and complexity.

The connections between Eastern martial arts and (embodied) philosophy are strong. Often ideas and associations involve images of calm detachment and tranquillity. Chapter Six deconstructs these images and the ways they function in contemporary discourses. It explores a range of connections and associations, from ideas of Zen Buddhist meditation to contemporary mindfulness and from Samurai to kamikaze themes as they have related to various kinds of militarism and the explicit outlook of Norwegian mass-murderer Anders Behring Breivik. It does so in order to demonstrate the ideological, political and ethical complexity (indeed, undecidability) of martial arts discourse vis-à-vis serenity, psychopathy, sanity and insanity.

But, after putting madness on the table, where can we go? How are martial arts regarded in the wider world, outside of martial arts contexts 'proper'? Derrida and other proponents of deconstruction would often engage issues tangentially or transversally, focusing on 'minor' or 'marginal' dimensions – things that lie on the outer limits of supposed relevance. Following this deconstructive approach, Chapter Seven examines conversations, dialogues and statements about martial arts in films that can by no stretch of the imagination be regarded as martial arts films.

The chapter takes this unusual focus in order to glean unique insights into the status of martial arts in mainstream popular culture. It is interested in the ways that martial arts are understood, positioned, and given value within the wider flows, circuits, networks or discourses of culture. Films examined include *Lolita* (1962), *Roustabout* (1964), *Rollerball* (1975), *The Wanderers* (1979), *An Officer and a Gentleman* (1982), *Trading Places* (1983), *Vision Quest/Crazy for You* (1985), *Full Metal Jacket* (1987), *Once Were Warriors* (1994), *Napoleon Dynamite* (2004), and *Meet the Fockers* (2004); and some discussion is given to 'limit cases' – action films such as *Lethal Weapon* (1987) and *The Matrix* (1999).

The analysis suggests that martial arts tend to be represented in non-martial arts films *audiovisually*, and that on the rare occasions martial arts are discussed they tend to emerge as improper or culturally unusual activities or practices. Because of their familiar yet non-normal (unhomely/*unheimlich*, uncanny) status, along with their entwinement in senses of lack and related fantasies and desires, martial arts in these contexts are frequently related to matters of sexuality, insecurity and the desire for plenitude. Accordingly, although occasionally associated with higher cultural values such as dignity, martial arts are more often treated as comic, uncanny or perverse aberrations from the norm.

After so many different approaches to issues in and around martial arts, the conclusion begins by reflecting on the diversity and range of directions from, into, around, out of, and out into which studies could develop. It poses the question of how and why, where and when we draw lines in our studies, whether of/around 'martial arts' and/or any other subject. In deconstruction, the question of drawing the line is often treated as contingent, conventional, consequential and political. It is often thematised as 'violent' in its own right. Nonetheless, for multiple reasons, 'drawing the line' is both necessary and inevitable. Accordingly, the conclusion sets out some of the key implications relating to where, when, how and why academics draw the line in their foci and approaches, specifically in martial arts studies, but also in critical, intellectual and academic endeavours more widely.

CHAPTER 1

The Triviality of Martial Arts Studies

Introduction

Eyebrows raise. Sometimes there are sniggers. Glances are exchanged. Some people look confused. Some say, 'What?' People seem surprised. 'Martial arts?', they ask, incredulously. 'Why?' Or even, 'Martial arts *studies*? What is that?' These kinds of reactions come from all sorts of people – whether academics or not. No one ever just nods and says, 'Oh, ok', the way they would if you had just said Romantic poetry or urban planning or philosophy or music or fluid dynamics, or the way they might even if you'd just said that you 'do' one of the many obscure and often peculiarly named branches of modern science (whether neuroparasitology, nutrigenomics, cliodynamics, or something even more unexpected).

Sometimes there is surprise and delight. Sometimes there is shock. A lot of it – whether shock, delight, dismay, concern, or confusion – should, on reflection, be unsurprising. On the one hand, people are used to hearing about the familiar subjects of the arts, humanities, and social sciences – the old, traditional fields. On the other hand, when it comes to the sciences, people almost expect to hear of new and unintelligible fields with exotic Latinate names, involving odd prefixes combined with all kinds of 'ologies', 'ographies', 'omatics', 'otics', 'amics', and 'omics'. We measure our social progress through this ever-rising spiral of technical specialization.

But *martial arts* as a field of academic study? Martial arts *studies*? This kind of thing sounds highly dubious to most ears. It doesn't seem to need explanation as much as it needs justification. What reason could there be for the existence of something so...so what? Words come out of the woodwork: iffy, dodgy, nerdy, niche, weird, boyish, hobbyist, or – of course – *trivial*.

What triviality is martial arts studies? What indulgence? What narcissism, navel gazing, nothingness, even naughtiness is this? These questions may seem hyperbolical. But recall a rhetorical question posed by Stuart Hall about

How to cite this book chapter:
Bowman, P. 2019. *Deconstructing Martial Arts*. Pp. 19–32. Cardiff: Cardiff University Press. DOI: https://doi.org/10.18573/book1.b. License: CC-BY-NC-ND 4.0

cultural studies in the very early 1990s, in an essay written at the height of the era of the full horror of the AIDS epidemic. Hall asked: 'Against the urgency of people dying in the streets, what in God's name is the point of cultural studies?' (Hall 1992, 285). Hall posed this question to illustrate the marginality and ineffectuality of academics who saw themselves as working in a field that sought to make a real difference *to* the world, a real difference *in* the world – because, as another famous thinker famously put it, surely the point is not merely to *interpret* or understand the world, 'the point is to change it'.

Is this so for martial arts studies? Karl Marx believed that philosophy should not merely seek to interpret the world but to change it. Does martial arts studies seek to 'change' things, or is it 'mere' interpretation? There are other interpretations of our academic obligations than a kind of quasi- or pseudo-Marxian radicalism, of course (Wetzler 2015). One does not *have* to struggle to change the world if one is working in academia. Indeed, one caricature of the academic figure is someone who retreats from the world, someone who hides in books, who is indeed incompetent in the 'real world'. Nonetheless, whether our understanding of our academic activities boils down either to trying to interpret the world or to trying to change the world, what in God's name is the point of martial arts studies?

Shortly after publishing my first book on Bruce Lee in 2010 (Bowman 2010d), as a relatively junior academic I was obliged to discuss my future research plans with a senior colleague. I stated my interest in developing further some of the lines of enquiry opened up by my work on Bruce Lee. (No one was talking about 'martial arts studies' then. It wasn't yet a 'thing' [Farrer and Whalen-Bridge 2011].) In response, my colleague said, with a kind of paternal or avuncular concern that suggested he thought I might be making a big mistake, 'Yeah, but that's just a bit...' and with a wince and a shrug and an expression that said, 'Don't make me say it: You know what I mean, don't you?', his sentence tailed off, inviting me, obliging me, to finish it in my head myself. One word leapt up for the job: Trivial. 'That sort of thing is just a bit (trivial)'.

Of course, I knew where he was coming from. Two places. A nexus, or chiasmus. Two forces converged, driving his opinion. Two fields of legitimation. The first force is the general force that has been exerting itself on the arts, humanities, and social sciences since at least the 1960s. This might be called the force of the political. Specifically, it is the force of the increasing consensus that grew to a crescendo by the final decades of the 20th Century, which held that *the way* to study something, *the way* to justify giving attention to something, *the way* to redeem something and to elevate it to legitimacy in the university, was to show that it was political (Young 1992; Readings 1996).

The second force in play in my colleague's words was the age-old sense that, to borrow a phrase, 'that just ain't how we do things around here'. In many departments, the obligation to work within the paradigm of the political has been interpreted and assumed in a very particular (literal and direct) way, and Bruce Lee and martial arts do not obviously or self-evidently fit within that space.

This is not to say that Bruce Lee or martial arts were *necessarily* anathema to that space. But such objects of attention were always likely to be filed as 'niche'. In a heavily politics- and journalism-focused school of 'Journalism, Media and Cultural Studies', Bruce Lee and martial arts *could* be made to 'fit in' – as part of the general non-journalism background of media and culture; just not as a particularly central part, even of them. Bruce Lee or other things related to martial arts could always fall into the subcategories of 'film', on the one hand, and 'popular culture' (or, 'worse', fan/subculture), on the other. Indeed, such foci would arguably fall further, into such unspoken or unspeakable sub-subcategories as *non-serious* film, and playful – or trivial – popular culture.[1] Even the historical study of these subjects tends to focus on questions of the 'social' and 'local', rather than the more prestigious (and properly political) categories of military, diplomatic, or national history.

The problem is that the kinds of things that the subjects of martial arts seem to open out onto are exactly the kinds of things that a few decades ago caused problems for the image and reputation of the fledgling fields of media studies and cultural studies. They are the kinds of things that once caused people to regard media studies and cultural studies as 'Mickey Mouse subjects' – i.e., non-serious, non-central, non-important: trivial (Young 1999). For similar representational reasons, areas like the sociology of sport or the academic study of other recreational pursuits or leisure activities never seem to carry the same prestige as 'serious' topics like economic class or religion.

The salvation or salvaging of the reputations of media studies and cultural studies came in the form of the quiet victory within the university of the idea that more or less everything is contingent and hence more or less political (Mowitt 2003). Politics – or, more precisely, 'the political' – became the sign under which certain previously excluded, overlooked, ignored, or disparaged things could justifiably and hence legitimately be studied (Marchart 2007). Women's things, ethnic minorities' things, postcolonial things, working class things, local things, new things, controversial things, and so on.

Unfortunately, it takes about three stages of argument to persuade the uninitiated that things to do with martial arts, like, say, Bruce Lee, are in some sense political and hence in some sense important and hence worthy of at least some kind of academic time and attention (Bowman 2010d). This means that, even if everything is equal in the eyes of the paradigm of the political (because everything is in some sense political), it is still a hell of a lot easier to show that *some* parts of media, culture, and society are 'self-evidently' political and hence more important than others. Such self-evidently important things include such

---

[1] People who are into things from popular culture – and even people who study such things – are regularly regarded as 'fans'; but people who are heavily into, say, broadsheet journalism or politics or news media are never called 'fans'. You rarely have a 'fan' of *The Times*, the labour movement, cancer research, etc.

'obviously political' parts of media, culture, and society as, say, serious news journalism, serious policy debates, protest, and so on.

So, things like journalism, news media, and protest, along with matters of gender and race and disability in representation, and so on, are easy to perceive as proper objects or fields to be privileged. This is because they are easy to regard as being somehow closer to politics or the political – or 'more political' – than certain other kinds of media and other kinds of cultural practice – like, for example, martial arts.

The fact that all things are potentially equal within the paradigm of the political does not mitigate the fact that it will always take about three argumentative steps to prove or persuade someone that martial arts are political (and 'therefore' valuable) in any number of possible ways. On the other hand, it takes little to no effort to show that political foci and political projects are political. They already seem political because they already seem political – even if it is actually possible to argue that they are not (Žižek 2001a; Bowman 2008).

Accordingly, senses and forces of propriety and impropriety vis-à-vis academic foci take hold. Recall my opening anecdote, which involved a senior colleague conveying a judgement that may be regarded as, intentionally or unintentionally, subtly seeking to discourage a junior colleague from pursuing a certain style or orientation of work or focus. Norms and values are being implied here: Good things to do and less good things to do. Of course, this anecdote is just an anecdote. But it could be followed up with quite a few others. In fact, the opening words of this chapter were a distillation of many possible anecdotes. Yet, what is the status of such anecdotes? And what of the innumerable possible counter-balancing anecdotes that could be considered?

In a rightly renowned essay called 'Banality in Cultural Studies', Meaghan Morris proposes that anecdotes 'are not expressions of personal experience, but allegorical expositions of a model of the way the world can be said to be working. So anecdotes need not be true stories, but they must be functional in a given exchange' (Morris 1988, 7). In this approach, anecdotes seek to say something about the way at least some parts of the world can be said to be working; in this case, in relation to the academic study of martial arts. Of course, the world of human interactions and conversational exchanges can be seen as an almost infinite ocean of potential anecdotes, so are we merely singling out only the reactions that suit our purpose? Indeed, are we maybe being a bit too sensitive to any perceived criticism of our shared field of work, whether real or imagined, no matter how slight the sleight may be, when evaluated according to more objective yardsticks? Do we protest too much?

Maybe so, but even if this is hyperbolic, or making a mountain out of a mole-hill, there will nonetheless be some value in the exercise of reflecting on the problem posed. Indeed, it is arguably the case that any and all serious, rigorous, and sustained academic treatments of anything must necessarily magnify and intensify the object of attention's status – and, in other words, make a mountain out of it, even when we know it is not a mountain, even if it really is a molehill.

To someone seriously studying molehills, a molehill is at least a mountain, if not bigger and more significant. In fact, to someone studying molehills, a mountain may be entirely insignificant.

To put all of this in slightly different terms: Is there an issue here that is larger, more far reaching or significant than these anecdotes themselves and their local interpretations? How do they connect with ways that the world might be working, and what might be the significance, importance, or consequences of that?

Elsewhere in 'Banality in Cultural Studies', Morris discusses the dynamics of the then relatively new (and very Japanese) term 'boom' – as in, 'economic boom'. As Morris notes via a variety of examples, in a period of boom, a certain kind of explosion in activity often goes hand in hand with another kind of limitation or prohibition. In her words, a boom involves not only 'passion and activity' but also 'a pre-emptive prohibition and limitation of activity' (Morris 1988, 5). As such, in a boom, there are ample opportunities for the exploration and expansion of activities that are popular (or booming). But, by the same token, any attempts to engage in non-boom activities are likely to be met with blank stares, closed doors, and dead ends.

In thinking about the features of a boom, Morris argues that there is a significant 'difference between the Japanese concept of cultural boom, and the older European notion of "fashion"' (Morris 1990, 4). Relating it to academia, she observes:

> The notion of 'intellectual fashion' … is usually used to denigrate passion and enthusiasm as 'fickle' – in order to imply that real, solid scholarship is going on somewhere in spite of the market, within which it will nonetheless find its true place of recognition once the fuss of fashion subsides. A boom, however, overtly defines and directs what can be done at a given moment. [Indeed] booms positively shape the possible, by stabilizing a temporary horizon in relation to which one cannot claim a position of definite exteriority, [meaning that] it also becomes possible to think more carefully the politics of one's own participation and complicity. (Morris 1990, 5)

So, if and where there is a boom, there is possibility, facility, propensity, energy, ability. If and where there is not a boom, there is resistance, apathy, confusion, skepticism, and so on. Indeed, as well as the lack of interest that may face any non-boom activity, there may actually be a lack of ability to imagine why anyone could be interested in it.

What, then, is the situation vis-à-vis martial arts studies? Is martial arts studies facing a boom, or facing its opposite – which is surely not a 'bust', as martial arts studies hasn't yet had its day in the sun, but rather some kind of 'pre-emptive prohibition and limitation of activity'? What would be the larger, only dimly perceived, intellectual trends which define this gravitational horizon?

One possibility is that martial arts studies is currently emerging thanks to the ground opened up by the victories won by subjects like cultural studies, the success of which is attributable in part to the demonstration of the political dimensions of culture and the contingency of norms, hegemonic values, and institutional investments. While not compiling a comprehensive list here and now, we might say that the movements of which cultural studies was a part revealed the extent to which our educations and our institutions were white, Western, male, heterosexual, Eurocentric, and upper class (Storey 2000). All of these things were deemed to require redress on ethical and political grounds. And a windfall-gain of the general deconstruction of elitist tastes, values, formations, and practices in so many of their incarnations was the attendant ability to revalue hitherto devalued things – not only non-white and non-male things, but also things that had been regarded as supposedly low-brow, popular, low-class, and – hence – trivial. Things like martial arts in their many incarnations, as well as the media, history, and training methods that accompany them.

So, in one sense, the emergence of martial arts studies owes a lot to the intentional or unintentional redemption or salvaging and revaluation of the supposedly secondary, inferior, inauthentic, non-serious, and trivial that took place in and around cultural studies. But, on the flipside, perhaps this is also a source of problems for martial arts studies. For, thanks to it, martial arts studies becomes an heir to the most problematic inheritance of the deconstruction and reconstruction of academia – namely, the trivial. This is why martial arts studies should expect to attract as much perplexity and even vitriol and vituperation as subjects like media studies, audience studies, fan studies, game studies, fashion studies, and so on – all of which have for a long time easily drawn flak for sounding like so many different names for something that should really just be called *Triviality Studies*.

As many people intuitively know, these kinds of problems might always be circumvented or deferred by sheltering or smuggling martial arts studies under more established umbrellas, as in such formulations as: 'I'm an anthropologist, and I research…'; 'I'm a historian, and I research…'; 'I'm an ethnographer, and I research…'; 'I'm a sociologist, and I research…'; and so on. In this way, the ground is prepared for the introduction of martial arts as a more obviously legitimate object of studies by framing it as merely one of the many possible objects of an already valid and valued field. Or, alternatively, the martial arts might be transformed from a dependent variable (the thing examined) to an independent variable (an explanatory factor) within a better-established research programme.

Such an approach has its virtues. Indeed, how many of us could actually say that we work in schools or departments of martial arts studies, or that we principally teach modules, courses, or degrees in martial arts studies? And for those handful of people in the world who could say something like this, what exactly is it that they are working in or teaching? Both of these questions point to a problematic that I tried to tackle in my book *Martial Arts Studies: Disrupting Disciplinary Boundaries* (Bowman 2015a). This problematic boils down to the question of whether martial arts studies could be said to exist as an academic field, and what it means to say that it does, or to operate as if it does. Phrased differently: We already know that martial arts studies can emerge parasitically, and exist as a kind of supplement, sub-field, or focus within other umbrella disciplines and departments. That has never really been in doubt. Many scholars have touched on the martial arts over the decades. Yet, might martial arts studies exist somehow independently? Is it possible to invent martial arts studies as an independent or discrete entity, and what would it look like if we were to try?

It soon becomes apparent that posing such questions very quickly opens out onto a whole range of questions about academic subjects, inspiring questioning which could – perhaps should – ultimately open out into a far reaching reflection on what a university subject (or discipline or field) *is*, what university disciplinary and managerial divisions and subdivisions are, why they exist, what they do, whether we 'need' them, what sort of interests and outcomes they serve, and whether we might dispense with them, or at least move them into different relations and dynamics.

I spent quite a long time on this (which I still think is a fascinating and important) subject in my 2015 monograph, so I will not tarry too long in the same terrain here. Instead, let us try to move things along by maintaining a focus on the question of triviality, and specifically the triviality of martial arts studies, before coming back to questions about the possible forms of existence of martial arts studies.

Triviality Studies

The *Oxford English Dictionary* says a lot of things about the words *trivia* and *trivial*, as well as the word *trivium*, from which they all substantially derive. As the *OED* tells us, trivial once referred to belonging to the trivium of medieval university studies, or 'the lower division of the seven liberal arts, comprising grammar, rhetoric, and logic'. We could make a lot of this, but to do so would involve sophistry. This is because when people say trivial today they do not intend to mean anything related to this, unless they are having a specialist discussion on the subject of the medieval university. Nor do people mean triple or threefold. Nor do they mean 'placed where three roads meet'. But they may mean 'Such as may be met with anywhere; common, commonplace, ordinary, everyday, familiar, trite', or – more likely – 'Of small account, little esteemed, paltry, poor; trifling, inconsiderable, unimportant, slight'.

There are other technical meanings for trivial that are used in fields like zoology and a range of sciences, but none of these relate to what is most commonly meant by trivial. However, one meaning of trivial that comes from mathematics is suggestive to the point of being poetic. In it, trivial means: 'Of no consequence or interest, e.g. because equal to zero'. So, we might say, trivial most often evokes something that is so ordinary, commonplace, familiar, or inconsequential that it is effectively deemed equal to zero. Or, if not nothing, then at least very little, almost nothing.

Again, we could make much of this and use all of the kinds of arguments made in cultural studies, gender studies and postcolonial studies and so on to argue for the revaluation, redemption, or reclamation of martial arts. But I will not do this here, because we should all already know how to do this. I'm sure I am not the only one who has, on many occasions – as I did in response to my anecdotal colleague – persuaded others of the value of martial arts studies by playing the political card. In one chapter in *Theorizing Bruce Lee*, I actually ran through a check list of many of the key themes and problematics that organise not only cultural studies but also many other fields – such as ethnicity, postcoloniality, polyvocality, polysemy, multimediality, cultural translation, intertextuality, sex/gender identity performativity, postmodernity, enculturation, hegemony, commodification, resistance and subversion, and so on – and showed the extent to which Bruce Lee ticked all of such fields' boxes. In *The Creation of Wing Chun* (2015), Benjamin N. Judkins and Jon Nielson engaged in a similar exercise, tackling themes such as imperialism, resistance, modernization, marginality, nationalism, and social violence.

There are other ways to argue for the legitimacy of studies of martial arts, of course: Legitimation by numbers (just look at how many people in the world do martial arts), legitimation by money (just look at how big a range of businesses martial arts are), legitimation by area (just look at how central martial arts are to nationalism and national identity-building projects, particularly across Asia), legitimation by UNESCO (if it's good enough for UNESCO to call it 'intangible cultural heritage' then it's good enough for a study, right?), legitimation by demographics, pedagogics, identity politics, ideological orientation, discursive status, and so on and so forth.

But existing scholars of martial arts, culture and society know all of this. If Judkins' wide-ranging and field-defining blog *Kung Fu Tea* has taught us one single thing, it is this: That, nationally and internationally, martial arts are *massive*. But lots of things are massive. Narcissism, nose-picking, and trainspotting, for instance, might all be said to be massive. The question is whether such things might warrant an academic field and/or whether such a field might be deemed trivial.

To move things forward, perhaps what is needed here is to note that one vital thing the *OED* does not tell us about the notion of the trivial is that it is radically relational and that reflection on what a given perspective, person, or situation deems to be trivial constitutes something of a royal road to the unconscious biases or unthought regions of that perspective, person, or situation itself.

So, if we are in a conversation with our critic, we can deconstruct any criticism of our position that proceeds according to the argument about something's triviality. Or, better, we can engage in discussion and win the argument and persuade our interlocutor of the validity or non-triviality of martial arts and martial arts studies. And so on. In fact, as just suggested, there are a range of options.

But whatever we decide to do, it is both theoretically and practically useful always to proceed in full awareness of the fact that all of us are very often going to regard certain other things as trivial. Moreover, some people, hostile to this or that academic focus or approach, are often likely to be inclined to wield whatever they think *is* properly important like a kind of sledgehammer to try to smash whatever it is they think is trivial. At cultural studies conferences it is a common (perhaps therefore apparently trivial – certainly frequent) occurrence for any session of presentations on more or less any subject – anything at all – you name it – to provoke a member of the audience to cry out, in exasperation, something along the lines of, 'Why are you all wasting your time with *this*? *What about the war*?!'

Wars are serious. When measured against the seriousness of an ongoing war, and people dying in the streets, academic studies of more or less anything, in any discipline, will almost always seem somewhat trivial.

Of course, the irony is that some people working in martial arts studies may well have compelling, informed, intelligent, specialist, rare, or valuable insights into questions of war and violence. But a further and more pertinent irony is that experts and specialists on modern war or social violence are actually likely to be in the minority in martial arts studies. This is so even though 'martial' has to do with war. Nonetheless, the peculiarity is that – for a whole host of linguistic, cultural, and historical reasons – many of us mostly seem to forget the most literal meaning of the word 'martial' as soon as it is combined with the word 'art'. This is why the very term 'martial arts studies' is rarely-to-never decoded, translated, defined, or interpreted as meaning anything like 'studies of the art of war' – even and perhaps especially within martial arts studies itself. Indeed, the tendency of the field today exhibits a definite bias towards studying armed and unarmed *embodied* fighting – or the very thing that Peter Lorge has suggested Chinese military experts throughout history have long regarded as being 'a developmental rather than a functional skill in the army' (Lorge 2012, Loc 3506).

The myriad other realms and components of the arts of war (or rebellion or riot) are rarely centralised or foregrounded in martial arts studies. Indeed, if the term 'martial arts studies' really meant 'studies of the arts of war' to us, this would make the field into a very different kind of thing – something that arguably already exists, under a range of different names: War studies, conflict studies, peace studies, security studies, and suchlike. But do war studies, conflict studies, or peace studies really capture or cover what we tend to think martial arts studies is or should be? And if so, why the new name, the new demarcation, if martial arts studies is just another version of something or some things that already exist? What the hell is martial arts studies supposed to be anyway?

I have argued many times against the drive to *define* martial arts and hence thereby to demarcate martial arts studies. I will do so again in the next chapter. As I have suggested on several occasions and will suggest again (in Chapter Two), such an orientation is naïve in a number of ways. And I will add here and now, in this context, that succumbing to such an orientation (the drive to define, or the 'definition drive', if you will) would achieve the opposite of what most pro-definition academics hope for: Rather than conferring scientific seriousness onto the field, it would most likely guarantee the marginality and triviality of any martial arts studies generated or facilitated by imposing a strict definition of martial arts. Or, to put it slightly differently, such a move would tend to isolate martial arts studies from the critical questions of the day, rather than asking what our hard-won understanding might contribute to the conversation.

We will turn to this more fully in the next chapter. At this point, let us consider an argument made by Mark Singleton about the word 'yoga' (Singleton 2010). Specifically, in a fascinating study of yoga, Singleton notes that, over the centuries, and in different contexts and different minds, the word 'yoga' has long existed; but it has always referred to ever-changing and very different things – ideas, practices, ideologies, orthodoxies, orthopraxies, and so on. In the face of such polysemy, rather than adopting a position that would force him into feeling the need to specify anything like 'this is real yoga but that is not real yoga', Singleton instead proposes that we always treat the word yoga as a *homonym*.

Homonyms are words that are both spelled the same and pronounced the same but mean different things. When I say 'martial arts' and you say 'martial arts', we may well be thinking of very different things, with different forms, contents, places, roles, functions, associations, implications, and so on. But we will undoubtedly be able to talk about this difference, because an interesting thing about these homonyms is that the meanings tend to cluster together, overlap each other, interact together, reflect (and reflect on) each other, and so on.

This is why not only 'we specialists' but also all practitioners and, most importantly perhaps, myriad non-practitioners and people who simply know as close to nothing as is imaginable about 'martial arts' will all have an immediate pre-critical inkling of what the 'martial arts' of 'martial arts studies' is most likely referring to. This is because the term 'martial arts' is a *discursive achievement* – a *construct*, not a trans-historical *datum*. It is a type of popular conversation (rather than a singular thing) that is already familiar to all.

Despite having a long history, 'martial arts' is nonetheless a comparatively recent term within English language popular usage. That is to say, it is a *current* term. Yes, it *also* has a long history. But to claim that the English language term 'martial arts', in the ways we use it today, is much older than the late 1960s is much the same as claiming that when people say 'trivial' they are referring to the disciplinary demarcations of the mediaeval university or that they are referring to 'where three roads meet'. That is to say, it is a claim that overlooks the words' *currency*, or *current-ness*. Martial arts has a certain currency *now*, in Anglophone cultures and societies. Again, it points to trends and conversations much more than to things.

Perhaps this widespread current currency is why studies of martial arts have so definitively broken free from anthropological or area studies paradigms, in which many research programmes are organised by notions of the rituals of groups. As popular as such approaches continue to be, postcolonialist deconstruction has taught us that, while subjects such as anthropology and area studies continue to invent their objects in terms of ideas about rituals and groups, white Western thinkers tend not to be quite as keen on the idea that white Western cultures and societies are themselves organised by groups and rituals. That kind of thing is easier to see in and as the societies of the others, not us and ours (Fabian 1983; Spivak 1993). So, if it's something 'we're into', something that's happening here, it surely can't be the traditional indigenous ritual practice of natives, now can it?

Nowadays, the flipside of this situation is never too far away. This is the belated realisation that the *apparently* 'ancient' traditional ritual practices of the natives 'over there' always turn out to be complex discursive formations and constructions, or a heady mix of 'orientalisms' and 'invented traditions'. There is a lot that can be said about the ideological invention of history in the present. But here, in terms of the earlier discussion of the field of martial arts studies, of 'currencies' and 'booms', one thing that seems significant is the currency of theoretical terms like 'orientalism' and 'invented tradition' in the generation and organisation of so much research. How adept we seem to be at finding 'our' orientalism and 'their' invented traditions. And so we should be: Scholars have been making these kinds of discoveries over and over again since the 1970s.

Discussion of all of this could take us far afield. But the point to be made here is that, as much as so many of us are so ready, willing, and able to carry out discursive or conjunctural analyses of our objects of study these days (as long as our objects of study are *others*: The practices of natives, the practices of tribes, or subcultures, or working classes, or bourgeoisies, and so on), surely we have an attending obligation to consider the question of how and why we ourselves are doing what we do in the ways that we do it.

The question is one of what the discursive conditions of possibility for today's emergence of an academic thing called martial arts studies are or have been. I have suggested that part of our enabling conditions relate to the revaluation of erstwhile trivia by former trailblazing projects like cultural studies. Might another key component relate to the enormous productivity of notions like orientalism and invented tradition? These terms have been available since the late seventies and early eighties, yet they show no signs of fatigue, which suggests that their work is not yet done (unlike countless other once fashionable or once booming theoretical terms that seem to have evaporated today but are presumably still skulking in the shadows or waiting in the wings – like the Baudrillardian ideas of 'banal strategies' and 'fatal strategies' that Morris' essay notes were dominating cultural studies in the 1980s. Are we still thinking about banal strategies and fatal strategies? Is that problematic even remembered today?).

However, some might worry that reflections such as this – reflections on our enabling and organising terms – take the entire field of martial arts studies too far afield – away from 'martial arts' *proper* and into a kind of self-reflection that is narcissistic, or trivial. It is easy to disagree with such an idea. There is immense value and opportunity for mastering and improving our practices if we learn more about the forces that mould and shape our activities. We may not want to apply the notion of 'invented tradition' to our own activities, but we ought to think about why that is and why we are happy to apply it elsewhere.

In fact, as much as I am often fascinated by the kinds of objects of attention that are emerging in martial arts studies, I am possibly even more animated by the challenge of thinking about where we are now. This is not simply to do with the 'newness' of the field, but rather with what can be seen to be happening right now in terms of discursive creation, writing, construction, invention, and the articulation and stabilization of martial arts studies as a 'thing'.

We are still close enough to 'the start' that the publication of a new book generates widespread excitement and gets everyone talking, and for the announcement of a conference in the near future to get everyone looking at their diaries and hoping that they might be able to afford to go. New English-language publications on martial arts are not yet merely felt as a drop in the ocean. Their status as 'a contribution' is still easily palpable.

Obviously, as this process continues and grows, the status of each new conference, paper, article, chapter, journal issue, book collection, and monograph will undoubtedly change, and maybe ultimately seem to diminish. The field will be elaborated and will proliferate, and in time it will surely mutate and reposition. But my hope (and sense) is that this will not be until after something has happened. For something has already started to happen. Something is happening. We have, at the very least, already resoundingly answered at least one question that haunted so many of us for so long: *Will martial arts ever be a valid object of academic study?* Remember how often and how pessimistically this question was posed? But now the answer is: *Yes, look, it can be, it is, and look how diversely and dynamically connected with so many other things martial arts always turn out to be!*

So, to use a well-worn question form: If martial arts studies is a thing, then what kind of a thing is it? What is it a case of? And, again: If something is happening, then what kind of a something is it – and what kind of a happening?

To take any or all of these questions, in isolation or at the same time, any answer would always involve asserting that martial arts studies is emerging to answer a demand – not just an academic demand, whether by 'academic demand' we mean in the sense of 'knowledge for knowledge's sake' (i.e., a demand to fill a perceived hole in the field of knowledge, simply because we have perceived that a hole is there) or in the pejorative sense of being a 'merely academic' matter. Rather, martial arts studies is emerging because an untold number of conditions have been met that now allow into the university the kind of ongoing and widespread intellectualisation of martial arts that has been taking place for many years outside of the university (Bowman 2015a, 2017b, 2017c). It is critical not to forget that intellectual discourse and scholarship on martial arts has long taken place, but mainly outside of standard university channels, and outside of the West. So, in this sense, Anglophone martial arts studies is *belated*. Nevertheless, finally, today – and helped in large part by having organised itself around and in terms of the questions, concerns, languages, vocabularies, and purviews of established fields like cultural studies, anthropology, history, and sociology – academic scholars have begun to find a way to legitimise martial arts as an academic field.

This kind of legitimisation is principally at the research level. Wherever martial arts studies has so far been instituted at the pedagogical level – that is, as a unique or discrete degree level subject taught to undergraduates – this has principally taken the form of practical and vocational orientations, i.e., as degrees involving learning martial arts and learning about them in terms of physical education delivery and self-defence pedagogy or industry (Wile 2014).

So, there is a difference between the research field and the pedagogical field. Of course, that's not to say there are not connections and crossovers. But the point is that there have so far been different orientations and modes of legitimation in which the research field has been legitimating itself via questions and concerns of critical, social scientific, and historical theory, while pedagogical instantiations of the field have proceeded according to a range of vocational, physical education, and industry questions and concerns.

The relations between these two levels are always going to be complex, and often fraught. But the homonym 'martial arts' that organises all levels and orientations can and will facilitate many leaps and links and crossovers and connections; it could indeed coalesce at times and in places into enormously exciting and genuinely multiple and heterogeneous experimental interdisciplinarities.

From any academic perspective, there is little to no triviality in this. Similarly, if money talks, there is no triviality in securing research grants, establishing research centres, or setting up modules and courses and degrees. There is no triviality in cross-disciplinary discourses that have the capacity not merely to enrich but to alter the disciplines from which they began. Nor is there triviality in transforming the wider cultural discourses on martial arts – in, say, demonstrating orientalism, or debunking myths, or revealing the inventedness of traditions. Orientalism and myths and invented traditions are big business. The stakes are high. So, this kind of work has the capacity – perhaps the obligation – to change things.

These are just some of the levels, some of the contexts, some of the scenes and sites of struggle and activity of the emergence of martial arts studies. All in all, when thinking about martial arts studies, we should perhaps take the famous phrase of Pierre Bourdieu that 'sociology is a martial art' and intensify it, by accepting that, in so many ways, *martial arts studies is a martial art.* The challenge is to understand both putative entities here ('martial arts' and 'martial arts studies') at the same time and in ways that are adequate to the complexity, forces, violences, vicissitudes, promises, possibilities, and potentials of their 'passion and activity' without any 'pre-emptive prohibition and limitation of activity', by reducing, simplifying, defining, or consigning either element to triviality.

CHAPTER 2

Theory Before Definition in Martial Arts Studies

Dealing with Disciplinary Difference

The matter of value that was broached in the previous chapter demands further interrogation. To do so here, let me begin with an anecdote. I was once invited to contribute a chapter to a collection being prepared on martial arts and embodied knowledge. When all the draft chapters were in and the editors were happy with the collection, the entire manuscript was then sent off to be assessed by two academic reviewers. Of my own contribution, one reviewer said that the chapter by Bowman was terrible, not publishable, and should be rejected. The other reviewer said that the chapter by Bowman was the best contribution to the volume, and greatly enhanced and enriched it. Faced with two diametrically opposed views from two presumably equally reliable peer reviewers,[1] the editors themselves held the casting vote. They decided that they liked the chapter overall, thought it had value, and wanted to include it. But they elected to share the reviews with me and invited me to make any changes I thought appropriate in light of them.

The experience of receiving such polarised views was educational. I share this anecdote here to introduce a cluster of interrelated issues. These start

---

[1] At the time, the emerging field that we now call martial arts studies was yet to be established, and the editors later commented that they had actually struggled to find suitable academics to act as peer reviewers who were not already contributors to the collection itself. Today, there would be peer reviewers aplenty for such a collection. This could be taken to demonstrate many things, including the proposition that the establishment of an academic field involves not only the establishment of (new) shared objects of attention, shared problematics and shared methodologies, but also the production of (new) academic subjects – i.e., individual scholars with a recognisable disciplinary identity, conferred or established reciprocally in the process of emergence of the discourse itself.

How to cite this book chapter:
Bowman, P. 2019. *Deconstructing Martial Arts*. Pp. 33–59. Cardiff: Cardiff University Press. DOI: https://doi.org/10.18573/book1.c. License: CC-BY-NC-ND 4.0

with the matter of how to establish value in an emergent academic discourse, the problematic of bias attendant to all acts and processes of evaluation and verification, and the fact that the shape, form, borderlines, organisation and orientation of academic fields are neither natural nor inevitable. Rather, these emerge in negotiation with decisions made by a host of agents and agencies, including academics, editors, reviewers, research councils, funding bodies, and publishers, all of whom make their evaluations with reference to established criteria and values. Accordingly, decisions as to what good or bad work looks like, and what 'deserves' to be published, are themselves reflective of values tied into interpretations of what good, correct or proper academic work in this field 'should' look like.

This does not mean that everything is already decided or overdetermined by pre-established 'structures' or 'systems'. Rather, it means that senses of pro-priety, validity, appropriateness, fit, and so on, are always *establishments* or *achievements* that are ongoing, in negotiation, subject to dispute, up for ques-tion, challenge, revision and review. Such negotiation and renegotiation can be perceived in all academic disciplines, but it is inevitably more cacophonic in newly emerging fields, where senses of tradition and tacit agreements about convention have yet to be set.

This is the situation of martial arts studies today, in which huge discipli-nary differences are palpable from one work to the next. Such vast differences are present because even though the emergence of the field is being driven by a sense of shared and communal investment in an object ('martial arts'), this shared interest is not yet matched by anything like a shared approach. In other words, the shared academic interest in 'martial arts' is currently drawing together academics from many very different fields. Yet the deceptiveness of the term 'martial arts' combined with the diversity of this community, with its myriad premises, multiple perspectives, methods and orientations, seems to necessitate the creation of some kind of consensus around the object, field and approach to 'martial arts'. Hence, understandably, people feel the need to *establish a definition of martial arts* (Jones 2002; Lorge 2012, 2016; but see also Judkins 2016b).

Because of this perceived necessity, at this point, many works would move directly into a discussion of definitions, attempting to settle the matter of which definition of martial arts should and should not be used, and where and when (Channon 2016; Lorge 2016). However, rather than entering into the discus-sion about how best to define martial arts, in what follows I will instead argue that the question of the definition of martial arts is both a distraction and a red herring for the emerging field of martial arts studies. The more pressing task, I argue, is not the establishment of a consensus around the definition of our object. Rather, it is the establishment of a shared, circumspect, literate, ana-lytical and theoretically informed critical discourse with rigorously formulated problematics that can contribute in diverse ways to both academic and public debates.

In short, I argue (somewhat against the current of recent debates, and even against the grain of many academic approaches) that we do not need to define martial arts at all. Rather, I propose that we need to theorise the entire field or nexus of research, including the place, point and purpose of definition within it. Indeed, my contention is that if we allow ourselves to be animated by defining martial arts without both theorising and constructing the field, then martial arts studies may founder and fail, like so many past attempts to establish an academic field of study for martial arts.[2]

Approaching Martial Arts Studies

Before following through on this, some further reflection on my opening anecdote seems called for. Ironically, even back at the time of this brush between my work and two border guards at the gates of a then unclear and embryonic field, I had already long accepted Roland Barthes' argument that readers can and will have very different responses to the same text (Barthes 1977). But I had never encountered such symmetrically opposed opinions from scholars I had presumed must work to some degree in the 'same' area, or at least close enough – i.e., holding an academic interest in 'martial arts' refracted through one or another approach of the arts or humanities. Even though I already believed I knew that academic disciplines are spaces of argumentation and disagreement rather than consensus, the vastly differing verdicts nonetheless surprised me. Today, I am no longer surprised by the appearance of such difference in what is still a very young and uncertain field. Indeed, as mentioned, encountering extreme disciplinary differences is currently our daily bread. The question is: Is such diversity simply something to be either shrugged off or celebrated, or might it harbour a problem? What might it mean if the object and field of martial arts studies continues to be conceived of very differently by different people from different disciplinary backgrounds? In short, is it a problem that we are still frequently experiencing such widely differing approaches to the academic study martial arts?

On the one hand, no. There will always be disciplinary difference, and even vast differences in conceptuality and orientation within 'the same' discipline or field. Different academic origins and kinds of training bring with them differing questions, differing objects of attention, differing values, methods, and so on. And, for the foreseeable future, martial arts studies will inevitably be built

---

[2] For an important and valuable contrast to this argument, see Peter Lorge's recent work (Lorge 2016), in which he argues against using theory – because it is difficult and off-putting – and instead for the virtues of deepening and refining *historical* knowledge. As Lorge sees it, deeper historical knowledge can both enrich martial artists' practice and clearly illustrate to the academic community the value of martial arts as a valid topic of academic study. I believe it is possible to concede Lorge's points and still argue for the value and necessity of theory 'before' or 'beneath' this.

from work and approaches hailing from different disciplines. Moreover, no one will ever be surprised, for instance, if a study of martial arts as they appear in one or more works of literature differs significantly from a study focused on questions of experiments in or around pedagogy (compare Liu 2011 with Lefebvre 2016 for instance). So where might the problem come in?

Far be it from me to advocate any kind of unitary, univocal, mono-disciplinary or monoculturalist approach in martial arts studies. That would be neither desirable nor possible. Nonetheless, in order for a field or discipline to emerge and survive, there must be coherent and meaningful internal (community) and external (cross-disciplinary) discourses and exchanges. In order for this to happen, the matter of what we might call 'the approach' is important. There are stakes and consequences attached to the matter of the paradigms that organise our efforts.

To illustrate, one might briefly consider the possible reasons for the repeated failure of attempts to create a field of academic study of and for martial arts. Most famously, of course, Richard Burton in the 19th Century and Donn Draeger later in the 20th Century attempted to found and ground an academic discipline that they called 'hoplology' (for an overview, see Spencer 2011). However, this or these projects repeatedly foundered. The question is: Why?

Even more pertinently, perhaps, is the related question of why a connected field of martial arts studies took until today to begin to emerge at all. Consider the fact that over the last two decades it became increasingly easy to carry out online academic searches and to discover that all sorts of different kinds of studies of all sorts of issues involving martial arts are being carried out across a surprising number of different disciplines. Yet there have been few sustained dialogues and fewer dedicated spaces for the academic study of martial arts.[3]

My contention is that the matter of the *approach* or *paradigm* is central to both questions. It relates not only to all failed past attempts to establish any kind of martial arts studies but also to the stubborn non-appearance of martial arts studies until today, despite scattered studies of martial arts in diverse disciplines.

To consider the recent situation first: There is a sense in which the very heterogeneity of the ways of approaching martial arts – the very richness of the potential field – may paradoxically have played a part in preventing the creation of a single interconnected, interacting field. The logic of this proposition is as follows: The creation of an academic discourse requires the emergence of shared problematics and discussions around – at the very least – matters of which questions are to be asked and which methodologies are best suited for their exploration. Yet, in recent decades, although there have been a great number of academic studies on all manner of things to do with martial arts, no

---

[3] The long-running *Electronic Journals of Martial Arts and Sciences* is a noteworthy project that has attempted to construct such dialogues and spaces (http://ejmas.com/). I defer a discussion of this project here, however, in order to focus on more 'stark' examples for clarity.

single field or conversation has emerged, because of the very heterogeneity of approaches to radically heterogeneous questions. (Moreover, far from informing, enlivening and expanding academic discourses on martial arts, the heterogeneity of approaches and diversity of kinds of work actually seems to have prevented many people from reading, engaging, *or even being aware of* the plethora of academic literature being produced on martial arts across the disciplines. Works continue to appear that present themselves as if they are the first to deal with the martial arts. Whether proceeding by making grand proclamations to this effect or by lacking a basic literature review, the net result is the same.)

What seems key to disciplinary emergence is a sense of a shared project. But this does not mean that a field demands a unitary or univocal approach. Far from it. Taking too limited a conception of the object and of the field, particularly when this is combined with too limited or problematic an approach, can equally stymie growth. This might be illustrated by a consideration of perhaps the most well-known past attempt to establish a field for the academic study of martial arts – hoplology.

Hoplological Hopes

Hoplology is surely the most famous example of the failure of martial arts studies to attain a stable and sustainable academic presence. According to the website of the International Hoplology Society, hoplology was founded by Sir Richard F. Burton in the 19th Century. However, it then (says the website) 'remained dormant' until Donn Draeger picked up the baton at some unspecified point after the 1960s, a baton he carried until his death ('About the International Hoplology Society' n.d.). The International Hoplology Society is now based in Hawaii and presents itself as 'an independent, not-for-profit organization' which 'offers its services to scholars, universities, museums, collectors, private and governmental organizations, writers and publishers around the world' ('About the International Hoplology Society' n.d.).

Given this evidence of its continued and current existence, readers may be surprised by my claim that hoplology is a failed academic project. Hoplology still exists. The published work of Donn Draeger itself is of mythic status in most narratives of the history of Western attempts to establish serious and reliable scholarly knowledge of East Asian martial arts. Nonetheless, what provides the clearest evidence that the project failed is the lack of any significant academic presence for hoplology. It is neither a discipline, nor a discourse, nor an unfolding research programme, nor an interdisciplinary nexus of debate. The fact that hoplology continues to haunt us in the form of the hopes and aspirations of its proponents does not change the fact that as a field of study it never really made it to where any such field of study most wants to be – the university. The university was always where Draeger and other proponents wanted hoplology to be. But it never really made it.

It 'never really made it' for lots of different kinds of reasons. There were of course both personal and 'political' elements at work that arguably hampered Draeger's attempts to get hoplology into a university (Miracle 2015). But my contention is that, more significantly, there have always been *fundamental* obstacles to its academic survival, and that these have always boiled down to its flawed conceptions of its object and its flawed theoretical orientations – in other words, its flawed paradigm and approach.

There are many possible ways to illustrate the conceptual and orientation problems at the heart of hoplology. For the sake of brevity and clarity, I will limit myself to one quick example. This is taken from the front-page text of the International Hoplology Society website,[4] which proudly trumpets the 'three axioms of hoplology'. These three axioms are:

1. The foundation of human combative behavior is rooted in our evolution. To gain a realistic understanding of human combative behavior, it is necessary to have a basic grasp of its evolutionary background.
2. The two basic forms of human combative behavior are predatory and affective. Predatory combative behavior is that combative/aggressive behavior rooted in our evolution as a hunting mammal. Affective combative behavior is that aggressive/combative behavior rooted in our evolution as a group-social animal.
3. The evolution of human combative behavior and performance is integral with the use of weapons. That is, behavior and performance is intrinsically linked to and reflects the use of weapons. ('About the International Hoplology Society' n.d.)

From any academic point of view, the fundamental problem with these axioms is that they are not academic. Rather, they are *tenets*, *beliefs*, and *assertions*. They may appear scientific on first glance, but they are actually scientistic. Specifically, they reflect an attempt to align hoplology with the controversial (and equally dubious) field of sociobiology (Wilson 1975), which itself has long been accused, among other things, of scientism and biological determinism (Schreier et al. n.d.; Bethell n.d.).[5] The function of these scientific-sounding

---

4   Although focusing on such an example may be open to the criticism that it has not been taken from a properly academic context and so should not be subjected to academic critique, nonetheless this example has been selected because these are words that have been placed 'front and centre' and presented as expressing the heart of the hoplological academic project.

5   The semi-autobiographical pseudo-academic book *The Professor in the Cage: Why Men Fight and Why We Like To Watch* by Jonathan Gottschall is perhaps the most well-known recent iteration of this kind of deeply problematic approach (Gottschall 2015). The book, appropriately, starts from the failure of an English professor's ongoing project to persuade anyone to use ideas from evolutionary biology in literary studies. From this failure, Gottschall turns to his stagnating academic career and the birth of his interest in MMA. In all of this, the book applies simplistic sociobiologistic ideas to the subject of 'fighting'. There is much that might be said about the limitations and skewing effects of all such pseudo-, crypto- and actual sociobiologistic approaches, and they warrant sustained critique. But such critiques should

'axioms' on the homepage is to gesture to the society's declared commitment to scholarship and research. Unfortunately, this gesture actually demonstrates the opposite: It reveals its constitutively doctrinaire orientation. As such, the text commits quite a few academic crimes, which all effectively add up to a kind of unintentional (but certain) self-ostracising and auto-abdication from the world of serious academic debate and discussion.

Of course, neither Burton nor Draeger authored these words. But it is clear that the table was set and the door opened to welcome them in advance by the kinds of approach common to hoplology since the beginning. The problem is that this is such a limited *raison d'être*, articulated with reference to and in terms of a very limited and problematic deployment of an already problematic set of contentions, that it will always be highly unlikely to pass as academic in any field or context. Few, if any, 20th or 21st Century academic journals, for instance, would accept any allegedly academic article that proceeded according to such 'axioms' (as illustrated by the aforementioned case of Gottschall [2015]).

Rather than this, in order to thrive within academia, what is required is something very different. Specifically, martial arts studies must emerge as a coherent communicative and self-sustaining field of meaningful and productive exchanges and interactions that might be diversely relevant. To achieve this, it will be necessary to undertake a sustained and explicit examination of, and engagement with, the stakes and consequences of the different conceptualisations, orientations and methods available to the field. This implies a sustained reflection on premises, remits, orientations and methods, along with ongoing dialogues with other disciplines and the principled awareness of other established and unfolding approaches across academia. Any conceptualisation of the field that starts out as an apologetic exercise for only a single set of assumptions or methods by definition cannot do this and will be highly unlikely to attract wider academic interest.

This chapter now seeks to contribute to such a reflection by moving away from failed projects like hoplology and discussing instead some significant recent contributions to the crucial debate about what martial arts studies is and how it might elaborate itself and develop. Before engaging with these contributions, however, it will be worthwhile to give some more attention to the matter of the significance for academic discourses of differing approaches and values.

Moving from 'Thing Itself' to 'Field Itself'

One helpful way to understand why differences of opinion and orientation will always occur within academic disciplines and discourses is proposed by Jacques Derrida (Derrida and Ferraris 2003). Derrida proposes that academic

---

be careful to avoid being dragged into a scientistic *cul-de-sac*. There are far better approaches to 'fighting' available than those which rush naively and crudely to ideas of evolutionary advantage (see, for examples, Jackson-Jacobs 2013 and Gong 2015).

fields are essentially always at war with themselves. The reason for this is that they essentially construct *both* their own objects and approaches *and* their own yardsticks for evaluating them. In this sense, a discipline essentially 'constructs the object of argumentation and the field of argumentation itself' (Arditi 2008, 115). There is no immutable or incontestable fixed point outside of the discipline's own discourse from which to adjudicate anything that takes place within it. But what takes place within it depends on a host of variables, including preferences in terms of premises, protocols, practices, procedures, and so on. Therefore, Derrida proposes that:

> A field is determined as a field of battle because there is no metalanguage, no locus of truth outside the field, no absolute and ahistorical overhang; and this absence of overhang – in other words, the radical historicity of the field – makes the field necessarily subject to multiplicity and heterogeneity. As a result, those who are inscribed in this field are necessarily inscribed in a *polemos*, even if they have no special taste for war. There is a strategic destiny, destined to stratagem by the question raised over the truth of the field. (Derrida and Ferraris 2003, 13)

Any academic field is 'a field of battle because there is no metalanguage, no locus of truth outside the field'. This 'makes the field necessarily subject to multiplicity and heterogeneity'. Hence, when faced with divergent opinions or evaluations of any given approach, argument, assessment or experiment within a field, there can be no simple appeal to any higher authority outside the field.[6] After all, how could anyone outside of a field be universally acknowledged as existing or operating in an informed, experienced or expert enough fashion to adjudicate on what takes place within the field? Do scientists ask philosophers to adjudicate on and decide the value of their methods and findings? Do lawyers? Kant thought that all fields could be interrogated and, in a sense, audited by philosophy. But do those working in fields other than philosophy agree? Indeed, do philosophers really (still) feel entitled, informed or expert enough to do so?

Of course, there are many crossovers and connections between certain fields. Work in one discipline often incorporates elements developed in other disciplines. Economics is often heavily involved in the use of mathematics, for instance. And the academic study of visual art regularly calls upon the approaches and insights of such fields as history, philosophy, cultural theory, sociology, and so on. But such crossovers, connections or collaborations are neither entirely free, nor inevitable, nor established without a battle

---

[6] During the 1980s, much was made of the fact that such a perspective reveals that there is always an *aporia* at work in the legitimation of knowledge (Derrida 1992), a kind of ineradicable tautology, and even what Lyotard called a 'legitimation crisis in knowledge' (Lyotard 1984).

or disagreement. Rather, such connections are contingent achievements, produced either through a sense of 'obviousness' or appeals to norms (as in, 'Of course the study of art and the study of history overlap and interact') or through the effort of making the case for the validity of their connection (as in, 'Perhaps recent advances in meteorology could be applied to help us learn more about cultural dynamics').

Currently, art history rarely appeals to mathematics for justification or corroboration of the knowledge produced in its own disciplinary space. Although it is not impossible or inconceivable, any move to make the discourse or discipline of art history reliant upon mathematics – or subject to any kind of mathematical validation – would be met with considerable resistance within that field. To propose that the academic discourse around fine art, art history, and so on, *should* be subject to mathematical procedures would provoke a vehement battle. But the point to be made here is that this battle would merely be different in scale or intensity, not in kind, from the ongoing day to day disagreements within the academic study of fine art and art history around such matters as whether, say, the psychoanalytic paradigm developed in the wake of the work of Jacques Lacan is of more use to art scholars than the sociological paradigm of Pierre Bourdieu, and so on.

Again, these are battles around the question of the paradigm or paradigms that structure a field. The choice of paradigm determines the kind of questions that can be asked, the type of work that will *seem* to 'need' to be done, and the ways in which such work will be approached.

Reflecting on the ways that academic disciplines and universities work, Derrida argued that what takes place within academic discourses involves 'not an opposition between the legitimate and the illegitimate, but rather a very complicated distribution of the demands of legitimacy' (Derrida 2003, 18). At the very least, then, the determination of such matters as best versus worst is no simple matter. It does not easily come down to a clear question of whether something is 'right' or 'wrong'. For, if there is no fixed point outside of and transcending the field, then the source of the determination of such values can only come from within the field itself – from among the paradigms constructed within it.

The problem is that because there will always be more than one paradigm in play (and in process), there will be no sustained consensus arising within the field. In a sense, there are only ever shared, modified or replaced problematics, and rarely any widely held consensus about the formulation of the object, the parameters of the problem, or the framework for any exploration or method of approach.

The proposition that academic disciplines are battlegrounds may either disappoint or delight. It may disappoint those who cleave to the idea that academic disciplines principally trade in the establishment of truth about reality, and that they find out and know more and more about truth and reality as time goes on and as the discipline progresses. Conversely, the idea of disciplines as battlegrounds may appeal to others, and for any number of reasons. However, it is important to point out that the type of 'war' being formulated by Derrida here is not some Darwinian or neoliberal notion of 'survival of the fittest'. Rather, Derrida is making a claim about the inevitable and inescapable emergence of pluralities of voices, positions and styles of attempting to establish or verify things within disciplines.

This depicts a condition of incessant and interminable disagreement, in which not only are there no absolute or eternal winners, there are not even agreed criteria for determining what notions like 'survival', 'demise' or indeed 'fittest' might possibly mean. (Has hoplology 'survived'? In what way? Is it 'the fittest'? For what?) In this kind of context, there will always be more to any disagreement than one matter or one issue. Indeed, 'disagreement', in this sense, can usefully be formulated as 'less a confrontation between two established positions – as in the case of a debating society – than an engagement between "parties" that do not antedate their confrontation. A disagreement constructs the object of argumentation and the field of argumentation itself' (Arditi 2008, 115).

In academia, the mode and manner of our argumentation, as well as the very object of our attention itself, must be understood to be particular kinds of institutional constructs. Our objects are 'disciplinary objects', essentially invented within, or at least 'worked over' by, our own discourses (Mowitt 1992). Our approaches to them are constructs too. This is so even though many people seem to believe that academic disciplines and fields *just happen*, that they are born spontaneously or emerge ineluctably in response to external realities of the world. However, this is not at all the case. Academic subjects are not born, they are made.[7]

The Paradigms of Martial Arts Studies

In light of this, it is important to realise that an early and essential challenge for the nascent field of martial arts studies was always going to be the field itself. That is to say, at the same time as exploring and engaging with problematics *within* the field, it is also necessary to more clearly and indeed securely establish martial arts studies *as* a field of study, that is, as a *legitimate* field of study (Bowman 2015a; Wetzler 2015).

---

[7]   There are many accounts of these processes. See, for example, Anderson on the formation of English Literature as a global discipline (Anderson 1991), Hall on the formation of cultural studies (Hall 1992), Fabian on how anthropology constructs its objects (Fabian 1983), Chow on the invention of film studies (Chow 2007), or, perhaps most famously, Foucault on the invention of psychiatry (Foucault 1989). Indeed, as one commentator put it to me: Why *should* there be a field of martial arts studies, distinct from the wider study of movement, performance and embodied knowledge?

This matter may not seem to amount to too much of a serious problem, given the abundant empirical evidence that martial arts studies is a field that is mushrooming internationally. There are currently conferences and publications appearing in many languages in many countries. But the fact that this is happening without much in the way of a conversation about *how* to study martial arts is troubling (Bowman 2015a; Wetzler 2015; Judkins 2016a). History is littered with failed attempts to establish any kind of coherent and sustainable academic discourse of martial arts studies. As I have been suggesting, perhaps this is in large part because of a lack of sustained communal effort to forge conceptual development via cross-disciplinary dialogues.

Moreover, in the present moment, we should not forget that until very recently one of the most frequently posed questions in and around these waters was: *Will martial arts ever be a valid topic of academic study?* If today we are hearing a resounding 'Yes!', there nevertheless remain not only 'strictly academic' but also 'pressingly practical' reasons for posing such *why* and *how* questions. Different answers produce differing conceptualisations of the aim, object and field, and entail different approaches. So, we need to ask: What are our aims? Which approaches best serve such aims?

In the terms of Thomas Kuhn's now classic approach to understanding the ways that academic knowledge is produced, established and transformed, the emergent field of martial arts studies would currently be classified as 'pre-paradigmatic' (Kuhn 1962; Nicholls 2010). This is because there is little to no consensus about its objects, orientations, methodologies or approaches. Some connections, crossovers and collaborations across disciplines are being formed, thanks to newly formed research networks, conferences and increasingly visible publications, but the wider field has long been confined to discrete islands of disparate disciplinary approaches in small enclaves. So, although some scholars are now producing works that engage with the question of the approaches and paradigms of martial arts studies, there remains much that still needs to be done to establish anything like a coherent topos.[8]

There is much to be said about this. But what I principally want to emphasize in what follows – in an argument that runs contrary or transverse to many discussions and impulses in and around the field – is that *none of this entails a 'need' to define martial arts.*

---

[8] Hence the importance of the question of the paradigms of martial arts studies. From the outset, we must pluralise the question because it is evident from the range of scholarship and avenues of enquiry currently beginning to be explored across the disciplines that differing conceptualisations of both *object* and *field* emerge reciprocally with different approaches and orientations. To establish the paradigms of martial arts studies, one approach would be to map current approaches, analyse their orientations and interrogate their current and potential interconnections, in order to generate an overarching awareness of the field in its multiplicity and heterogeneity. Of course, the question that arises here is that of the map itself: What are the characteristics of the lens through which the cartographer is looking?

Against Definition

As mentioned, there is a widespread belief in and around the nascent discourses of martial arts studies that a primary and orientating task must be to *define* martial arts (Monahan 2007; Cynarski 2008; Lorge 2012, 2016; Channon and Jennings 2014; Cynarski, Sieber, and Szajna 2014). The matter of defining martial arts has also prompted some valuable recent reflections on the many problems and issues that it raises (Wetzler 2015; Judkins 2016b; Channon 2016). However, I want to intervene by arguing that this very belief and orientation harbours problems (Bowman 2015a, 2017b). More precisely, my argument is that it is actually an error to think that forging definitions must be primary, or indeed even necessary, in academic work. Often, the belief in the necessity of definition is already an effect of a tacit acceptance that a certain manner, mode or register of academic discourse must be the proper, best or necessary method. Indeed, it arguably boils down to a belief that the only or best kind of academic work is scientific, and that science starts from definitions.

There are at least two problems with this. One problem lies with any attempt to make studies of human life, culture and society emulate science. In our case, this would take the form of trying to force the study of martial arts to conform to a certain (scientistic) conception of science. For it is important to be aware that scientific approaches are neither the only nor necessarily the best, assuming they are even viable, approaches. (Must we use scientific methods to explore martial arts in/and literature, film, music, gaming, philosophy, religion, gender, identity, or politics, and so on?) The second problem relates to the idea that science starts with definitions. This involves a misunderstanding of science. Science starts from theory. Scientific method always and only boils down to the attempt to test, verify or falsify a theoretical hypothesis.[9] Such work often *seems* to involve numbers, but science does not *necessarily* involve numbers. Some statements *about* science or elements of it *involve* numbers. But what is primary in science is *theory*.

On the other hand, or at the other end of the supposed spectrum of approaches, even putatively non-scientific approaches to any subject also involve theory – whether consciously acknowledged or not, and whether the theory is postulated explicitly (to orientate the work) or whether it emerges out of the work, through different kinds of encounters with 'objects', 'things', 'processes', 'phenomena' or 'stuff' – and regardless of whether we want to call such stuff 'text', 'evidence', 'material', 'archive', 'fieldwork', 'results' or 'data'. The

---

[9] One reviewer of this chapter challenged my use of the word 'verify' here, as it jars with scientific terminology. However, I have elected to keep the word, because my thinking is more influenced by Jacques Rancière than by scientific method per se. Rancière argues that attempts to establish, prove or argue for something – anything, anywhere – ultimately involve constructing ways of trying to verify (rather than falsify) the proposition, position or belief one is supporting (see for instance Rancière 1992).

belief that such encounters, or any results or statements about any of this, necessarily or properly begins or ends with 'definition' is a misunderstanding. As such, any approach that positions the matter of how to define martial arts as if it is a primary or somehow fundamental question is misconceived or badly formed.

As Alex Channon has recently reminded us (although he argues for the utility of principled moments of definition), definitions quickly produce hierarchies, and help to erect values, borderlines, norms and exclusions (Channon 2016).

For Theory

Fortunately, early work in the recently established journal *Martial Arts Studies* has, from the outset, attempted to move beyond the (dis)orientation caused by becoming trapped in the taxonomical labours associated with defining. Issue One of *Martial Arts Studies*, for instance, contained several different efforts to conceptualise the field and to work out ways that it could profitably and productively develop (Bowman 2015b; Wetzler 2015; D.S. Farrer 2015; Barrowman 2015b). Significant among these is Sixt Wetzler's 'Martial Arts Studies as Kulturwissenschaft: A Possible Theoretical Framework' (Wetzler 2015).[10] This article is a particularly notable contribution to the field, to which I would now like to turn.

In his article, Wetzler carries out a number of important tasks. He identifies the pitfalls that can arise when academics use the object-, folk-, or practitioner-language of the practices that they are taking as their objects of study. From here, he broaches the problem of adequate academic terminology, asking: What terms should scholars use when talking about this or that aspect of martial arts in/and/as culture, politics, history or society? He then argues that academic terms should surely not be the same as the terms and concepts used by practitioners themselves, either to characterise what they do or to carve up the conceptual spectrum of categories and hierarchies. This discussion moves Wetzler into a reflection on the well-worn problems of conceptualisation and – surprise, surprise – definition.

In an important move, however, rather than arguing for or against this or that definition of martial arts, Wetzler deconstructs and reveals the limits of a range of conventional and popular categories that circulate within martial arts discourses and points to the essential impossibility of establishing fixed referential categories in these waters (Wetzler 2015, 28). He proposes instead that martial arts studies analyses should be orientated by looking for and at

---

[10] My own contribution was entitled 'Asking the Question: Is Martial Arts Studies an Academic Field?' (Bowman 2015b) In this chapter, I stopped short of explicitly addressing the question of which particular theories or approaches the field might involve (even though my preferences are surely readily inferable).

the 'dimensions of meaning' attendant to any given construct of martial arts. To this end, he proposes five plausible but always provisional dimensions of meaning: Preparation for violent conflict, play and competitive sports, performance, transcendent goals, and health care. After making a case for these dimensions and inviting others to expand or refine his conceptualisation of them, Wetzler turns to the matter of how to conceive of, frame, and conceptually manage (in order to analyse and discuss) matters of martial arts studies without falling into what Derrida would call 'metaphysical traps', what cultural theorists would call 'essentialisms', and what Wetzler himself calls pitfalls of 'lexical illusion'.

The way to avoid making conceptual mistakes, Wetzler argues, is to find an adequate theory. The one he proposes as valid and viable for martial arts studies is Even-Zohar's polysystem theory. Wetzler quotes the following important passage from Even-Zohar:

> Systems are not equal, but hierarchized within the polysystem. It is the permanent struggle between the various strata … which constitutes the (dynamic) synchronic state of the system. It is the victory of one stratum over another which constitutes the change on the diachronic axis. In this centrifugal vs. centripetal motion, phenomena are driven from the centre to the periphery while, conversely, phenomena may push their way into the centre and occupy it. However, with a polysystem one must not think in terms of one centre and one periphery, since several such positions are hypothesized. A move may take place, for instance, whereby a certain item (element, function) is transferred from the periphery of one system to the periphery of an adjacent system within the same polysystem, and then may or may not move on to the centre of the latter. (Even-Zohar 1990, 13-14, quoted in Wetzler 2015, 28-29)

Wetzler goes on to explain how this theoretical paradigm might be used in martial arts studies:

> Transferred to the development of the Asian martial arts in Western culture within recent decades, this means: The total realm of the martial arts is the polysystem in question, which can itself be understood as a system within the ultimate polysystem 'culture'. The cultural meaning of the polysystem 'martial arts' is not monolithic, but instead consists of several systems that each have their own relevance within the polysystem. Such systems might be 'use for self-defence' or 'preferred way of combat for the silver screen', while the 'items' that occupy these systems are the individual martial arts styles. (Wetzler 2015, 28)

Furthermore, the theory seems to offer ways to conceptually grasp change within and across systems. Wetzler continues:

To clarify with an example: Upon its arrival in the West, karate was perceived mostly for the *Dimension 1: Preparation for Violent Conflict*, and thus at the centre of the system 'self-defence'. However, it has been driven to the periphery of 'self-defence' by other styles, especially by wing chun, which was then in turn driven from the centre by krav maga. Regarding the perception of *Dimension 2: Play and Competitive Sports*, karate was again driven from a centre, this time of the category 'tough combat sport', in this case by kickboxing, which was replaced by Muay Thai, which was replaced by MMA. However, not all is lost for karate. When the style held the centre of the self-defence system, it also had a connotation of being a pastime for bullies and hooligans. While losing the centres of those systems karate was able to gain ground in the systems including 'martial arts for pedagogical purposes' and 'self-perfection by Eastern practices' (both systems obviously representing *Dimension 4: Transcendent Goals*), whose centres it shares today with other Japanese budo styles, along with yoga, qigong, and various meditation practices in the second case. (Wetzler 2015, 28)

Wetzler's ensuing discussion of the insights that such an approach opens up is extremely suggestive and rewarding – even though it does not broach the matter of how anyone might ever establish what is at the 'centre', 'periphery' or other 'position' of this or that 'system' – *all* of which will surely *always* be in question. Nonetheless, it has already generated (or at least enriched) some highly significant work, most notably in the form of Benjamin N. Judkins' recent study of the *Star Wars* inspired phenomenon of Lightsaber combat (Judkins 2016a).

Using the 'five dimensions of meaning' that Wetzler proposes can be associated with martial arts practices in different configurations at different times and in different places, Judkins easily demonstrates that the perhaps unlikely pastime of Lightsaber combat training can in fact entirely reasonably be classed as a martial art. This is so even though such a conclusion might surprise or dismay certain scholars of martial arts and even if many of Lightsaber combat's own practitioners would not feel entirely comfortable making such a claim.

Judkins' approach to the quite possibly controversial example of Lightsaber combat, informed by Wetzler's intentionally rigorous (looking) framework, has the benefit of challenging quite a few different positions – including, most importantly, any essentialist or 'referentialist' approach that proceeds on the assumption that something is a martial art if it is somehow 'obviously' a martial art. So, such works as these by Wetzler and Judkins – along with the arguably even more radical approach taken in the recent work of Chris Goto-Jones, who argues that certain kinds of computer gaming can become martial arts practices (Goto-Jones 2016) – are all valuable, and not least because they foreground the limitations of any hasty attempt to *define* martial arts. Moreover, not only do such approaches all problematize the impulse to rush to definitions, they also do so without sidestepping or avoiding the issue of how to specify and handle martial arts as an object of academic attention.

For my purposes, a key value in this work is the demonstration of the primacy and productivity of theory before definition. Such frameworks clearly exceed the frames and orientations of hoplology, for instance, which is mired in inessential preconceptions and doxa. As such, it is in full support of Wetzler's efforts and in broad agreement with the orientations of such scholars that my present contribution to this debate about definition and theory aspires to be read. This is so even though my own contribution does involve criticisms of Wetzler's proposed theoretical paradigm for martial arts studies. But these are less like fundamental disagreements and more like questions for further consideration. Importantly, any criticisms I have will neither be 'anti-theory' nor 'pro-definition'. Rather, in what follows, I seek less to disagree with Wetzler and more to point out some potential pitfalls and problems attendant to any avoidance of theory or insistence on definition in martial arts studies.

Defining Problems: Relationality before Definition

A well-known part of the problem that arises when trying to define the objects or foci of martial arts studies is semiotic openness, slippage, instability and the incessant ongoing changes that take place across cultures, communities, societies, technologies and practices. Wetzler tackles this by proposing a framework for structuring academic enquiry and proffering a set of theoretical terms for grasping what he represents as 'systemic' but what I would prefer to call *discursive* change. I prefer to approach the world in terms of the language of *texts* and *discourses* rather than elements, functions, systems/polysystems, and so on, for ontological reasons that boil down to the primacy (proposed by poststructuralist theory) of *relationality* rather than notions of 'system' or even 'systematicity'. As Derrida writes of 'system':

> If by 'system' is meant – and this is the minimal sense of the word – a sort of consequence, coherence and insistence – a certain gathering together – there is an injunction to the system that I have never renounced, and never wished to. This can be seen in the recurrence of motifs and references from one text to another in my work, despite the differing occasions and pretexts … 'System', however, in a philosophical sense that is more rigorous and perhaps more modern, can also be taken to mean a totalization in the configuration, a continuity of all statements, a *form* of coherence (not coherence itself), involving the syllogicity of logic, a certain *syn* which is no longer simply that of gathering in general, but rather of the assemblage of *ontological* propositions. In that case deconstruction, without being anti-systematic, is on the contrary, and nevertheless, not only a search for, but itself a consequence of, the fact

that the system is impossible; it often consists, regularly or recurrently, in making appear – in each alleged system, in each self-interpretation of and by a system – a force of dislocation, a limit in the totalization, a limit in the movement of syllogistic synthesis. Deconstruction is not a method for discovering that which resists the system; it consists, rather, in remarking, in the reading and interpretation of texts, that what has made it possible for philosophers to effect a system is nothing other than a certain dysfunction or 'disadjustment', a certain incapacity to close the system. Wherever I have followed this investigative approach, it has been a question of showing that the system does not work, and that this dysfunction not only interrupts the system but itself accounts for the desire for system, which draws its *élan* from this very disadjoin-ment, or disjunction. On each occasion, the disjunction has a privileged site in that which one calls a philosophical *corpus*. Basically, deconstruc-tion as I see it is an attempt to train the beam of analysis onto this dis-jointing link. (Derrida 2003, 3-4)

Systems fail to be systematic; system is impossible. This also accounts for the desire for it, and the possibility of the deconstruction of it. Adding 'poly' to the word 'system' does not solve, resolve or dissolve the matter. Pluralizing merely defers acknowledging the fact that there may be no system other than in the 'lexical illusion' of the eye that wishes to perceive/believe that there is system-atic organisation and some kind of systematic process at work, even if we can only ever 'discover' (invent) it afterwards.

As an alternative to what Derrida would call 'metaphysical' thinking about systems, the poststructuralist notions of *text* and *discourse* provide alternative concepts, metaphors, vocabularies and paradigms (Laclau and Mouffe 1985; Mowitt 1992; Bowman 2007). Key here are the notions of *relation* or relation-ality, on the one hand, and *force*, on the other. It seems worthwhile to discuss these notions further, as they are important dimensions, but they are currently undeveloped, or at best underdeveloped, in Wetzler's proposed framework for analysis in martial arts studies.

To start with the matter of relation first: Can an identity ever be said to be anything other than relational? As Ernesto Laclau and Chantal Mouffe argued in the 1980s, 'identities are purely relational' so 'there is no identity which can be fully constituted' (Laclau and Mouffe 1985, 111; Bowman 2007, 18-19). Already this kind of perspective, with origins in Saussurean linguistics and semiotics, problematizes the notion of 'elements' within a 'system' and replaces the notion of 'entities with identities' with a much more fluid sense of their ongoing incompletion and irreducible contextuality.

Almost two decades after his influential 1985 monograph with Chantal Mouffe, in a dispute with Slavoj Žižek about politics and society, Laclau was still making the same arguments. In response to Žižek's now infamous (and what Laclau always regarded as ill-thought-through) adoption of a kind of crude

Marxist and quick Leninist position on the question of how to make radical political change in the world, Laclau argued that:

> We gain very little, once identities are conceived as complexly articulated collective wills, by referring to them through simple designations such as classes, ethnic groups and so on, which are at best names for transient points of stabilization. The really important task is to understand the logics of their constitution and dissolution, as well as the formal determinations of the spaces in which they interrelate. (Butler, Laclau, and Žižek 2000, 53)

Laclau pitched his argument about how to approach political entities, identities and processes in terms of the vocabulary and concerns of a poststructuralist and post-Marxist political theory, whose essential proposition runs like this: Because everything – and by 'everything' what is meant is *everything* – can be seen to be *contingent* and hence *conventional*, *everything* is therefore to be regarded as irreducibly *political* (Arditi and Valentine 1999; Marchart 2007).

There is much to be said about this argument (Bowman 2007, 2008). I return to it here not just as a rejoinder to Wetzler's metaphorical invocation of the putatively non-metaphorical notion of 'system' but also because I believe it is vital (and vitalising) to try, as Laclau urges us, 'to understand the logics of [the] constitution and dissolution [of entities and identities], as well as the formal [or informal] determinations of the spaces in which they interrelate'.

This is important not least because, if 'identities' can also be understood as 'complexly articulated collective wills', then to understand either 'wills' or 'identities' as arising 'systematically' could have a problematic impact on the way we understand such important matters as (for example) political struggle. Stated bluntly, to rely on polysystem theory might cause us to follow a line of thinking in which political struggles and political identities come to be conceived as somehow merely being the systematic unfolding of some kind of predetermined plan.

This is why the notion of *force* is also key. Entities and identities are not just matters of signification, or of systems, but also of force. Force is the other side of signification, a key part of the process of establishing meaning (Protevi 2001). This is why Laclau believes we should not be content with the moment of referring to entities and identities 'through simple designations such as classes, ethnic groups and so on': Because such terms 'are at best names for transient points of stabilization'. In other words, signification should not be studied in isolation from considerations of force.[11]

---

[11] Laclau's use of the word 'stabilization' here is significant. It seems to owe something to the fact that Derrida once emphasised the importance of the ideas of stabilization and destabilization in a published conversation with Laclau in the 1990s (Mouffe 1996). In his response to Laclau and others, Derrida said: 'All that a deconstructive point of view tries to show, is that since convention, institutions and consensus are stabilizations (sometimes stabilizations of great duration, sometimes micro-stabilizations), this means that they are stabilizations of something

So, Laclau's broadly deconstructive perspective challenges us to think about the *making* or *establishment* of any identity in a way that exceeds the lexical illusion of systematicity and emphasizes instead the complexity of contingent processes of articulation (Laclau 1994). This differentiated perspective – which replaces ideas of structures and systems with those of iteration, reiteration, dissemination, dislocation, and so on – forms the main part of my critique of the use of polysystem theory in martial arts studies, or at least my critique of Wetzler's advocation of it. However, to reiterate, making such a critique is not my primary aim here. Wetzler is a sparring partner, not an opponent. Rather, the matters that I ultimately want to challenge are somewhat different.

Changing Discourses

Specifically, I want to point out that Laclau's approach to discourse analysis involves rather different investments than thinking about the *academic definition* of any activity, entity or identity. Indeed, although Laclau's argument here includes the injunction that academics be rigorous and forensic in their conceptual grasp of their key terms, *it is not limited to this injunction.* Moreover, the position Laclau advocates does not merely involve the endless or supposedly 'useless' *problematizing* of terms (something deconstruction was once regularly accused of), whether to try to reconfigure and refine the definitions and distinctions that academics use in their work or those that practitioners use in their practice, *or* to show them to be impossible.

Rather, for Laclau – and indeed for the overwhelming majority of works of cultural theory developed through and since the 1980s – the fundamental point to be taken on board is not that *we* should work out how best to define something; it is rather that we must face up to the fact that 'things' are neither simply nor necessarily 'things', that all identities are at root contingent discursive *achievements*, or *establishments*, or – to use Laclau's words, 'transient points of stabilization'.[12]

---

essentially unstable and chaotic. Thus it becomes necessary to stabilize precisely because stability is not natural; it is because there is instability that stabilization becomes necessary; it is because there is chaos that there is a need for stability. Now, this chaos and instability, which is fundamental, founding and irreducible, is at once naturally the worst against which we struggle with laws, rules, conventions, politics and provisional hegemony, but at the same time it is a chance, a chance to change, to destabilize. If there were continual stability, there would be no need for politics, and it is to the extent that stability is not natural, essential or substantial, that politics exists and ethics is possible. Chaos is at once a risk and a chance, and it is here that the possible and the impossible cross each other' (Derrida 1996, 84).

[12] Accordingly, given that 'martial arts studies' takes its very name and focus ('martial arts') from what Wetzler deems to be the dubious and problematic realm of 'object language', there can therefore be no 'metalanguage' that is not contaminated by this fact. As Laclau and Mouffe argued in the 1980s, because there is never anything like a fixed centre, stable system or simple outside, there can be no metalanguage (1985).

Moreover, our shared use of a term like 'martial arts' or 'system' stabilizes *our* discourse. But it can also impose and project a fixed view – our present view – of all sorts of dimensions of culture and society, both backwards in time and outwards across different linguistic, geographical, cultural, religious and social contexts. So, the establishment of a shared and stable term has its benefits (predication and communication being among them). But it inevitably also comes at a cost – which we might render in a number of ways, including projection, simplification, hypostatisation, generalisation, transformation, or even cultural, conceptual or linguistic imperialism.

Wetzler calls this 'lexical illusion', as in: We say 'martial arts' in English here today, but did or do they say or mean anything like it there (elsewhere) or then (elsewhen), without difference or remainder? Or are we misrecognising the things 'out there' (and 'then') that we talk about in our terms, here and now? As an example, consider how frequently it is currently said that 'mindfulness meditation' has been practiced within Eastern movement traditions and martial arts for millennia. (Before we heard this claim being made about mindfulness, we heard the same claim being made about qigong [Palmer 2007]. And before that, it was said about yoga [Spatz 2015]. And so on.) Such propositions are all based on acts of fantasy and projection, back into a fantasized notion of 'long, *long* ago' (Fabian 1983).

Such acts of projection are clearly faulty. They also have any number of potential ideological dimensions and material and discursive effects. Consider a second example. On a tour I was given during a visit to the new Mecca of Taekwondo in South Korea, the Taekwondowon, our guide pointed to a picture of an old statue and said, 'Look, this is a statue of someone doing taekwondo. That posture comes from taekwondo'. The facts that (a) taekwondo was only invented in the 1950s (Gillis 2008; Moenig 2015) and (b) its patterns, or kata, were only subsequently changed from the Japanese martial arts from which it was derived would seem to problematize the idea that an ancient statue could possibly depict a taekwondo posture. The possibility that the taekwondo posture might have been invented deliberately to depict the ancient statue in order to strengthen the ideological claim that taekwondo is ancient was not really encouraged or entertained at all.[13]

Entities and identities are discursive achievements, produced through efforts and institutions, arguments, articulations, demonstrations, and indeed processes and acts of institution (where 'institution' is to be read as both noun and verb). What something 'is' emerges through forceful – often enforced – processes of narration and representation. 'Mindfulness' is an entirely modern construct. 'Taekwondo' is no older than the 1950s. The resignification of such

---

[13] After my visit, I blogged about this here: https://goo.gl/FXVF6T. I also went on to discuss it in 'Making Martial Arts History Matter' (Bowman 2016) and in *Mythologies of Martial Arts* (Bowman 2017b).

institutions as ancient is an effect of the contingent but motivated modes and manners of their discursive articulation and emergence.

Optimistic Relations

Theoretically, I have revisited some broadly poststructuralist points (all too) briefly here because I believe that remembering and taking into consideration these lessons in our various ongoing research projects into martial arts – and the international development of the field of martial arts studies – will allow us to move on, and specifically to move on from a certain kind of fixation on definition. (Neither Wetzler nor Judkins suffers from this fixation, however, and my comments about the problems with definition, though inspired in part by engagements with their work, are not directed towards either of these scholars.)

I am drawing attention back to poststructuralist theory because, rather than orientating and habituating us into an academic life of taxonomical labours centred on defining and demarcating, such approaches proceed from the proposition that identities are always irreducibly relational and incomplete, and hence contingent, open and ongoing. Identities are constituted by and within discourses, and they always emerge as points in clusters of moving constellations of related, contiguous, cognate, differentiated, associated, contrasting and oppositional terms, in all kinds of possible relations – linguistic, semiotic, lived, institutional, academic, legislative, and so on.

One point to be emphasised again is the role not just of lexical illusion but also of force within the construction of entities and identities. Whether using what Wetzler terms object language or what Derrida terms metalanguage, we always think through and with inherited terms, and hence conceptual differentials and differentiations – inheritances that we are more or less forced to work with and, to some degree, within (Derrida 1976).[14]

---

[14] Nonetheless, as Saussure taught us, when we are thinking about our linguistically instituted categories, first and foremost we must remember that there are only 'differences without positive terms'. Moreover, as Derrida went on to demonstrate, there are no easily specifiable or simply stable referents 'behind' these differences. The flipside of signification is force (Protevi 2001). There is no stability in signification without force. Furthermore, as Gayatri Spivak added, the institution of any difference in the production of an identity in discourse, the drawing of any demarcation that distinguishes and hierarchizes entities and identities, is essentially and irreducibly a *political* act, with more or less overtly political consequences (Spivak 1990, 1993). (Such poststructuralists sometimes even formulate dimensions of this in terms of violence [Bowman 2010a]. This means that, if we were to follow this logic through to one of its conclusions, it would become possible to argue that more or less any identity is in some sense 'martial' (it has either been fought for or fought against), as well as stabilized but conflictual.) Within martial arts studies, quite what these acts and their consequences may be remains to be seen. But hopefully such reflections as this may cause some hesitation, and possibly reorientation, before the battles continue over this or that 'correct' definition. I return to this point at the end of this chapter.

Now, although I am critical of the scramble for definitions, nonetheless, it strikes me that the growing prominence of the matter of definition does attest to a lot that is promising in the current stage of development of martial arts studies. It is evidently a reflection of the drive to found and ground and legitimate and build the field rigorously, and according to proper academic protocols. To this extent, despite the scientist features of some forays into this new terrain, our current moment is of great significance. So, we may be optimistic. However, in the current rush to try to define and establish 'things', there is always the risk that we labour under misapprehensions. My concern is that some of the misapprehensions we see arising today may come to constitute an obstacle or impediment in the development of the field tomorrow, pushing it towards becoming something dominated by what Žižek once termed 'naïve empiricism' or 'naïve cognitivism' (Žižek 2001a). Decades before Žižek, Derrida too had worried about something similar, which he called 'incompetent' and even 'irresponsible' empiricism (Derrida 2001).

What such thinkers mean in making claims like 'empiricism is naïve, incompetent, or even *irresponsible*' – is that there is a kind of untenable idealism and simplicity at the heart of approaches that begin from the premise that to make sense of the world we should simply look around us, focus on things, classify them and count them, and that, through a process of testing and disputing around categories, we might eventually get at the truth of reality and get it right. Their more or less opposite opinion is that, on the contrary, what we all always need is an explicit theory. I say *explicit* theory, and not just 'theory', because, arguably, everyone always has a theory, even if they don't consciously know what it is. By 'explicit theory' I am referring to anything from an overarching theory of ontology to an actively thought-through image or sense (to use Laclau's terms again) of how discourses and identities are constituted and the logics of their processes of establishment, stabilization, interaction, transformation, and dissolution.[15]

It is in this sense that I am arguing for more theory, an injection of theory, and the permeation of theory, before definition. But I am not proposing a return to the intellectual battles of the 1980s and 1990s, in which the introduction of Continental Philosophy into the humanities led to a state of trench warfare between those who 'did theory' and those who 'did empirical work' (Hall 2002). Furthermore, although I am arguing explicitly 'for theory', I want to be clear that I am certainly not therefore arguing 'against empirical work', or 'history', or 'reality', or anything like that.

Rather, I want to insist that it will be vital and vitalising for work in martial arts studies to embrace certain aspects of cultural theory, especially when – as in the current moment – people seem to feel an apparent '*need*' *to do something*

---

[15]   I use the word 'sense' here because I think that we can only ever get an image, sense or feeling for ontology anyway. I hesitate to say 'structure of feeling', though, for, as Derrida himself made clear, the very idea, term, notion or (possible) concept of 'structure' is rarely ever much more than a metaphor anyway.

properly academic, a need that so many people seem to believe is to be interpreted as *defining our object*. For, faced with the (apparent) challenge of 'needing' to define, as we have already seen, with even the tiniest bit of theory, we are able to pause to reflect on the fact that *before definition there is relation*. Words and meanings and practices and values travel and twist and turn and change and move in relation to larger and other forces and processes. These may or may not be systemic, systematic (Wetzler, Even-Zohar), conjunctural (Hall), discursive processes of articulation (Laclau), or 'dislocated', 'out of joint' or even 'hauntological' (Derrida 1994), and so on.

All such theories would concur that martial arts will always be relationally determined. Laclau and Mouffe theorised this in terms of 'discourse' and 'articulation' (Laclau and Mouffe 1985). Hall insisted on the need to establish a sense of what he called the 'conjuncture'; according to him, any analysis requires what he called 'conjunctural analysis' – that is, an analysis informed by an acute awareness of the historical moment and context as well as the forces and relations that produced it. Without this, we cannot really know or understand anything about any entity or identity, whether martial arts, class, ethnicity, or any other kind of identity or entity in process.

Of course, there may be many ways to characterise and analyse a conjuncture. As deconstruction sought to teach us, no context is ever fully closed (Derrida 1988). We might never know for sure that we know for sure everything salient about a context or a conjuncture. Maybe we can't really know for sure that we know anything at all for sure. Yet, what we can do is attempt to assess a context in terms of forces and relations, relative weights and gravities, and the ways in which forces and fields constitute, colour and condition entities, identities and practices. This may not be too far from Wetzler's proposed use of Even-Zohar's polysystem theory – or it may be a world away.

Alternative Discourses

In this chapter, I have so far proposed the necessity of theory for martial arts studies and entered into a critique of one proposed branch of theory. I have done so because part of what needs to be theorised is the orientation of the discipline's discourse, and I would prefer to steer that discourse as far away from anything approaching scientism as possible. My chief criticism of the tropes of 'systems' would be that this approach risks pointing the discourse of martial arts studies back towards a scientistic orientation.

Given this criticism, an obvious question is what, therefore, my proposed alternative approach would be. My answer relates to my ongoing arguments from poststructuralism about the need for attention not just to signification ('dimensions of meaning') but also to force, as in the forms of different relations to and entanglements within different kinds of social, cultural, economic and other forms of power.

In Britain, Raymond Williams long ago proposed that it is possible to formulate and look at entities, practices and identities and to assess them in terms of whether they are *dominant, residual* or *emergent,* and to ask whether they may be acting in ways that are either in line with a *dominant* or *hegemonic* ideology, or whether they may be *alternative* or even *oppositional* to such an ideology (Williams 1977). This may seem like quite an old and crude paradigm. This kind of approach has certainly been significantly refined and developed over the decades (Laclau and Mouffe 1985; Laclau 1994; Butler, Laclau, and Žižek 2000). But I draw attention to this seminal paradigm here because, even as simple as it is, it offers a viable and flexible framework through which many different kinds of studies of martial arts and society might be initiated. All of these are happily liberated from the stifling imperative to define and demarcate without any real sense or sensitivity to the complexities of matters of time, place and the interplay of forces that both produce and transform meanings, practices and contexts.

To illustrate the value of this framework, we might quickly consider one final example: The deliciously marginal or problematic case of taijiquan. Using Williams' approach, we will be able to reconfigure discourse and debate about taijiquan from a sclerotic fixation on the question of whether it can even be 'defined' as a martial art or a combat sport, or self-defence, or a form of what we now insist on calling 'mindfulness meditation', etc., and to an understanding of what 'taijiquan' *has been* and *has done* and *might be* and *might do* in a given conjuncture.[16]

As Douglas Wile has argued, taijiquan *emerged* in a discursive foment in which China was threatened ideologically, economically and politically (Wile 1996). Its 19th Century proponents elaborated its philosophy along obscurely yet immanently nationalist lines, so that taijiquan came to stand in stark opposition to any and all things Western or European (see also Lorge 2016). In this process, *residual* Taoist ideas and principles were mixed into a growing *alternative* worldview that was *oppositional* to everything supposedly non-Chinese. This is also precisely why Maoism tolerated taijiquan, of course, and why it 'survived' the Cultural Revolution: It amounted in its elaboration to a collective, combined, non-Western, non-competitive, non-individualistic calisthenics avowedly rooted in a non-religious worldview. But this was 'survival' via a formalisation that amounted therefore to a mutation on a genetic level. So, in a sense, post-Mao, the term taijiquan essentially had a transformed meaning referring to a transformed practice (Frank 2006).

In its journey to the West, as we know, taijiquan was ostensibly deracinated from any nationalistic inflection or valence, and became articulated to

---

[16] Note again the way that we now 'see' 'mindfulness' everywhere, from meditation in modern America to martial arts in ancient China, even though even a few years ago we wouldn't have seen *anything* as mindfulness, anywhere, because no one, other than a few specialists, was using the term.

(connected with) a range of open-ended discursive configurations or conjunctures, from the counterculture to new age ideology and onwards into therapeutic and even medical culture (Frank 2006). In all this, it becomes differently articulated or constructed at different times and places, often existing with utterly contradictory and heterogeneous (non-systemic, non-systematic) partial, immanent or potential meanings at the same time. Furthermore, any of those involved in taijiquan in any of its different times and places will believe themselves to be either or both learning a martial art, either or both for sport or for self-defence, and/or involved in healthful calisthenics, and/or preserving or changing a culture, and/or involved in a religious or mystical practice. And so on.

We can multiply our examples to look at the ways in which certain words and moves have drifted and disseminated and flipped and mutated all over the place, around the world, through time and space, and examine the processes of their emergence and development within each new context, the ways they become mixed up and mixed in with existing concerns and outlooks, and reciprocally modify and move existing situations. This may or may not be systemic or systematic.

I have mainly referred to the theoretical models of people like Laclau, Derrida, Hall and Williams here. And I have done so mainly because I believe that there is – to a greater or lesser extent – a kind of theoretical ontology that connects their outlooks, despite their many other differences. This outlook is essentially poststructuralist or postfoundationalist (Sedgwick 2003).[17] And as much as many people may still have a distaste for so-called 'high theory', I maintain that martial arts studies will only benefit from a sustained engagement with what there is to be learned from high theory – as much as there is to be learned from engaging with the most intimate ethnography, the most detailed historiography, the most multi-layered sociology, and so on.

Some of the first lessons relevant to us here would relate to an awareness of the slippage and vicissitudes of signification that require us to pay very close attention to the shifting and drifting apparent referents of our focus, their different meanings in different times and places, the genetic mutations and quantum leaps that occur in 'cultural translation' from one time to another, one place to another, one language to another, even one utterance or instance to the next, and the rather frustrating fact that, despite our eternal desire to see unity and simplicity, cultures and practices are always 'in bits', always in process, incomplete, disputed and contested. There is no unity to the lexical illusion that guides us, whether it be martial arts, combat sports, self-defence, culture or society – apart from that which seems to be conferred by the use of such terms themselves.

---

[17] Interestingly, Sedgwick (2003) also sees an affinity between poststructuralist and Buddhist ontologies, and she ponders whether she is drawn to the former because of her interest in the latter or to the latter because of her agreement with the former.

Discussing such entities often has much in common with discussing unicorns, fairies, justice, Father Christmas, or how many angels might fit on the head of a pin or through the eye of a needle. Discussing such things can create a 'reality effect' that can lead people to believe these are actually existing real and unitary things (Bowman 2012). All meanings, all practices, are stabilizations. The questions to be asked then surely include explorations of why certain stabilizations take place at certain times in certain ways, why some people often become so fixated on fixation or stuck on stabilization, and what it is that both stabilization and destabilization are 'doing' in any given context at any given time.

The Stabilization of Martial Arts

Martial arts as a cluster of familiar ideas, motifs, images, and as a category has certainly achieved stabilization in contemporary discourses, even if it lacks both precision and a stable referent. Nonetheless, it is a relatively stable term – perhaps no more or less stable or precise than any other familiar term, such as 'society', for instance. That is to say, despite its familiarity, the term 'society' could have a number of different conceptualisations and configurations, and it could mean different things within different configurations.

This 'semiotic openness' around even the most familiar terms is interesting. Even more interesting is the fact that the most widespread scholarly response to semiotic openness and instability is not to embrace it and explore it, but rather to try to close it down and eradicate it, by such strategies as imposing definitions and insisting upon strictly demarcated meanings. Such responses seek to eradicate or banish predicative instability, in order to try to be clear. Accordingly, such an impulse is understandable. Nonetheless, one problem with it is that academic definitions and strict meanings often give short shrift to the ways that terms actually circulate and function in the discourses of the everyday lives of the people who use the terms out there in the world. Consequently, this form of stabilization may come to be problematic, especially if we are indeed interested in the things as they exist 'out there' rather than as they might be made to seem to exist within a scholarly discourse.

Of course, the meanings and definitions generated in scholarly discourse often come to inform, enrich and even transform the meanings of terms as they circulate in wider cultural discourse. But self-reflexive scholarship ought to interrogate this relation rather than just assume everything is straightforward. It may turn out to be valuable to work out where a term and its meaning came from – was it inherited from 'folk' or 'popular' discourse, or was it generated in a laboratory, so to speak? And what are the consequences of either inheritance? There is always drift and condensation and displacement going on. We think through and with inherited terms, and hence conceptual differentials and differentiations, that we are more or less compelled to work with and within (Derrida 1976). But, as Saussure taught us, when we are thinking about our linguistically instituted categories, first and foremost we must remember that there are only 'differences without positive terms'. Moreover, as Derrida went on to point out, there are no easily specifiable or simply stable referents 'behind' these differences. The flipside of signification is force (Protevi 2001). There is no stability in signification without force. Furthermore, as Gayatri Spivak added, the institution of any difference in the production of an identity in discourse, the drawing of any demarcation that distinguishes and hierarchizes entities and identities, is essentially and irreducibly a *political* act, with more or less overtly political consequences (Spivak 1990, 1993). But what is being stabilized, and in what ways? This question supplements the next chapter.

CHAPTER 3

Martial Arts and Media Supplements

Martial Bodies

As described in the previous chapter, when we speak of martial arts, we are never referring to a simple, stable or fixed entity. Rather, 'martial arts' is a constellation conjured up from clusters of ideas that play, drift, transfer across and transform within different media. Our senses of martial arts refer to what early semioticians like Roland Barthes might have termed 'martial art-ness' (Barthes 1972; Bowman 2017b; Wetzler 2017; Judkins 2017), and this derives from key coordinates of a contemporary cultural discourse: Reiterated images, signs, tropes, conventions, clichés, and of course innovations, interminglings and hybridizations, moving from one medium to another, across geographical, linguistic, generic and other borders.

Perhaps the key anchor (or what theorists from Jacques Lacan to Ernesto Laclau called the key '*point de capiton*' [Laclau and Mouffe 1985]) in discourses about martial arts is *the body* – or rather, a range of contingent, conventional, motivated or interested constructions of the body. Certainly, the notion of 'the body' has an overdetermined relation as both foundation and keystone of 'martial arts'. The body is seemingly *always* implied in the term 'martial arts'. This is so even though a long and powerful line of thought, from Sun Tzu's *The Art of War* to Chris Hables-Gray's *Postmodern War* and beyond, all but ignores the individual body and focuses only on all of the other technical, technological, tactical, logistical, strategic, political and ideological arts of war-craft (Gray 1997; see also Cooling et al. 1972 and Turner 1997). Yet, when we evoke 'martial arts' today, the term almost always implies the body.

We should pause to reflect on this contemporary configuration of meaning. Has the term 'martial arts' really always referred to the body? Or is this a false universal – an example of a false sense of eternality that Althusser regarded as the very definition of an ideological view? Of course, we might nonetheless note that, even in works that seem to take a far broader view of the art of

How to cite this book chapter:
Bowman, P. 2019. *Deconstructing Martial Arts*. Pp. 61–73. Cardiff: Cardiff University Press. DOI: https://doi.org/10.18573/book1.d. License: CC-BY-NC-ND 4.0

the martial, the body is not actually absent (Gray 1997). It is always strongly implied. And if there is always reference to a martial body when martial arts are evoked then we might enquire into the forms that the martial body takes.

Studies of the figures of what we might call 'the martial body' as they emerge and circulate in different discursive contexts would be extremely rewarding. To refer this back to my argument in the previous chapter, I would propose that exploring such constructions and figurations would be more worthwhile in martial arts studies than the production of any more definitional lists and hierarchies of what supposedly is and what supposedly is not a martial art. For, if we were to pick out the contour lines of the discursive figures, configurations and representations of martial bodies in different contexts, then we would be able to reflect on how these constructions reflect back on or illuminate the contexts in which they were produced. Or, put differently, such textual analyses might help us glean more about the ideological contexts and discourses within which the texts and figures have been produced – much more so than dreaming up and trading in disputations around definitions.

Figures and figurations of the martial body are multiple. Yet, they may not be all that numerous. Figures of the martial artist vary from place to place, but they frequently include the following familiar figures and forms. First, within Western orientalist discourses, we have the martial artist as the oriental (Iwamura 2005; Frank 2006). Then, we have the martial artist as the soldier, police officer, or agent of the law (Chong 2012; Bowman 2015a; Barrowman 2015a, 2019). (This figure appears in many, perhaps even *all*, cultures). Also, the martial artist as underdog is a staple of both Hollywood and Hong Kong traditions (Morris 2001). Then there is the martial artist as the wanderer or drifter (Bowman 2013b). We also have the figure of the woman warrior, from Yim Wing Chun to Buffy the Vampire Slayer and beyond (Funnell 2014; Channon and Matthews 2015). And then the warrior monk, a figure that has been much appropriated in Western orientalist texts and discourses but who is not exclusive to them, as it is also popular in Eastern cultural texts and discourses (Iwamura 2005). We also have the gangster, whether triad, yakuza, mafia, or generic 'hard man' (Park 2010). And a cluster of intermingling figures that might be called the shaolin ninja Jedi superhuman, along with the cousin species, the superhero (Judkins 2016a; Goto-Jones 2016). There is also, of course, the competitor, ideally the Olympic athlete (Channon 2012), and the bodybuilder (at least in the modern Western imaginary the martial body has long been connected with athleticism, which itself has even longer been connected with often impossible images of mesomorphism [Spatz 2015; see also Krug 2001]). Then, conversely, the flipside of the hyper-visible martial body: The invisible man or woman, the surprising, unexpected expert, who has skill without physical markings, the master of pure technique rather than muscular hypertrophy.

There is also another figure that interests me quite a lot: The Janus-faced figure of the martial artist who also amounts to a kind of psychiatric patient-in-waiting. I am thinking here of the 'troubled' or 'damaged' figure who needs the 'therapy' of pugilistic training to be 'saved' (think of a figure like Robert Downey Jr. here, whom I have written about before [Bowman 2017b]). But, at the same time (on the opposite face of the Janus-mask), we also have the supposedly serene hippy, the new ager, or the modern mindfulness practitioner, moving and meditating via taiji and qigong but whose need for such practices ultimately suggests the presence of a previous or underlying problem – for who needs therapeutic practices to attain serenity unless serenity has been missing or lacking? (I reflect on the problematic discourse of 'martial arts as therapy' more extensively in my book *Mythologies of Martial Arts* [2017].)

The figures on this surely incomplete list might be categorised and organised in many ways, perhaps clustered into three groups. First, people in films; second, people of moral fibre; third, degenerates. Such a grouping seems apt to conclude or summarise the list – encompassing as it does, first, media or representational simulacra; second, figures of supposed social improvement; and third, supposed agents of social decay. And if the figure of the martial body can encompass such a range then it should be possible to pose and test many hypotheses about whether martial arts are (to be) regarded as socially righteous or socially deleterious, and also to come up with any number of possible conclusions.

Martial Movements

However, being attentive to the construction of such figures via reiterations and reconfigurations of imagery and textual features that travel across cultures and across media suggests that the study of martial arts requires a different kind of attention. One kind of attention would be the approach that Rey Chow proposed in her 1995 essay 'Film as Ethnography; or, Translation between Cultures in the Postcolonial World' (Chow 1995). In this essay, Chow advanced both a theory and a method that she proposed any scholar of film, cultural, media or literary studies concerned with questions of cultural crossovers or cultural translation should take on board.

To develop it, Chow reads (among other things) Walter Benjamin's essay 'The Task of the Translator' (Benjamin 1999) with a view to instituting premises and protocols of cultural analysis that grasp from the outset the extent to which 'translation between cultures' already takes place a great deal of the time in our 'postmodern', media-saturated 'postcolonial world'. Crucially, Chow proposes that translation between cultures takes place neither simply nor even primarily by way of conscious or linguistic translation. Rather, *cultural* translation, in the sense Chow conceives it, proceeds by way of the movement across borders and from context to context and media to media of material objects, commodities, techniques, technologies and practices (Chow 1995; Bowman 2013a). She does this 'in order to highlight the problems of cross-cultural exchange – especially in regard to the commodified, technologized image – in the postcolonial, postmodern age' (Chow 1995, 182).

When it comes to the question of the relations between martial arts culture and media culture, this kind of approach is arguably not merely desirable but necessary. For, in the (notional) West, at least, and accelerating exponentially throughout the 20th Century, 'martial arts' have arguably always been both mediatized and overwhelmingly represented as 'Asian' (Farrer and Whalen-Bridge 2011). Their emergence and proliferation throughout the 20th Century was always bound up with their media representations, and these overwhelmingly tended to make at least some reference to their putatively Asian 'origins' or 'character'. Indeed (and although there may be exceptions), it seems reasonable to propose at the outset that, in many cases, and certainly for most practitioners (other than, say, police, security and military personal), media representations of martial arts came first, and that these representations very often involved reference to 'Asia'.[1]

However, there is more to the global spread of 'Asian martial arts' than a simple anticipatory structure of orientalist desire. That is to say, there is more to this than seeing, then wanting, then doing. For, if we consider the global dissemination of what we might term for convenience 'East Asian martial arts', one thing to note would be *all of the other things – everything else –* that is carried, transported and transferred along with them. Asian martial arts bring with them modified worldviews, outlooks, philosophies, ideologies, exercise principles, posture modifications, dietary considerations, lifestyle changes, sartorial choices, ethical norms, aesthetic tastes, cultural and intellectual interests, and so on. In fact, so much 'baggage' comes along with Asian martial arts that it is effectively impossible to disambiguate the primary from the secondary, the essential from the add-on, or the inside from the outside. Inevitably, therefore, the question always waiting in the wings is that of what we even think we are referring to when we refer to martial arts or when we evoke the movement of Asian martial arts from the East to the West (Chan 2000).

Despite saying this, I do not want to return to the debate around how to define martial arts discussed in the previous chapter. As I have already argued, academic study does not oblige us to plough all of our efforts into the taxonomic and judgemental labours of deciding what is in and what is out, what is good and what is bad, what is right and what is wrong, etc. Rather, because 'martial arts' is always essentially a *discursive construct*, it seems better to explore the *ways* that martial arts are constructed in discourse – the ways they are evoked, tacitly understood, recognised, represented, talked about, fantasized, stereotyped; the ways practitioners self-identify, how they dis-identify and differentiate; what it is that fans or practitioners (think and/or say they) are

---

[1] Such reference of course is neither essential nor eternal. Even quite quickly after the demise of Bruce Lee and the first 'kung fu craze' of the 1970s, Western martial artists and actors began more and more to disassociate themselves and their representations from 'Asia'. Sylvia Chong, for instance, discusses the exemplary example of Chuck Norris, who moved from discussing his films in terms of Asian martial arts towards discussing them in terms of the tradition of John Wayne movies (Chong 2012; see also Krug 2001 and Bowman 2015a).

fans or practitioners of; and so on. From such a perspective, it seems reasonable to suggest that when people say 'martial arts' they tend to think of a relatively limited range of images: Either of people, wearing something like white or black pyjamas, in training halls, practicing punches, kicks, holds and throws, or other intelligible or perhaps inscrutable movements; or of the dramatized representations of skilled fighters in action film, comic book or computer game contexts. Between these two realms – between the one we might witness or experience at the local sports centre and the one we might witness and experience on TV – I propose that more people will regard the former (the lived practice) as 'primary', 'real', 'true' or 'actual', and therefore think of the specific scenarios of people training, or trained people fighting, as being the principal object of or referent for 'martial arts'. The common belief might therefore be formulated like this: Martial arts reside immanently as skills and propensities within trained people and they are revealed or actualised only in certain spectacles, such as fights (dramatized, sporting or spontaneous), or when people train (practice, repeat, reiterate, explore and experiment) in self-defined martial arts movements, techniques and principles, in pedagogical environments and relationships. Conversely, therefore, my proposal is that most people will therefore regard the media images of martial arts as 'secondary', 'false', 'fake', 'parasitic', or, at best, 'supplementary'.

I indulge in such generalising statements not in order to legislate or adjudicate anything, but rather to show why the types of complex, material, technological, textual and often deconstructive approaches of scholars like Chow (in a different context), Tim Trausch, Chris Goto-Jones, Benjamin N. Judkins, and others, can help us to move on from simple schemas like Eastern versus Western, past versus present, or the inside versus the outside of 'martial arts'. For, in line with their broadly deconstructive approaches, I want to reiterate: 'Martial arts' cannot actually be neatly circumscribed or demarcated, nor can 'primary' be simply or neatly separated from 'secondary'. (Nor does this matter – although showing how and why we should move on from this discussion is an important and consequential matter, as discussed in the previous chapter.)

Moving from Primary to Supplementary

As mentioned, from the beginning, if we evoke the global spread of East Asian martial arts such as judo,[2] taekwondo and styles of karate and kung fu, then we inevitably evoke much more than the spread of specific training techniques, practices and skills in isolation. Rather, the movement of the practices went hand in hand with the movement of clusters of ideas, values, ideologies, and

---

[2] Judo, however, was a very 'Westernized' innovation from its inception, at least to the extent that its founder both studied and advocated Western(izing) and modernizing principles in its development (Law 2008).

myriad material objects, either directly or indirectly associated with martial arts – whether taking the form of a taste for green tea or kimchi, meditation or *wuxia pian* in film or literary tastes, as well as different fashion, design and other aesthetic and lifestyle choices, from haircuts to tattoos to ways of speaking to comportment to demeanour.

Moreover, if we organise our thinking according to the terms of the familiar import/export or 'movement' narrative, in which East Asian martial arts were 'exported' to the West – or 'Eastern things' moved West – then we should be aware of the possibility that there were at least two other attendant movements – and that these movements were not simple or unidirectional transfers. Rather, these *transfers* involved *transformations*. For, first, as mentioned, other things also moved West, along with 'martial arts', and second, correspondingly, things moved (transformed) in the West. Such movement/change can be regarded as both a precondition and consequence of the importation, adoption or appropriation of 'East Asian martial arts' in the West (Krug 2001; Barrowman 2015b).

As poststructuralist political theorists would say, we must enquire into the 'conditions of possibility' of any event or situation (Derrida 1997; see also Laclau 1996). What conditions of possibility enabled the emergence of such things as Chinese or Japanese martial arts classes in the West? One of the key ingredients for the possibility of the emergence of martial arts classes in the West was the prior circulation of images and ideas. The idea of doing karate or kung fu came first, for most non-military Westerners. And such ideas always come from images: Media images; images in newspapers; images of exotic Asia; images in comic books, travellers' tales, war stories, serials and novels.

The two themes I have so far picked out – the strange primacy of the supposedly secondary image and the inextricability of 'martial arts' from their entanglement in clusters of putatively peripheral objects, practices and values – can be approached fruitfully according to some of the arguments offered by Jacques Derrida. The two most relevant aspects of Derrida's thought for approaching martial arts and (or within) media culture are his intertwined arguments about what he called 'supplementarity' and the 'metaphysics of presence' (Derrida 1976, 1982, 2001). These are relevant in terms of this discussion of martial arts because, although we tend to prioritise and hierarchize in terms of what Derrida regarded as our ('metaphysical') presuppositions or ('metaphysical') biases – in which we place living, embodied presence first, and non-living, non-embodied non-presence second (or last) – it often turns out on closer analysis that the things we had deemed secondary, derived, supplementary or inferior are in fact strangely primary. Think here of all of the things 'around' martial arts that we so easily regard as 'peripheral', inessential, extra, added-on – or, in other words, supplementary. Where would we be without them? They constantly refer to, evoke, conjure up, allude to something else, some other essence or entity, somewhere else: Martial arts. Martial arts paraphernalia constantly refers away from itself, (as if) to that certain something else, somewhere else, that thing that 'really is' martial arts. But if we try to look for this essence, this evoked essential entity, we can never seem to find it. It's always somewhere else. Even one instance or example of it is not fully or truly or decisively 'it'. Derrida famously called this effect *différance*.

Différance is even active in what we might like to think of as reality. In other words, it's not just martial arts paraphernalia and quirky consumer goods that incessantly refer away from themselves to the elsewhere and elsewhen of some true essence and identity of martial arts. Différance is also active in the realms of actually-existing martial arts practices themselves. This or that dojo refers incessantly to Japan, this taiji class refers relentlessly to China. But which or where or when 'Japan', and which or where or when 'China'? This martial arts style or club or that martial arts practice does not seem to encapsulate or cover everything that seems essential or proper to 'martial arts'. But they allude to it, they try to approach it, to actualise it. Yet, what is the 'it'? It's never quite there and never quite that.

This is the very definition of différance. Mostly, rather than a referent, a sense of a 'spirit' is conjured up: Spectres of Funakoshi haunt us, spirits of Zhang San-feng inspire us, and so on and so forth (on 'haunting' in this sense, see Derrida 1994). In other words, always absent presences are conjured up in the rituals, rhetorics, concepts, imaginings, objects, evocations, terms, and other paraphernalia of the practices. But, more than this, it is surely even the case that any one dimension of the cluster of practices only ever refers to the others, needs the others, and none can ever, in and of themselves, amount to the essence of the practice, entity or identity. At this point, everything starts to seem secondary, supplementary, peripheral, partial, incomplete…. This is why critics of deconstruction argue that it is problematic to follow such a style of thinking all the way: Because deconstruction seems to make everything impossible. However, this is a nihilistic way of relating to deconstruction, because, rather than denying things, deconstruction merely insists upon the supplementarity of things – their constructedness, the contingency of their constructedness, and hence the potential for transformation and change in all things. In this sense, deconstruction is essentially optimistic and always interested in constructive change. To quote Derrida on this point once again:

> All that a deconstructive point of view tries to show, is that since convention, institutions and consensus are stabilizations (sometimes stabilizations of great duration, sometimes micro-stabilizations), this means that they are stabilizations of something essentially unstable and chaotic. Thus it becomes necessary to stabilize precisely because stability is not natural; it is because there is instability that stabilization becomes necessary; it is because there is chaos that there is a need for stability. Now, this chaos and instability, which is fundamental, founding and irreducible, is at once naturally the worst against which we struggle with laws, rules, conventions, politics and provisional hegemony, but at the

same time it is a chance, a chance to change, to destabilize. If there were continual stability, there would be no need for politics, and it is to the extent that stability is not natural, essential or substantial, that politics exists and ethics is possible. Chaos is at once a risk and a chance, and it is here that the possible and the impossible cross each other. (Derrida 1996, 84)

At the very least, deconstructive interrogation is useful to the extent that it asks us to challenge, test and sharpen the otherwise rough and ready hierarchies that it is easy to come up with, and so easy to be led by, in our thinking. This is relevant here because, as I have been suggesting, it is all too easy to assume that when we say 'martial arts' we are primarily referring to the living embodied formal pedagogical practices of conscious, living, striving human beings. To think like this is fine, in one sense. But the problem with such an assumption is that it necessarily carries the implication that therefore we are not referring to computer games, media fictions, cuddly toys or comedy caricatures. We may regard our image of the proper practice as primary and most of the paraphernalia that goes around it as secondary, derived, inferior. Obviously, we assign some of the 'paraphernalia' a different status: Training swords, staffs and other weapons, punch bags, kick shields, sparring mitts and so on are easily regarded as proper to the proper object or practice, whereas toy swords, foam nunchakus, and inflatable *Kung Fu Panda* punch bags are less easily regarded as proper to (nor the proper property of) the proper object or practice.

I am aware that these more or less deconstructive formulations around the idea of what is proper and what is improper to, or the property of, something may sound convoluted.[3] But I want to propose that ultimately they can help us to see further and more clearly, because thinking along such lines asks us to examine what we deem to be proper or primary to an object, field or practice, and what we conversely deem to be improper, secondary, derived, and inferior, or indeed a digression from, a perversion of, or aberration away from the proper (Bowman 2001). Asking such questions helps to reveal both our own and others' values, biases and orientations more clearly.

It is likely that there will long be a need to draw attention to the important status of 'media supplements' in studies of martial arts practices and discourses. This is because many of the disciplinary fields within which scholars operate and carry out studies of different aspects of martial arts remain 'metaphysical' in Derrida's sense – that is, subject-centred, often 'Cartesian', and quick to move on from the complicating dimensions that the media supplement threatens to introduce into any study of martial arts culture. So, this is a perspective that remains worth reiterating, repeating, and insisting upon. Indeed, without impressing upon people the strength of these arguments time and again,

---

[3] In another context and with another focus I have written explicitly about the determination of senses and values of propriety and impropriety (Bowman 2001).

'media studies' and 'cultural studies' will always remain consigned to the status of being regarded as second-class academic citizens rather than as 'serious' subjects, 'proper' subjects, or fields in which proper things are studied properly. Not sociology, not history, not psychology, not politics, not economics, not anthropology – media and cultural studies have long been cast (out) as 'Mickey Mouse subjects' (Bowman 2003).

Much as those who work in media or cultural studies may baulk at the accusation of working in a 'Mickey Mouse' field, my argument here is that a strong response from media and cultural studies to such an accusation would not be to deny or disavow the place of 'trivia' like cartoons/animation, movies, enjoyment, playfulness, fantasy, childhood or childishness, consumerism or cuddly toys, and so on. Rather, there is a value in embracing the accusation and arguing strenuously for the importance and power of all the 'Mickey Mouse supplements' that we are surrounded by.

Such supplements are everywhere, and they are both big business and transformative of many things, including societies, histories, individual and group psychologies, politics, economies, and all manner of anthropological areas. To mention a few examples: We know that Bruce Lee films are responsible in large part for the global popularity and proliferation of wing chun, just as we know that they are equally responsible for the recent revisionist filmic hagiographies of Ip Man (Bowman 2013b). We know that the 1982 film *The Shaolin Temple* was directly responsible for a massive and immediate increase in international tourism to the Shaolin Temple and other areas in China (Frank 2006). And so on. In fact, it is easy to point to example after example of films intervening into – and even dramatically changing – other areas of reality, in all sorts of ways. I have discussed before the 'rediscovery' – in actual fact, the complete invention – of a new 'ancient' martial art in China, in the immediate aftermath of two key events: First, the massive international success of the Disney animation *Mulan* (1998), and second, the Chinese government crackdown on Falun Gong, the suppression of its practice and the arrest of many of its practitioners (Palmer 2007). As Adam Frank notes in his study of taijiquan in Shanghai (Frank 2006), after the crackdown on Falun Gong, hundreds and hundreds of practitioners of a hitherto unknown art called Mulanquan were literally bussed into Shanghai and other cities in China to perform it in the public parks, as they would otherwise have been empty, having been evacuated of qigong and Falun Gong practitioners by the police (I discuss this more fully in Bowman 2015a).

The impact of a media text is massive here. The choice of 'Mulan' as the name of the simulated and ersatz martial art of Mulanquan strongly suggests a deliberate Chinese state attempt to cash in on the success of the orientalist Hollywood film by supplying the demand it sparked in potential Western tourists for a new/ancient 'feminist' and hyper-oriental(ist) practice. Furthermore, the very fact that there was a perceived need – or strategic value – in ensuring the continued presence of a certain style or aesthetic of martial arts practice in China's parks speaks volumes too. (As Adam Frank argues, the aesthetic of taijiquan appears to have been elevated to the very symbol of Chineseness – a key part of the 'brand' that puts a new twist on the meaning of the 'PR' in 'PRC'.) Clearly, martial arts fictions, fantasies, simulations and simulacra are big business; they impact on policies of all orders – not just Chinese policies, but those of other countries, as well, more and more of which have begun to elevate their 'indigenous' martial arts to 'national sport' or 'national treasure' status, following the lead set by UNESCO, with its attributions of 'intangible cultural heritage' to practices like wing chun kung fu in Hong Kong, and so on.

From this perspective, it is apparent that we have hardly begun to scratch the surface of the possibilities of media-focused martial arts research. Works in the emergent field of martial arts studies to date have begun the exploration and examination of martial arts as they exist within and across some, but not all, contemporary media texts and technologies, and have begun to unearth several rich seams and reserves of martial arts tropology that permeate and even orientate key dimensions of contemporary transnational media culture. But there is more to do. Without a principled focus on such supplementary matters, studies of martial arts could continue to ignore, downplay or exclude the media supplement and hence be skewed by a kind of myopic realism.

The obverse of this situation is equally problematic: Many film, TV, gaming and other media studies scholars are not prepared to take the step out of text-focused disciplinary discourse and into an exploration of the implications and consequences of their text- and technology-focused studies and insights in other contexts, such as lived bodily practices, social relations, para-textual ideological constructions, embodied martial arts practice, and so on. In a world in which cosplay and battle re-enactment enthusiasts have begun to research, study and develop discourses around such matters as how to use Jedi weapons like the Lightsaber properly, there is clearly room – and obvious starting points, staging posts, or gateways – for media studies to leap across and to become new and other forms of cultural studies (Judkins 2016a).

But there is a reluctance to do so. The people who are looking into cosplay martial arts from academic perspectives are currently less likely to be media studies researchers than they are to hail from disciplines such as history, dance or theatre studies, or scholars and hobbyists with a focus on such topics as Historical European Martial Arts (HEMA). But such innovations are opportunities, linking points, potential bridges, between the supposedly discrete realms of media and body, or between textuality and corporeality. As such, they are crying out for the attention of creative thinkers, experts, researchers, scholars and analysts of media.

In other words, the situation arguably remains effectively the same as it was when I proposed – as a call to arms – in a 2014 journal issue editorial (Bowman 2014a) that if film, media and cultural studies scholars do not jump into this new field then it will be hegemonized by approaches that more than likely will downplay or exclude the media supplement. By this I meant, and mean, approaches that are limited by the absence of, and that often even actively militate against, any kind of deconstructive, media or cultural studies paradigm or approach.

The key question is: Why is there reluctance – even palpable resistance – to crossing boundaries such as those between the media on the one hand and embodied practices on the other? Just as I have often grumbled that sociological studies of martial arts rarely venture seriously into the realm of the film and media that are obviously at the origin and heart of martial artists' fantasies and orientations, so the reverse is also true: Martial arts film studies rarely ventures into sociology. Forces of resistance are evidently active on both sides of the divide. Accordingly, we should give the divide itself some serious attention.

Disciplined Movements

For, what is the divide between, say, film studies and sociology, anthropology or psychology? It is a divide between disciplines. It is a disciplinary divide. This is why scholars are reluctant to traverse it: They have been *disciplined* in quite particular ways (Foucault 1977). As disciplinary subjects, they want to stay where they know that they know what they know and where they know how to find out and how to know what they don't yet know. This is what disciplines give us, and make us: Ways of knowing, ways of doing, ways of being. Different disciplines do things differently. Crossing into a new field is always a new beginning, it is always to start from scratch. Few of us have the patience, time, humility, or even desire to take such steps.

True interdisciplinarity has long been understood by theorists and those who have attempted to do it as being genuinely conflictual, and often conflicted (Mowitt 1992; Bowman 2003, 2007, 2015a). Academics and researchers cannot simply traverse disciplines the way that bits and pieces of Bruce Lee imagery, signs, ideas and tropes can traverse multiple texts and technologies in almost any media, region or language of the world. The movement of academics across fields is not quite like the movement of martial arts across media – even if the movement of some academic points and perspectives may have similar abilities to travel (and translate): Bits and pieces, fragments, terms, concepts, can be picked up and redeployed in multiple contexts. Just think of the afterlives of once-critical/theoretical terms, like text, discourse, postmodernism or, indeed, deconstruction. All of these words have had precise academic formulations in certain texts, and such terms and their meanings have been picked up, fleshed out, contested, expanded or contracted, modified and transformed, in various academic fields. Some have proved suggestive in other contexts – from journalism to cultural commentary, photography, dance or even more distant disciplines and fields; or, indeed, with words like 'deconstruction', in culinary conversations and cookery programmes (where we now have dishes like 'deconstructed apple pie', and so forth).

This suggests that the fruits of academic labours may indeed traverse myriad regions and realms. However, the form and direction of that movement is outside of the control of intentional agents (such as the nuncupators, neologists or theorists of the terms that travel). Moreover, their movement from one context to another and one medium to another inevitably involves transformations, both in the meaning of the term and in the context of its deployment. (It is doubtful that Derrida would ever have intended or accepted that 'deconstruction' could to refer to a dessert served inside out, for instance.)

Nonetheless, it seems likely that one of the reasons why terms like text, discourse, postmodernism, and deconstruction caught on in so many ways and in so many places is that they seemed useful and appropriate in helping to conceptualise and describe things. One of the things such terms help us to grasp and express is precisely the fragmented and porous character of contexts in a media-saturated (postmodern) world. This is doubtless why – even though disciplines still have fights at and about their boundaries – we currently seem to be living through the effects of the deconstruction of the erstwhile hermetically sealed or at least well-policed and sacrosanct borders of academic disciplines. People now talk about disciplines, like many other parts of life, as being more 'fluid' or 'liquid' (Bauman 2005). Some have proposed that we are now fully moving into an era of 'post-disciplinarity'.

'New' media technologies are clearly prime movers in some of this disciplinary deconstruction. The emergence of para-academic blogs, for instance, such as Benjamin N. Judkins' hugely popular *Kung Fu Tea* (which he has been publishing since 2012 at www.chinesemartialstudies.com), and a few others, including perhaps my own martial arts studies blog (http://martialartsstudies. blogspot.com/), have been key in drawing together both academic and non-academic researchers from multiple fields and disciplines in remarkably convivial and collegial discussions about martial arts and how to study them. So, whereas before the era of such blogs academics would operate in more isolated academic islands, today it seems hard not to perceive what others are doing. And, perhaps because the institution of the blog always stands midway between 'proper' academic scholarship and 'personal opinion', more readers seem more prepared to read more open-mindedly, for curiosity and pleasure. Hence such blogs have helped to generate a new sense of community. In the emerging field(s) of martial arts studies, disciplinary differences that might otherwise have precipitated antagonisms and passionate disagreements seem currently to be taking a back-seat to the shared interest in, love of or fascination with all aspects of martial arts – whether 'proper' and 'primary' or 'improper' and 'peripheral'.

Perhaps this is because of the newness of the field. Or perhaps it is because of the strange situation in which there is an obviousness and consensus around what is meant by 'martial arts' combined with a peculiar impossibility in terms of defining them rigorously, and despite the persistence of so much scholarship that always tries to define, demarcate, hierarchize and legislate on what martial arts are and what they are not. For, despite such orientations, we all just feel that we know what martial arts are and what martial arts stuff is. There is, to use Raymond Williams' term, a 'structure of feeling' around martial arts in media culture; or, as many academics now prefer to say, economies or fields or structures of affect (Highmore 2011). Martial arts have many manifestations within shifting and multiple discursive formations. We understand the terms and we recognise the manifestations because there are regularities and repetitions, serial structures[4] and more or less predictable forms and contents, albeit often combined with newness, innovation, hybridisation and unpredictable aspects, in all of the iterations of martial arts signs, symbols, supplements, tropes, signatures, events and contexts, across the multiple institutions and discourses that supplement and are supplemented by martial arts in media culture.

This perspective raises questions about the status of some more established terms in the study of martial arts, such as 'the body', 'embodiment' and 'embodied knowledge'. It is to these questions and problematics that we turn in the next chapter.

---

[4] For fascinating work on the force of 'seriality' in modern culture, see the work of Ruth Mayer (2013).

CHAPTER 4

On Embodiment

Introduction (Trigger Warning)

'Embodiment' is a very current term. Many academics talk about it, and they do so very fluently, comfortably and easily. However, this chapter proposes that embodiment is a uniquely challenging problem for certain traditions and approaches to scholarship, particularly those that are implicitly or explicitly organised by the aim of establishing meanings. Such an orientation is exemplified by semiotics, but this chapter argues that even approaches designed to critique semiotics and other forms of 'logocentrism' (or approaches that focus on words and meanings) ultimately struggle when trying to deal with aspects of embodiment. Even Derridean deconstruction – which was developed as a strident critique of logocentrism – struggles to move beyond the focus on words and meanings. So, the question becomes one of whether scholars interested in embodiment should reject or move beyond these kinds of approaches.

Drawing on a loosely autobiographical narrative that touches on aspects both of my academic training and my investment in martial arts and other physical cultural practices, this chapter argues that it is not simply possible to 'reject' or 'move beyond' the logocentrism of traditional 'search for meaning' orientations. I argue instead that, even though this may seem relatively passé to some scholars, 'embodiment' is still very productively conceived of as 'embodiment of' – i.e., as the embodiment of *something else*; specifically, as the performative and interpretive elaboration of something *other* that is received, perceived, felt, constructed, believed, assumed or otherwise lived as being either an aim, ideal, desire, objective, fantasy, or as a norm, or indeed as the warding off of something undesired or feared.

The chapter poses questions of how to 'capture', 'convey' or 'communicate' embodiment in words, and it interrogates the necessity of the current hegemony of the written word in academia. However, it seeks to avoid any kind of evangelism about new approaches or understandings of embodiment, and

How to cite this book chapter:
Bowman, P. 2019. *Deconstructing Martial Arts*. Pp. 75–90. Cardiff: Cardiff University Press. DOI: https://doi.org/10.18573/book1.e. License: CC-BY-NC-ND 4.0

twists around at the end to propose that even certain forms of what we perhaps too quickly regard as 'enlightening' or 'emancipating' practices and techniques of embodiment might be regarded as traps, or indeed prisons.

In other words, please be aware that in what follows I am at times going to be quite shamelessly autobiographical. But this is not merely self-indulgent. Rather, it is because I think that personal anecdotes can offer an economical way of getting a lot of concerns on the table quickly, by conveying the ways that some key problematics around 'embodiment' have arisen in relation to my research and thinking, and the ways they have both vexed and stimulated me.[1] However, when I say 'me' I do not just mean me as some kind of unique, isolated individual; rather I mean 'me' as an academic who has searched for theoretical and practical academic ways out of many of the problems discussed. So, my hope is that when you read about 'me' here, you will think less about *me* and much more about 'we'. Either way, please have patience with the autobiographical aspects of what follows. They are doing some heavy lifting.

A Brief History of No Body

I have always loved martial arts and I have always loved writing. I loved martial arts films as a child. As a teen, I tried to learn how to do the flashy moves that I saw on screen. At the same time, I found writing essays for school to be one of the easiest things I'd ever been asked to do. So, although I far preferred other subjects (economics, geography, art), it transpired that, with no effort at all, for some reason, I started to come top in English. In due course, without really knowing anything at all about what it meant, I was advised to apply to go to university. Following a path of least resistance, I pragmatically elected to take a subject I was 'good at' and found easy, simply because I was good at it and found it easy (and because it had the added attraction of minimal contact hours and maximal assessment by essay). So, I studied English. The irony was that I came from a barely literate working-class family in which no one had ever passed a written exam. I was regarded as a kind of freak of nature by my father and brothers, because I could and would read and write, I was left handed, and I spent most of my time doing things that they did not do and did not understand or regard as 'proper activity', because none of what I did involved visibly making, fixing, altering, tinkering, moving and obviously *doing*.[2]

---

[1]   As mentioned earlier, in the influential essay 'Banality in Cultural Studies', Meaghan Morris argues that 'anecdotes for [her] are not expressions of personal experience, but allegorical expositions of a model of the way the world can be said to be working. So anecdotes need not be true stories, but they must be functional in a given exchange' (Morris 1990).

[2]   We could easily psychoanalyse this, of course. It all sounds very Oedipal. But we could also 'sociologize' it too: The supposed lack of comprehension of 'intellectual work' by working class subjects is a very Bourdieuian way to illustrate 'habitus' – as in, 'How can you say you are "at work" when you are in your dressing gown reading a book?'

At university, I genuinely loved literary theory from the moment I met it (formalism first, then structuralism, poststructuralism and – my favourite at the time – semiotics) but I was increasingly bored by literature. After my degree, a friend told me about a subject called cultural studies. I looked into it. I did an MA, using erstwhile 'literary' theory (now redubbed 'cultural' theory) to look at more interesting things than literature – such as martial arts films, music videos, the rise of body consciousness in men via bodybuilding, and the political possibilities of stand-up comedy. I was invited back to do a PhD. What did I want it to be on? Something about 'theory' had hooked me. I chose to interrogate the political theory of Ernesto Laclau and Chantal Mouffe (primarily Laclau and Mouffe 1985). There was no 'body' there. Just words, institutions, mechanisms, political processes, hegemonies, relations of articulation, power/knowledge, semiotics, interpellations,[3] conflicts of interpretation, and so on.

Throughout my PhD studies and in the years immediately thereafter, I kept writing about problems in political and cultural theory using poststructuralist approaches (see Bowman 2007). But, all the while, what I wanted, more and more, was to write about a completely different thing – martial arts, in terms of what we now call 'embodiment'. However, the problem was that I was immersed in the world of problematics and approaches and paradigms that were primarily kitted out to deal with very different things – principally, the philosophical critique of, in Derridean terminology, logocentrism and the metaphysics of presence, conceived of as key parts of the wider ethico-political deconstruction of essentialisms of all kinds.

Being Haunted by The Body

It is probably worth remembering that Jacques Derrida (the so-called 'father' of deconstruction) was always widely denounced and defamed by opponents as someone who did not believe in and who tried to deny the existence of reality, or the reality of existence (for discussion see Derrida and Weber 1995). I mention this unfair critique here not because it is correct but because there is something close enough to a spectral or chimerical grain of truth in it to illustrate the predicament I was in. For, if deconstruction does not simply deal with 'things' – 'real things', like, say, our bodies – then surely trying to use Derrida to think about embodiment is a bit like trying to use a chocolate teapot to make tea. Nonetheless, when I did eventually, tentatively, (re)turn to trying to write about embodiment, I did so via the only means I knew: Derridean deconstruc-

---

[3] The Althusserian theory of 'interpellation' of course very strongly and directly involves a body that is 'turned' by being addressed by another embodiment of power (such as a police officer). But the type of cultural theory I was immersed in at this stage was much more interested in the power effects within a world conceived as a world of power relations than in the bodily effects in a world conceived of as a world of bodies.

tion, poststructuralist discourse theory, and Barthesian textual analysis (Bowman 2008, 2010d).

This may sound a bit like trying to dig your way out of a hole, or like Slavoj Žižek's joke about searching for a lost key under the light of a streetlamp rather than in the surrounding darkness where you actually lost it because you can't see anything over there in the dark. But you start from where you are, you think with the tools and in the terms you have learned to think with, and you write the way you know how, about things that interest you. So, my first attempt to deal with the impact and importance of martial arts on the lives and minds and bodies of people (like me) took the form of using the approaches of Derrida, Laclau and Stuart Hall to account for the emergence and to assess the significance of the 'kung fu craze' of the 1970s. My very first attempt was a conference paper called 'Enter the Derridean' which reflected on the impact and enduring significance and effects of Bruce Lee films on people's imaginations, activities, lives and loves.

At the same time, however, it was important to me not to consign 'Bruce Lee' and 'martial arts' to the status of being treated as *mere examples*, to be (ab)used only in order to unproblematically 'prove' a certain theory – in this case, the theory of 'discourse' as developed by the likes of Laclau and Hall, following on from Michel Foucault (mixed with a lot of Antonio Gramsci). So, as the title of my first paper on this ('Enter the Derridean') hopefully suggested, the work was also attempting to assess the emergence not only of what might be too easily dismissed or categorized as the kung fu 'craze' – or some kind of 'subculture' – but rather the emergence of the 'discursive formation' of cultural studies, cultural theory, and deconstruction themselves. After all, all of these things took off during the same kind of period, yet we tend not to regard academic movements as being crazes or subcultures, do we? We tend rather to connect them to wider issues and problematics and to dignify them with labels like 'intellectual developments'. Reciprocally, I wanted to accord the same dignity to figures like Bruce Lee and to cultural changes such as the uptake of 'Asian martial arts' in Western popular culture. I did not think these were mere crazes. Nor did I accept that they should they be categorized as 'subcultures'. Such designations keep the scholarly gaze that creates them safely free from the same kind of scrutiny that it applies to everything else.

Papers like that (which was eventually worked up and worked into the first chapters of my book *Theorizing Bruce Lee* [2010]) were my first baby-steps into working towards matters of embodiment. So, I suppose you could say I followed an eccentric route into such waters. (Or maybe I wasn't even in the waters yet, but still stuck on the rocks, looking around me for a viable sandy route down to the water.) For, overwhelmingly, my approach was *textual* (principally organised by looking at films, books and magazines); it was self-consciously part of a tradition (cultural studies) that had a strong commitment to redeeming so-called 'popular culture' from the stigma of being branded trivial and inconsequential and it was informed and organised by paradigms that focused on macro-political discourses. And (while Barthes' approaches extended to audiovisual culture, Derridean deconstruction and much poststructuralism was principally a critique of 'logocentrism') my approach, despite my best intentions, was arguably very much focused on words and pictures.

In The Beginning Was The Word – and Pictures

Of course, things are not so simple. In the history of the notion of 'discourse', the work of Foucault looms large. And there are two obvious sides to Foucault, first his studies of the effects of arguments, ideas, texts, legislations and institutional operations on, second, the human subject, in mind, body, flesh, blood, muscles, skills and disciplines. So, there are clearly at least two directions that a Foucault-inspired or informed 'discourse approach' could go. One is macro-historical and/or institutional. The other is focused on minds and bodies and persons and people. All of my prior training (indeed, all of my *disciplining*) had been in the world of the first orientation. So, when I tried to turn to the question of things like non-logocentric knowledge and embodiment, my efforts essentially took the form of conceiving of embodiment *as embodied discourse*. That is, I understood embodiment as always and necessarily involving discursive factors and forces (words and pictures). These forces found their actualization in and as aspects of embodiment via what may be called 'performative elaborations' or 'performative interpretations'. (I take these terms more from Derrida [1994] than Judith Butler [1990].) Accordingly, embodiment in my thinking was always likely to be associated with wordy or audiovisual discursive *injunctions, imperatives, ideals*, and so on.

So, my approach could be accused of believing that 'in the beginning was the word'. And pictures. But pictures translated into words. And actions. It is definitely the case that I have always read many 'words and pictures' as being – or becoming – *injunctions* (or Foucauldian discursive statements), such as 'Aspire to be like this' or 'Desire this'. Doubtless this orientation is a residue of the influence that Barthes' arguments in *Mythologies* (1972) had on my thinking. Indeed, I still regard almost any deliberately selected and crafted audiovisual textual image of people, places and things to be injunctions – aspire to this, desire this, be like this – or their obverses – avoid this, reject this, be disgusted by this.

This is hardly a radical position to take. Many others go much further. In a different context, and in a slightly different direction, Andrew Barry goes significantly further than this. In *Political Machines*, he notes that even the 'factual' world – the world of 'facts' – is constructed and works in terms of injunctions. Neither 'data' nor 'information' are ever neutral. As he puts it: The existence of data about, say, smoking and mortality, or diet and diabetes, and so on, implies a subject who 'needs' that 'information' and who *should* respond to its implications and act accordingly because of it – give up smoking, lose weight, etc.

(Barry 2001). This is relevant to embodiment because it would mean that any subsequent actions undertaken in light of the 'facts' or 'information', leading to body modification or enskillment (running skill, say, or the production of a 'yoga body' [Singleton 2010]) would amount to the embodiment or performative interpretation or articulation of a certain kind of discursive injunction.

In my approach to bodies, embodied knowledge and bodily practices (specifically, to martial arts), I have tended to prioritise cases of the 'translation' of visual material (say, moving or static pictures of someone like Bruce Lee) into being a kind of injunction ('Be like this!' 'Desire this!') or indeed a Foucauldian 'statement' (Foucault 1970), and, from here, on into the transformation of lived practices – and hence the transformation of bodies, bodily skills, lifestyle norms, values and sensibilities, and so on (Bowman 2010d, 2013b). But the key point has always been that, in the case of moving or static pictures of Bruce Lee, such 'messages' were not solely translated into words. Rather, in the case of words and pictures about martial arts, such cultural 'messages' were and are often translated by people into *physical practices* – the taking up of new activities or living life according to new values and different orientations. The 'creation myth' image here is one of children and teens seeing a martial arts movie for the first time and leaving the cinema making Bruce Lee catcalls and trying to do flying kicks (the exemplary work on this creation scenario is Brown 1997). Over the coming days and weeks and months, how many such erstwhile spectators went on to seek out a martial arts class? The evidence (or at least the accepted narrative) says many. This means that embodiment is also often *supplemented* by media spectacles – or, in other words, *mediatized* – as discussed in the previous chapter.

In turning to the impact of martial arts films on people and on popular culture, I was trying to step away from the world of institutionally and macropolitically focused poststructuralism and to start thinking and researching the ways that cinematic images have functioned effectively in and as fantasy identifications and other forms of psychic/psychological processes to inspire and induce certain embodied practices. My first focus was Bruce Lee and I was interested specifically in martial arts practices. Of course, this means that I was still entirely subjected to thinking of 'culture' and 'subjectivity' (embodied or otherwise) in the terms of *poststructuralist semiotics*, in which everything becomes signifiers sending messages and pointing to other signifiers, and so on (see Silverman 1983). Consequently, I don't really think that any of this work actually or simply got to the matter of 'embodiment'. It focused on the nexus of media representation, identification and fantasy, conceived as a kind of motor that *inspires* and/or *sustains* physical practice.

Phrased like this, it all sounds very technical and grand. Yet, maybe we don't even need the trappings and baggage of the language of psychoanalytical cultural theory to describe it. Maybe we could just as easily talk about people's *beliefs* or *hopes* or *ambitions* being the things that generate and sustain their practices. If we think of the common case of running, for example, people can (and do) talk a lot about *why* they run (for health, to lose weight, to raise money for charity, for a sense of wellbeing, or because they are 'addicted', and so on). But none of these words give us any insight into any matters *of* embodied running, from anything about the *experience* to any other kind of (non-wordy) insight. Rather, such conversations about running are often chiefly about *reasons for* running or problems and achievements in terms of *measuring* the activity. When we try to probe the experience of running itself, our words often come up short. There seems to be a dearth of terminology, of vocabulary, of concepts. There are shared 'technical' phrases, and shared descriptions: We can speak of muscle cramps, how we might feel like we can't get enough air into our lungs, how we hit the wall, and so on. Past that, the experience of running in the discourse of runners often seems to find its way out into speech and language as nothing other than euphemisms and value judgments about something that cannot otherwise be expressed. The experience of a run was *great* or *terrible* or *hard* or *easy* or *exhilarating* or *harrowing*, and so on. But what was the 'that' that we are saying was good or bad or hard or easy or fun or challenging?

How To Do Things With Guts

Before we rush headlong into saying that we are now in the realms of phenomenology, we should note that what we are facing here is a *general* problem of signification. To translate something from an individual experience into words and meanings always requires a move away from the perceived essence or heart of the matter via a necessary (invented, poetic) connection with another coordinate. An experience is *like* one thing, and *not like* another thing; it can only ever be evoked through comparison, analogy, metaphor, contrast, and so on. Admittedly, the communication of a non-linguistic event, phenomenon or experience is a particularly knotty kind of semiotic problem, but it is a semiotic problem nonetheless. Like everything, attempting to signify 'that thing' will always involve composition, construction, and a perhaps ultimately impossible or forever unsatisfying effort of *translation*.

All of this has been reflected upon since at least the time of Charles Sanders Peirce. People have found fascinating ways out of this abyss, or ways to bridge it, or bypass it. But I have always insisted on remaining frustrated by any apparent solution or attempt to dissolve this problematic. I have always felt the need to hold onto the tensions, gaps, disjunctions, aporias, absences and irrelations between experiences and words. This is because trying to keep ahold of this tension imposes a gnawing, generative problematic. Loïc Wacquant expressed it well, I think, when he wrote, on the subject of learning boxing:

> How to go from the guts to the intellect, from the comprehension of the flesh to the knowledge of the text? Here is a real problem of concrete epistemology about which we have not sufficiently reflected, and

which for a long time seemed to me irresolvable. To restitute the carnal dimension of ordinary existence and the bodily anchoring of the practical knowledge constitutive of pugilism – but also of every practice, even the least 'bodily' in appearance – requires indeed a complete overhaul of our way of writing social science. (Wacquant 2009, 122)

For a long time, this passage stood out for me as a near perfect statement of a problem that animated – or, rather, agitated, aggravated, frustrated, sometimes paralyzed – me. I still don't feel like I have actually *resolved* it.

Wacquant himself says his attempt to solve the problem took the form of adopting a strategy of mixing different styles of writing, different modes of address: Sometimes literary/descriptive, other times confessional, emotional, ethnographic, analytical, and so on. The purpose of using different modes of address and manners and conventions of writing when talking about his experiences of learning boxing (Wacquant 2004) was his attempt to find a way to capture and convey as much about 'the comprehension of the flesh' as possible in the medium of words. Different modes and conventions of address could be said to capture and convey different dimensions, so Wacquant's 'solution' is one of mixed modes and multiple voices. Such an approach both acknowledges and attempts to outflank the kind of abyss that often seems to exist between (the experience of) embodied know-how and the communication of that embodied knowledge in words.

A few things always jump to mind when I think about this. One is the expression 'one showing is worth a thousand tellings'. Another is 'that which cannot be said can be shown'. Another is 'he who knows does not speak, he who speaks does not know'. And still another is from a scene in a David Lodge novel in which someone considering studying psychology at university (because they want to know how people's minds work) is advised by a literary scholar that if they really want to gain an understanding of human psychology they'd be better off studying novels.

These fragments spring to mind here because Wacquant's adoption of different literary modes acknowledges that the attempt to convey embodied knowledge via words will always require different conventions: The academic, philosophical or phenomenological will be helpful, but partial and incomplete; as will 'thick description'; as will poetic, emotive, rhetorical and otherwise literary language. Taken together, perhaps the effect will be more rounded than one style of writing alone, or in isolation. But, still, all will in some sense *fail*. This is because the act of moving from the guts to the intellect requires a *leap*, an act of *bridging*, connecting different worlds, *translation*, and *catachresis*. Catachresis refers to 'drawing a face on that which does not have a face', or indeed embodying that which doesn't really have a body (e.g., the cliff *face*, the table *leg*) (Sacks 1978; Spivak 1990).

Viewed from here, even Wacquant's choice of the word 'guts' can be regarded as hugely metaphorical and poetic. It was doubtless chosen precisely because of its complex historical and cultural *overdetermination*, i.e., its residual, resoundingly emotive, evocative force. For, the word 'guts' has a range of mythological associations, all of which suit Wacquant's purposes. These associations range from conjuring up senses of 'the body' to 'bravery' via 'the abattoir' and even 'peasant food' or 'working class fare from days of yore', and so on. So, it sounds gritty and earthy and manly and basic and essential and real. Yet, the embodied knowledge of pugilism both is and is not a knowledge of, from, or centred on or in 'the guts'. Guts are *involved*, but that still doesn't actually capture what we are trying to convey here, or what 'guts' evokes (catachrestically, rather than metonymically or synecdochally).

For, what is Wacquant trying to convey with the word guts? I think he is talking about a specific kind of enskillment and that general kind of enculturation that he refers to via Bourdieu's theorisation of 'habitus' (Bourdieu 1979; Wacquant 2013). Of course, probably more literally important than 'how to go from the guts to the intellect' would be 'how to express such things as balance, proprioception and timing skills in written words'.[4] But none of these terms sound quite as good as 'guts' *as a contrast to 'intellect'*.

Rather than doing something like designating Wacquant a sophist or dualist or anything like that, it seems more reasonable to acknowledge the inevitability of imprecision, evocation and contrast, and to acknowledge that, in going down the line of trying to escape poetic language by trying be literal or specific, we quickly become ensnared in the paradox of *blason* poetry. As a lover's hymn for the woman he desires, the *blason* attempts to itemise and wax lyrical about each and every part of the desired lady's beautiful body – to try to isolate and comment on precisely why and how it is so beautiful and attractive. The problem is that in attempting to do so the overall image that is created becomes heterogeneous, improbable, often ugly, always literally preposterous, and just generally ridiculous. In *blason* poetry, women come to be made up of the cobbling together of things like flowers, apples, milk, silk, oceans, precious stones, music, landscapes, stars, planets, feathers, and so on – or indeed 'sugar and spice and all things nice'.

Nonetheless, just because something requires a work of translation in order to be expressed or communicated, this should not deter us from trying it. Derridean deconstruction essentially held that a true, complete or adequate translation was ultimately impossible. But this never stopped dyed in the wool Derridean deconstructionists from translating the texts of Derridean deconstruction into language after language. Similarly, embodied knowledge need not be regarded as something ineffable, inexpressible or mystical, as if it were the Tao of Taoism or indeed the divine in any kind of negative theology.

---

4   Practitioners and aficionados of Chinese 'internal' martial arts may disagree and retort that in many respects the 'guts' are indeed *literally* the key area to discuss, as deep in the guts is where we find the *dantian* (*dantien*, or *tantien*).

So, despite its problems, Wacquant's statement of the problem stands as a challenge. His proposed solution of mixed modes and manners of expression even seems reasonably acceptable. But if we accept it then our questions should henceforth become something like: *What concepts, metaphors, images, vocabularies and genres and conventions of writing are best able to convey embodied knowledge, skill, technique, experience?*

This is one viable and valuable line of exploration. But, before rushing into it, maybe there is further cause for hesitation. For, in posing things in this way, maybe we are still being unnecessarily blinkered. Maybe we are not seeing the bigger picture – or, once again, perhaps we are insisting on looking for our lost keys under a streetlight rather than in the surrounding darkness where we actually lost them – or trying to dig our way out of a hole. If we were to take a slightly broader view, perhaps the real question would be: *Is the written word actually capable of communicating any of this, or* (more modestly put) *might other, newer, media be better?*

Simulacra and Stimulation

The recently established *Journal of Embodied Research* gives resounding and unequivocal answers to these questions: No, the written word can't be, or isn't simply, the best, and it should now be regarded as inadequate and inferior when assessed in relation to the potentials or propensities of new audiovisual media technologies. The latter far outpace and utterly reconfigure the possibilities for capturing, conveying, communicating and developing knowledge and discourse about embodiment. Ben Spatz theorised this in his important book *What A Body Can Do* (2015), and it was principally he who went on to establish the agenda of the *Journal of Embodied Research* in light of his earlier work.

As someone who remembers Jean Baudrillard's arguments about the supposed loss of the real, *in and because of* the audiovisual image, I delight in the inversion and displacement of the gauntlet thrown down in the editorial manifesto of the *Journal of Embodied Research* inasmuch as its argument seems to be precisely the opposite of the Baudrillardian hypothesis of the loss of the real. Rather, proposes the journal, it is actually going to be by exploring and developing the capacities and propensities of audiovisual media that academics and other researchers will be able to establish a kind of 'royal road' to the body, in terms of audiovisual studies of embodiment, skill, practice, experience, and the establishment of embodied knowledge.

The Body of Knowledge

Unfortunately, to argue that new media technologies trump the written word when it comes to establishing, documenting and discoursing academically on embodied knowledge (thanks to the creative and innovative audiovisual texts that they can allow us to construct) produces a whole new problem. This is the problem of the *legitimation* of different kinds of texts, such as audiovisual media texts, in the face of the ongoing absolute hegemony of the written word, as representing the pinnacle and yardstick of academic propriety within academia.

That is to say, despite innovations here and there, academia (like other institutions) continues to produce principally *written* documents. So, innovations like the *Journal of Embodied Research* are posing a direct challenge to this hegemony, not by *rejecting* writing but by attempting to massively expand the range of possibilities for new kinds of academic writing – including inscription, analysis and discourse, not just 'documenting'. (For a compelling discussion of this, I encourage readers to read the final chapter of Spatz's *What A Body Can Do* [2015].)

To restate all of this via a deliberately naïve rhetorical question: If we want to translate from embodied experience and into some other mode, manner or medium, why do we continue to single out and prioritize *writing*? We live in an audiovisual age, one that has been called 'post-literate', as it is characterised by the waning of older kinds of literacy, and the emergence of newer kinds of literacy (Chow 2012; Bowman 2013a). Indeed, even the word 'literacy' reveals the residual hegemony of the written word. Yet, *book reading* is increasingly being supplanted by different kinds of interaction with different kinds of audiovisual text or platform, many of which can hardly be called 'reading' anymore, even if we still treat them as if they are. The era has passed in which the dominance or hegemony of the written word was unquestionable and necessary, in which knowledge and skills centring on written cultural forms such as the novel or poetry equalled both the yardstick and the pinnacle of *necessary* learning.

Like the once-presumed imperative educational value of teaching children to be able to locate countries and cities on a map of the world, certain forms of 'cultural literacy' wither and die.[5] Educational imperatives and values always in some sense reflect the concerns, orientations, technologies and values of their times and places (Young 1992). Despite Prime Minister Margaret Thatcher's attack on the arts and humanities, I grew up believing in the almost unquestionable and surely timeless value of 'English literature'. It always felt like there might be 'something about class' involved in learning to love it (Bourdieu 1984), but it was only much later that I learned of the Eurocentric colonial-management basis of the subject's origins and development (Anderson 1991).

Of course, we are definitely now not simply or directly talking about embodiment here. We are now talking about the ways that attempts to advance the study of 'it' (singular or plural, noun or verb) reciprocally challenge established conventions that ostensibly have nothing to do with bodies, the body, or

---

[5] When I was growing up, the older generation bewailed our inability to populate blank maps of the world with country and city names. But the British Empire was no more. Former educational imperatives were now redundant. So we weren't forced to learn them.

embodiment. But my sense is that this will (maybe even should) always be the case. The body isn't simply one thing. We so easily say 'the body' – but there is not just *one* body. And there are not just lots of different ethnic and gendered and sexualised and classed and interpellated and self-identified bodies either. So 'politically correct' pluralisation doesn't get to the heart of the problem either – because nor is there simply one body for one person. All of this and more is why the word embodiment, for me at least, will continue to imply at least a sense of referring to 'the embodiment *of something else*'. As mentioned earlier, maybe the fact that I think and see it in this way is a symptom of the eternally returning force of my schooling in poststructuralism and deconstruction. Nonetheless, I also think that much scholarship on the body, on bodily learning, embodied skill, and so on – at least in and around the area of martial arts that I most frequently read – supports my sense of this inevitability. In fact, if embodiment *doesn't* mean 'embodiment of', then I struggle to see what it *does* mean.

In a way, this is fine. I am unlikely ever to renounce my 'secondary habitus', which involved my schooling or (antidisciplinary) disciplining in all things poststructuralist. So, I am quite content to discover that when reading studies that are ostensibly about embodiment I actually find that I am reading just another book or article about nationalist projects, institutional structures, pedagogical relations, ritualistic fetishizations of orientalist fantasies, and so on. I'm happy because often this is great scholarship, and it feels really stimulating and important.

But, thinking about it now, one thing that strikes me is that, as I become more and more immersed in reading and researching 'the body' in different ways, the force of the problematics that first captivated me have lost some of the once powerful hold they had on my imagination. For instance, I can *remember* the extent to which I used to wonder and worry and fret and work away with the 'guts to intellect' problematic on my mind, in my mind, but, as I have dug down into various schools of scholarship that have engaged with embodiment in various ways, this problematic has lost its prominence, albeit (for me) without ever having been *resolved*.

Maybe this is what 'becoming disciplined' is like. It is as if, by reading more in ethnography, anthropology, performance, and so on, and becoming more literate, more circumspect, more informed about the work being done in these fields, the prominence of this once agonising problematic has more and more *settled down* (rather than having been *resolved*); as if I have simply and without really realizing it just become used to it and stopped seeing it, or stopped *feeling* it. Surely this is what 'discipline' is, or does – it *gets you used to* things, so that a thing that once seized hold of your soul ceases to be quite so striking, shocking, disruptive, forceful, jolting, deforming, transforming.

Or perhaps it's just that new and equally fascinating problematics have arisen and seized hold of my soul: Questions of how embodied practices (such as martial arts *kata, forms, patterns* or *taolu*) emerge, stabilize, stay the same over time or mutate, deform, transform, and so on; questions of how bodily skills and types of knowledge are conveyed or communicated from one person to another, how or whether that happens without omission, addition, or transformation; whether certain types of practice are isolatable or abstractable from larger formations, and whether 'elements' or 'components' of supposed entities are 'portable', and, if so, whether they stay the same, or, if not, what they become. I know there are many in-depth studies of the complex stabilizations, transformations and deformations of complex cultural practices (some of my favourites include Wile 1999, Frank 2006, Singleton 2010, Sieler 2015, and Judkins and Nielson 2015, but there are many more), but, on a smaller, more personal, level, I often find myself consumed with questions about whether you could learn taiji push-hands 'properly' without learning taiji forms and/or qigong standing postures; what the borders and boundaries are between, say, qigong and yogic pranayama breathing; whether the training ethos and values of taiji practice could or should be applied in escrima training, or whether there is an absolute and necessary divide, how and where and why this applies if there is, and so on. These are the kinds of questions that currently consume me.

Yet, as all-consuming as such questions sometimes feel, I always seem to want to keep them *amateurish*. I want to keep them rough and ready. As soon as they are too easy to articulate, or as soon as an academic idiom steps up and presents itself as being totally able to handle, conceptualise and communicate the problematic, I tend to feel like they have vanished. To resurrect Paul de Man's phrase, I tend to cleave to the idea that the real should involve at least some 'resistance' to theory (de Man 1986). If there's nothing resistant there, no friction or drag, then it starts to feel like I'm no longer dealing with something real, and maybe just completely immersed in a kind of non-referential theory.

In this and other ways, my amateurish and principally autodidactic (or at least iconoclastic) physical training informs much of my intellectual and academic thinking and writing. More precisely, my *worries* about my physical training practices inform many of my academic reflections and ruminations. And I do worry deeply and profoundly and at length about my physical training. Questions that keep me awake at night and wake me up in the morning tend to take the form: *Can* I combine this with that? If I do this then do I *have* to do that? What happens if I *add* this but *omit* that? And so on. Yet, despite obsessing over so many questions, I almost never ask an authority figure to tell me the answer. This is less because I fear reprimand from former martial arts teachers for asking heretical questions or abusing traditions with the way I am doing things now and more because my academic studies have alerted me to the very real likelihood – indeed, inevitability – that even the most 'authentic', 'traditional' and 'masterful' of authentic, traditional masters – on some fundamental level – *do not know 'the truth' and are inevitably either making it all up themselves or religiously repeating something that was really basically just made up.*

Somebody had to make it up. It had to come from somewhere. And, despite what people like to believe, it almost certainly hasn't come from some unbroken millennia-long tradition. If it wasn't made up by your teacher, it was almost certainly modified by them (Bowman 2016b). So, where does that leave us? Or rather, where does it take us?

Perhaps if I were entirely content and confident that what I were doing in my physical practices were right or true or correct or best or essential then maybe I would not worry so much about whether, say, a Lacanian language (of symbolic lack and imaginary plenitude, and so on) or a Deleuzean language (of affect and rhizomes and reterritorializations, and so on) were more or less appropriate for capturing or expressing the truth or reality or relevant features of my embodied experiences. But I am not. I do not have complete faith in the truths and axioms and tenets of either realm – neither my martial arts practice nor my academic practice.

For Better or For Worse, In Sickness and In Health

I suspect (sometimes I worry) that my irrepressible skepticism might make me a better theorist but a worse martial artist. The promiscuity of my martial arts practice has definitely broadened my perspectives and enabled me to grasp and to feel confident enough to talk about a wider range of practices. But if I had been more faithful to fewer martial arts then I would surely be a much better practitioner. However, I have never been able to limit myself to one established set of practices, or one paradigm. I do one thing and then I worry that I am not doing another, and inexorably I flip over into practicing that other thing for a period of time, until I worry that I am not doing something else, so I flip across to that; and then I flip back, a bit like the Chinese elements, or rock-paper-scissors, each thing overcoming another and being overcome by another. If I am obsessing about taiji and qigong, all of a sudden I will find myself consumed with worry that I am not engaged in enough hard-core pugilism or grappling and I will flip over to that. Then I will worry about the damage I feel I am doing to myself and flip into more therapeutic practices, like yoga. Then I will worry about strength, and flip into weightlifting. Then I will worry about losing my taiji sensitivities and flip back into that. So, perhaps my embodiments, the things I could be said to embody, seem to involve worries about what I am not doing and constant crises of confidence and faith.

Yet, despite my eternally-returning skepticism and rhythmically predictable crises of faith, this does not mean that I lack faith or that I am somehow emancipated from belief. Rather, I am constantly plagued by doubts and worries. Worries about some vague, unspecified Terrible Thing that might happen if, for instance, I were to stop doing my taiji forms, or to stop doing standing qigong, or the associated stretches that are said to be *necessary* supplements to the practice of the standing postures. Or worries about what might happen if I were to stop sparring.

These are, of course, my own personal existential matters, which might perhaps only be connected to my own sense of self and my own sense of identity.

Certainly, you could psychoanalyse me and easily diagnose me as screwed up in any number of ways. That is entirely possible. But, as I said at the beginning, although I am talking about myself here, I believe the implications of what I am discussing extend beyond my own personal idiosyncrasies or neuroses. The connections between physical practices, senses of identity, and wider discursive movements and ideological formations are not just related to psychology. They are a large part of anthropological, ethnographic, sociological and cultural studies approaches to embodiment. I mention crises of faith, anxieties, worries about sticking to one course or taking another, taking a bit of one course and combining it with another, and so on, because I think it suggests something important about 'embodiment'.

For instance, I have a weird relationship with taiji. I have practiced taiji for nearly two decades, yet I no longer feel like I 'really believe in' taiji as a martial art. I also don't particularly rate it as a physical exercise or health-giving practice. (I would rate qigong, yoga and weightlifting far higher.) And yet I *cannot* bring myself to stop practicing taiji at the same time as I find myself unable to articulate clearly and directly what my investment in the forms is.

For me, this casts a very real kind of light (or shadow) on Peter Sloterdijk's recent argument that religions are essentially misrecognised or 'misinterpreted anthropotechnic practice systems' (quoted in Spatz 2015: Loc 517) inasmuch as it suggests that taiji has the status of a kind of religion for me. Or, worse, a very particular kind of relationship to religion: The relationship of a non-believer who still goes to church. The automatism of the form seems to have produced a compulsion to repeat. Here we are in the orbit of Althusser, Pascal and Freud, and of the profound effects of institutions and ideologies on pathologies (Althusser 1971). The forms are pleasurable, to be sure; they definitely used to mean certain things to me, and I definitely used to believe that they were, if not 'actual' combat, at least *about* combat. But what are they to me now? They seem to have the status of a kind of 'warding off' of something terrible that might happen were I to stop doing them, a kind of gently pleasurable yet inexorably compelling exorcism ceremony that I feel drawn to and feel I *have* to perform.[6] (This thought about taiji practice as 'warding off' something terrible that might happen if I were to stop doing taiji often intrudes to bother me when I am performing the taiji move called 'ward off'.)

I raise all of this at the end of this chapter because I think it is important not to be too evangelistic about the possibilities of embracing embodiment, in academic study and in daily life. It is definitely marvellous to be 'in touch' with one's body, to become differently encultured, enskilled, enabled, even emancipated from many problems that can plague people who are not 'in touch' with their bodies. But, at the same time, we need to realise that our forms of embodiment

---

[6] For more on the relationships between martial arts and exorcism, see Scott Park Phillips' fascinating recent study *Possible Origins: A Cultural History of Chinese Martial Arts, Theater and Religion* (Phillips 2016).

can also become our bondage. I remember reading an article about the effect of nicotine on the body in a 'how to give up smoking' article. The author wrote that smokers feel like nicotine *gives* them something. But what smokers need to realise is that nicotine has actually originally *stolen* something from them, and they are driven to return to nicotine in order to temporarily remember what it is like to be reunited with the stolen thing: Namely, the feeling of calmness and not-craving-nicotine that non-smokers don't even realise they always and already have and that smokers miss and attempt to recreate by smoking another cigarette.

That article certainly helped me to establish a perspective that helped me to give up smoking. And that's definitely good, right? Smoking is definitely bad, right? But what if the nicotine-effect extends to other things? I remember as a teenager and twenty-something feeling compelled to go to the gym to lift weights. I *had* to. I felt like a bicycle tyre with a slow puncture, and that I would deflate to nothing if I did not keep going and pumping up my muscles. Strength training and bodybuilding was certainly very enabling for me. But it also trapped me. I'm still not sure that I have actually escaped from the clutches of that particular affliction. But the same is also true with taiji, qigong, yoga, sparring. In some respects, they feel like a life sentence. And like the 'lifers' in *The Shawshank Redemption* (1994), my worry is that I would not (will not) know how to cope, what to do, how to be, without it, or outside of it.

Maybe I need a coherent and overarching philosophy. Perhaps Taoism would be most appropriate. With this in mind, the next chapter attempts to examine Taoism, the philosophical worldview with which the most quintessentially Chinese and/or esoteric martial arts are often said to be aligned.

CHAPTER 5

Taoism in Bits

A Bit of Orientation

I would never claim to be an expert on Chinese thought, culture or philosophy. In fact, I would never claim to be an expert on anything. I tend to object to discourses organised by the notion of 'expertise'. This is because the notion of expertise is often invoked as a way to exclude, subordinate or de-legitimize non-professional voices from discussions. Rather than being an 'expert', at best I am a scholar of cultural studies, popular culture and ideology with a life-long interest in martial arts. Almost everything I have learned about Chinese thought, culture or philosophy, I have learned through and in relation to martial arts and popular culture. As such, some may question what I could possibly have to say to anyone about Taoism; they may contest my authority to hold forth on such a complex subject and challenge the legitimacy of any claims I may make. However, any claims I could make in this respect relate to my long-term research interests in ideology and popular culture. In other words, this chapter will principally draw not on my 'expertise' but rather on my research (and) experience in these areas.

For this reason, this chapter begins from what might be called two 'popular' propositions. First, the proposition that it is widely understood that Taoism is Chinese. Second, the proposition that there was a veritable explosion of interest in Taoism in Western popular culture in the wake of (and arguably in response to) some of the major wars of the second half of the 20th Century, particularly WWII, the Korean War and the Vietnam War (Watts 1990).

To flesh out the second proposition briefly: In particular, different kinds of Western interest in Taoism can be seen in the interests and orientations of the Beat Generation, the counterculture and, of course, hippies everywhere. It is often said that these interests had much to do with different kinds of rejection of, or protest against, the institutions that carried out the wars. In other

How to cite this book chapter:
Bowman, P. 2019. *Deconstructing Martial Arts*. Pp. 91–106. Cardiff: Cardiff University Press. DOI: https://doi.org/10.18573/book1.f. License: CC-BY-NC-ND 4.0

words, Western institutions and their ideologies were regarded by the Beats, the counterculture and the hippies in particular as being inhuman and driven by a machine-like rationality involving industrial-scale, exploitative instrumentality, all of which came to be regarded as something to be rejected (Clarke 1997; Heath and Potter 2006). In contrast to the dominant Western religions, philosophies, ideologies and worldviews, Taoism always seemed very different: A philosophy of the moment, the present, the experience, the natural, the ecological, and the ethical relation to the other. So, among other Eastern worldviews and philosophies, Taoism is often regarded as offering a genuine alternative to the outlooks driving the dominant status quo.

As for Taoism *itself*, there are many things to say about it. But these first two points – on the one hand, that Taoism comes from China, and, on the other hand, the Western interest in it – will structure much of what follows. In many respects, this chapter will chiefly be exploring the theme of the interest in Taoism in the West and the connection of this with martial arts. But all of this will be referred back and related to the subject of Taoism in China.

A Bit of Taoism

Because of the 'macro' perspective that my framing has just set up, the coordinates that are already being used in this chapter are the highly problematic notions of the supposed *East* and the supposed *West* (Hall and Gieben 1991). As problematic as these terms have often been shown to be, there is worse to come: Sometimes I am going to talk about China, sometimes East Asia; sometimes I am going to talk about Europe, sometimes America; and other times I am going to talk about some nebulous monster called Euro-America. The reasons for using such shifting and mostly unsatisfactory and imprecise coordinates boil down to familiarity, convenience and the effort to produce an effect of clarity, even at the cost of a huge lack of specificity.

Given the use of such problematic, shape-shifting and crude mirages as East/West coordinates, one might reasonably hope for more precision regarding the object of attention itself, namely 'Taoism'. However, the problem here is that an implied distinction between 'Taoism in China' and 'Taoism in the West' has already been generated, as if there were two different things with one name. However, there may be considerably more than one understanding of 'Taoism'. As this preliminary distinction already suggests, there may be at least one Eastern one and at least one Western one. And these may not be the same. Yet, if such a proposition is unproblematically accepted and assumed, this is going to have consequences. For instance, such a binary may lead us to leap to a predictable conclusion, one that has two faces. First, it will become both possible and likely that we will be inclined to presume that it will obviously be the case that the *Chinese* Taoism is the one that must be regarded as the original and therefore authentic and therefore superior or true Taoism. And second, that therefore any 'Western Taoism' must necessarily be secondary, derived, inauthentic, ersatz or inferior.

A deconstruction would unpick these assumptions at both ends, in terms of the complexity of the situation 'in the real world' and in terms of an awareness of the fact that this very binary was effectively invented (*constructed*) within this present argument itself. Although the kinds of assumptions that this argument reflects are certainly very familiar, a deconstructive approach would not follow this line of thinking at all. This is because this type of 'binary' thinking is saturated with all sorts of problems and introduces all sorts of prejudices (Chow 1995; Bowman 2010c). So, it is important to deconstruct and avoid them. At the very least, what should be borne in mind throughout is the possibility – or inevitability – that, instead of believing that there is one Chinese Taoism and one Western Taoism, there are inevitably going be multiple (even myriad) different understandings and interpretations of Taoism in both East and West, including many which totally undercut, eradicate or dissolve the supposed border between East and West.

In other words, this is not going to be a discourse about a true Taoism of China versus a false Taoism of the West. Readers should be aware that there will be intricately sophisticated, nuanced and effectively authentic incarnations of Taoism in the West. Conversely, at the same time, there will be multiple modulations of Taoism in China, some of which may well have been invented recently, perhaps with motivated ideological ends or agendas.

Taoism's Travels

It is important to reflect on all of this because it is vital to be vigilant against certain types of thinking and the unexamined bias(es) harboured within them. To help with this, there are multiple reasons, at the outset, to dispense with the idea of 'authenticity' (Heath and Potter 2006), as might be implied in an attribution of highest value to some idea of the 'original'. If we try to stop fetishizing ideas of original and authentic (perhaps because we are aware of the extent to which such ideas are themselves so often *contemporary inventions*), however, what might be the alternative?

One option is to replace the overvaluation of ideas of original and most authentic with the premise of any supposedly stable and unitary entity actually being elaborated over time and space in ongoing, open-ended, partial, and always in some sense incomplete iterations. Conversely, the search for authenticity implies a journey 'back to the source', and such thinking can be mired in ideological preconceptions exemplified by the idea of 'the original and best' versus 'most recent and least authentic/most inferior'. As Rey Chow has shown in her analyses of Chinese literary and cultural studies, for instance, the ideological and political effects of such styles of thinking can produce highly exclusionary hierarchies in which, for example, former colonies like Hong Kong are not

regarded within Chinese studies as being 'properly Chinese'; hence the literature and culture produced in such areas are not deemed worthy of study within
Chinese studies and excluded from the curriculum. The net result is a fetishistic
fixation on ancient Chinese literature and culture – the older the better.

In this sense, the race to the origin is a race to a kind of mythically-
manipulated past, and the search for the 'most authentic' can become a project that hierarchizes, orders and excludes many recent and very real forms of
practice. Rather than this, cultural studies can be oriented with considerably
more diverse and dynamic kinds of questions and perspectives. So, when it
comes to questions about Taoism and culture, for example, one might consider
beginning from a thoroughgoing questioning of what the 'it' is that is being
referred to whenever we refer to 'Taoism'. *Which* Taoism, where and when?
Does 'it' stay the same over time? How? Why? Is it the same when it moves?
Can such an 'it' travel? Can it travel intact? What conditions are required for
the smooth transition of something like Taoism from one place to another, one
time to another, one linguistic and cultural context to another, without it falling
to pieces, breaking up, becoming something else altogether?

As can be seen in the previous paragraph, in challenging simplistic understandings, deconstruction has always tended to complicate things – arguably
deconstruction often tends to overcomplicate matters. In this case, in a reflection on Taoism's travels, we might pause to explore whether the movement of
'Taoism' from culture to culture, context to context, is a relatively straightforward or complex case of cultural movement or cross-cultural communication.
Any enquiry will be required to address the question of what Taoism 'is'. Given
everything said so far, this may well turn out to be tricky, to say the least. Nonetheless, as with so many things, it is actually quite easy to come up with a rough
outline of answer. For instance, as with so many other things, you can start
simply by carrying out a cursory internet search.

The first result in the list generated by my Google search was the Wikipedia
entry for Taoism. Admittedly, there are many reasons to doubt the reliability
of every Wikipedia entry. So, I cross-referenced the Wikipedia entry with the
second page listed in my search results, which was the BBC pages on Taoism.

(Many may baulk at my admitting something like this. However, part of the
point of this exploration is to examine the general or popular cultural understandings of such a term. To do this requires referring to the main sources of
information about it. Wikipedia and the BBC can be regarded as mainstream
sources of information. Hence, there are multiple reasons to start from such
webpages.)

The first paragraph of the Wikipedia entry on Taoism reads as follows:

Taoism (/ˈdaʊɪzəm/), also known as Daoism, is a religious or philosophical tradition of Chinese origin which emphasizes living in harmony
with the *Tao* (道, literally 'Way', also romanized as *Dao*). The *Tao* is a
fundamental idea in most Chinese philosophical schools; in Taoism,

however, it denotes the principle that is both the source, pattern and substance of everything that exists. Taoism differs from Confucianism by not emphasizing rigid rituals and social order. Taoist ethics vary depending on the particular school, but in general tend to emphasize *wu wei* (effortless action), 'naturalness', simplicity, spontaneity, and the Three Treasures: *jing* (sperm/ovary energy, or the essence of the physical body), *qi* ('matter-energy' or 'life force', including the thoughts and emotions), and *shén* (spirit or generative power).

Specialist or expert academics could perhaps challenge such accessible characterisations. Nonetheless (and as unreliable as Wikipedia may sometimes be), this entry squares not only with the BBC pages that I cross-referenced it with but also with many other texts that I have read on Taoism before. For instance, as with other things that I have read on the subject, the Wikipedia entry concurs that: Taoism feeds from and back into lots of different kinds of Chinese intellectual and spiritual traditions; that it doesn't quite fit into Western categories, yet it is not utterly alien to them; that in Western terms it straddles or flows between familiar Western conceptual categories like religion and philosophy; that it has specific theories, specific ideas and specific principles, but that there are different interpretations, different rituals and different obligations in terms of ethics, norms, mores and injunctions, in different approaches to Taoism, even within and across China.

If such a definition refers heavily to China, let's flip perspective now and consider Europe or America. What does Taoism look like here?

If Taoism has a range of different incarnations in China, it seems fair to say that in the West it is mostly present only in bits. There is not much explicit or highly visible Taoism in the West. Of course, there is *some*. But, as the BBC website notes, the ritualistic and religious dimensions of much Chinese Taoism are almost unheard of in the West.

At the same time, a central symbol of Taoism, the yin-yang (or *taijitu*), is not at all uncommon. It is all over the place. Of course, when yin-yangs occur in the West, their status is unclear. Yin-yangs most commonly occur in what I will call for convenience subcultural contexts, or in the form of tattoos, or on children's stickers, or in posters for taiji lessons at the local community or sports centre. Books, pictures and paraphernalia can be found on sale in hippy shops, head shops, and alternative lifestyle shops. But Taoism rarely appears in the West as part of a fully formed institutional existence.

Words and phrases involving the yin-yang occur frequently in explanations of how martial arts like taiji or bagua 'work' (sometimes also Japanese arts like aikido or even judo), and in relation to the practices of different kinds of qigong. But the Taoism of the West seems to manifest principally in or as *bits* of Taoism.

Indeed, to many, Taoism may still seem exotic or unusual – even though it is far from new to the West. There are several centuries long traditions of Western intellectual engagements with Chinese and other East Asian philosophies and cosmologies (Said 1978; Clarke 1997; Sedgwick 2003). Many Western philosophers, theologians, theorists and thinkers have had many kinds of interest in many of the texts, traditions and practices of Taoism, along with other notable East Asian 'things', like Zen or Chan and other forms of Buddhism, as well as many less well-known shamanic practices, and so on.

The Circulation of Yin-Yangs

Given this, what is the status of Taoism in the West? As mentioned, in some ways, Taoism – or at least the trappings of Taoism – or at least bits of it – have become familiar in the West. The yin-yang symbol is certainly very well-known, even if an understanding of the logic, argument, principles or cosmology it implies is often absent. It has mostly found its niche in the West on the bodies and clothes and décor of certain 'types': Hippies, alternatives, crusties, teens, martial artists, New Agers and so on.

Further empirical cultural or sociological analysis of the contexts in which the images, trappings, paraphernalia and ideas of Taoism have been grafted into the Western world would be rewarding. But my hypothesis is that if we were to do a visual cultural analysis and look to see where we could find visual evidence of the signs and symbols of Taoism in the West, the study would reveal that the signs and signifiers of Taoism are most frequently grafted onto or into contexts that present themselves (or are regarded) as alternative, non-mainstream, often possibly oppositional or quasi-oppositional, frequently martial artsy, as well as New Age and orientalist. In other words: Marginal (Bowman 2017b).

Of course, no visual or material cultural study could tell us everything about the status of Taoism in the West. For instance, a study of visual culture would remain blind to the reach, scope, and influence of Taoism in books – books of Taoism and books about Taoism. Today, a lot of this kind of communication and discourse has moved onto blogs, vlogs, and podcasts. And, while there might be ways to measure the scale of online discourse about Taoism, it would still ultimately be impossible to ascertain the status, reach, influence or place of such discourse in any kind of convincing way. Nonetheless, my hypothesis about its discursive or cultural status in popular culture is that it emerged and exists along with a jumbled and often garbled collection of other often nebulous ideas and associations, many of which are taken also to refer and relate to martial arts. What I mean by this might be illustrated by a brief consideration of an example: The character of Caine (played by David Carradine), the lead protagonist in the early 1970s TV series, *Kung Fu* (1972-1975).

Although the actor who played him was white, Caine was meant to be from China (ethnically half Chinese, to be specific), a martial arts graduate monk of the Shaolin Temple and subsequent wanderer in the American 'Wild West'. It is a TV series that maps onto and encapsulates the peak of what is known as the 'kung fu craze' that swept the US, Europe and much of the rest of the world in the 1970s (Brown 1997; Prashad 2002, 2003; Bowman 2010d, 2013b; Kato 2012). And I actually think it also illustrates the form of one of the most significant recent bursts of Western interest in Eastern philosophy (Bowman 2010d).

For, Caine is not only invincible, he is also stoic, wise, modest, humble, good (see also Nitta 2010 as well as Iwamura 2005). He is a mishmash of the Confucian gent, the Taoist sage and – as certain commentators have noted – the West Coast/Californian hippy (Preston 2007). In fact, some of the most critical commentators have argued that the supposed Eastern wisdom embodied and mouthed by Caine has much more to do with Californian ideologies of the hippy era than with anything Chinese (Miller 2000).

This raises at least two interesting questions: First, if a major US TV network (along with Hollywood film companies) produces shows that champion Taoist philosophy, might this suggest that Taoism has (or had, or almost had) a larger, less marginal and more mainstream status in the West than we might otherwise have thought? But, second, if the brand of Taoism disseminated by this hugely popular and enduring TV series seems to hail more from California than a mythic Wudang Mountain, does this suggest that Western versions of Taoism will always be warped by or transformed into something else? There are other questions raised by *Kung Fu*, of course (Chong 2012; Bowman 2013b, 2015a), but these are the two that I would like to look at here.

Eurotaoism

Interestingly, philosophers such as Peter Sloterdijk and Slavoj Žižek have proposed that, far from being alternative or obscure, what they call 'Western Taoism' and 'Western Buddhism' are actually the hegemonic ideology of (or at least ideal ideological fit for) postmodern Western liberal consumer society (Žižek 2001b). Žižek's argument is that in situations of deregulated capital in a consumerist society the ideological imperative becomes one of not clinging and not getting too hung up on things. The first argument here is that things like consumerism and *feng shui* can be brought into alignment quite easily, via ideas like de-cluttering, deep-cleaning, updating, going 'out with the old, in with the new', and refreshing and reinvigorating by buying new stuff.

Indeed, Žižek proposes that a hybrid of ersatz Taoist, Buddhist and yogic ideas often blossoms wherever what used to be called yuppie conditions apply. For example, he argues that a chaotic life of stock market speculation or financial trading almost cries out for the calm of *feng shui* décor, early morning yoga, qigong or 'mindfulness meditation', as well as things like regular retreats (whether 'glamping' or in health spas). Most importantly, in such situations, Žižek argues, the yoga, taiji, qigong or 'mindfulness' practices enable the practitioner to console themselves with the belief that their meditative time is where they get in touch with the 'truth' of themselves – so that they don't have to face up to the fact that their work life *is* their 'real' life.

So, for Žižek, Taoism is a kind of 'spontaneous ideology' – not imposed from above but arising organically in response to the real conditions of economic life. By the same token (but on the other hand), the uncertainty, chaos and instability generated by deregulated capital is a prime breeding ground for the ethos of 'not clinging', of 'keeping moving', 'not stagnating', 'moving on', 'going with the flow', and so on. As Žižek puts it, the erosion of traditional rights and erstwhile certainties (such as fixed jobs and guaranteed pensions, etc.) is repackaged not as loss but as opportunity. A lost job is represented as an opportunity to retrain. Having no guarantee of a pension is an opportunity to invest. And so on. Ultimately, Žižek argues (in an almost Taoist move), the very victory of the Western economic global system has produced the emergence of what he calls the West's ideological opposite. Sloterdijk calls it 'Eurotaoism'.

Now, I am not at all sure that 'Western Buddhism' or 'Western Taoism' could be regarded as 'hegemonic' in any empirically verifiable sense, but I think the argument is interesting. It is possible to see how it might apply, where it might apply, and why it might apply. But whether, where, when, and to what extent it has been so is another matter altogether. Just because kung fu, yin-yangs, taiji, qigong and feng shui have been popular at different times and in different places, this does not somehow prove that Taoism or Buddhism are hegemonic ideologies.

Of course, establishing the facts of any matter has never stopped Žižek from making a sweeping statement or dramatic argument. And then there is the question of whether Žižek implies that we are supposed to regard this kind of Western Taoism as a *good* thing or a *bad* thing. The implication in the Žižekian argument is that, as an ideology arising within and because of changes in capitalism, this kind of Western Taoism must be a bad thing. But is it?

We could discuss this matter as long as we liked, but it might ultimately have the status of the exercises in which Mediaeval Christian theologians would reputedly debate how many angels could stand on the end of a pin. So, instead of arguing for or against Taoism, let us turn to our second question: The question of whether Western Taoism could ever be the same as Eastern Taoism.

A Bit of East is East and West is West

On this matter, answers might be divided into two camps. One camp regards the transmission of ideas from East Asian philosophy and thought into the West to be entirely possible. The other regards it as impossible. One great example of a writer who believed the transmission of ideas from East to West to be difficult but possible is Alan Watts. Watts rose to prominence in the decades after the Second World War with writings that tried to explain the spirit of Zen, Buddhism and Taoism to readers in English. Although not everyone has read Watts, one can often find traces of his accounts of East Asian ideas in the words of others. For instance, one of my own first encounters with the notion of the

Tao came via the writings of Bruce Lee, particularly his posthumous book, *The Tao of Jeet Kune Do* (1975). It was only much later that I read Watts.

As an ethnically Chinese martial artist, Bruce Lee was often called upon, when interacting with his Western students and other audiences, to play the role of the Taoist or Confucian sage. In fact, playing the wise man was a role that he often evidently relished, at least in his daily life (Preston 2007). In terms of his professional life, however, he sometimes complained about having been ethnically stereotyped and typecast in certain TV and film roles. But in books like his *Tao of Jeet Kune Do*, we find Lee using his most 'oriental wise man' tone of voice and mode of address. (Ironically, this is so even though what he advocates in that book is actually a totally iconoclastic, non-traditional, deracinated and revolutionary approach to martial arts.)

But, given that Lee was ethnically Chinese, and his first language was Cantonese, we might assume his Eastern philosophy to be authentic, right? The irony here is that recent scholarship and archival work on Lee's own personal library has shown is that he lifted most of his ancient Eastern wisdom straight from the pages of writers like Watts, along with other Western interlocutors (Bishop 2004). Famously, his favourite expression was the very Buddhist or Taoist sounding, 'Walk on'. But this was a phrase that he picked up from an early 20th Century English-language book on Buddhism, called *Walk On* (1947), written by the wonderfully named writer Christmas Humphreys (Humphreys 1947; cf. Bowman 2013b). I mention all of this here to give an indication of the complexity of ideas like 'transmission', and also, of course, 'authenticity'. I am not saying that Bruce Lee *only* read Western-authored English-language works on Chinese philosophy. But he certainly *also* did, and these informed his own discourse on Chinese philosophy. Whether such texts are right or wrong is a complex matter.

There are famous cases of radical misunderstandings of Chinese and Japanese history, society and culture – misunderstandings that have made their way into European consciousness as facts and truths. There have been controversies around the interpretations present in works such as Eugen Herrigel's *Zen and the Art of Archery* (1948), for instance, and in the supposedly authoritative and certainly enormous body of work on history, culture and civilization in China produced by sinologist Joseph Needham (Needham and Wang 1954, 1956, 1959; Needham, Wang, and Lu 1971; Needham and Tsien, n.d.; Needham and Bray 1984; Needham, Harbsmeier, and Robinson 1998; Needham, Robinson, and Huang 2004).

Martial arts historian Stanley Henning, for one, points out that at times Needham regards all Chinese martial arts as associated with Taoist health exercises. Hence – argues Henning – Needham radically misinterprets the complexity of the places of different martial arts in China in different places and different times. The effects of this misclassification of all martial arts as essentially being Taoist, Henning argues, leads Needham to fundamentally misunderstand some key aspects of Chinese culture and society (Henning 1999; Bowman 2015a).

So, there are risks in the face of interpreting across cultures and across times and places. And this leads us to the second camp: The people who do not believe that transparent translation across distant cultures is possible.

One interesting representative of this camp would be the infamous German philosopher Martin Heidegger (Heidegger 1971). Heidegger was very interested in Taoism. Some have even gone so far as to argue that Heidegger's own trailblazing 'Continental' proto-deconstructive philosophy was explicitly indebted to Taoism and other kinds of East Asian philosophy (May 1996). Heidegger even reputedly harboured dreams of producing his own translation of the key text of Taoism, the *Tao te Ching*, or *Dao de Jing*. (This work is sometimes known as the *Lao-Tzu*, after the name of its attributed author – an author who some argue almost certainly did not write it.)

What is perhaps most interesting about Heidegger's interest in Taoism is that he is said to have abandoned his dream of translating the *Lao-Tzu/Tao* because – even though this work is said to be one of the most frequently translated and re-translated texts in the world – some have even claimed that it is *the most translated* text in the world – Heidegger regarded the task of translating it as being too difficult. In fact, in the end, despite all of his interests in Taoism and what he often referred to as 'East Asian thought' (or indeed the 'East Asian lifeworld' *in toto*), Heidegger came to regard the East and the West as fundamentally, constitutively alien to each other. He came to conclude that, on a fundamental and unsurpassable level, 'East is East and West is West and ne'er the twain shall meet' (Heidegger 1971; Sandford 2003).

A Bit of Difference

Because of this ambivalent relation, what we might see in the case of Heidegger is interesting. In fact, what might be learned from Heidegger's relationship with Taoism is quite possibly exemplary of the matrix of possible relationships that Westerners have had with Taoism. Not just Taoism, of course. What I'm saying about Taoism could stand for Western engagements with a wide range of aspects or essences of Chinese and East Asian thought.

Many have been interested in all of this, and heavily involved in it, precisely because it all seems so different. But, if it is all so profoundly different, then perhaps (as Heidegger thought) it may be just *too* different, meaning that Westerners may never really 'get it'.

To many of us today, this is a familiar but problematic idea which sometimes sounds romantic but which often smells a bit too much of essentialism. Essentialism is one of the dirtiest of dirty academic words, even though essentialism in academia is not unusual. It is possible to find it all over the place, whether just below the surface or luxuriating in plain sight. There are *still*, for instance, academic studies being published that first propose and then explore the idea of the alleged fundamental difference or uniqueness of 'the Chinese mind'.

However, for the rest of us, to propose an essential difference between ethnicities (or ethnonationalities), and to reify or dignify such a proposition through any kind of consideration, is deeply problematic. It just smacks too much of colonialist (or indeed apartheid) anthropology and psychology, approaches that were premised on the belief not only of racial difference but also ('therefore') of racial hierarchy.

To those of us who work in or around cultural studies – with all of the refined (or mandatory) sensitivity to issues of identity that this entails (particularly in terms of class, race, gender, and sexuality) – the proposition of an essential difference (between East and West, or Europe and China) may appear crass to the point of being offensive. It is certainly not an idea we expect to find in our academic field. Here, scholars are more interested in cultural 'crossovers', 'encounters', 'communications' and 'relations' than they are in ideas of 'absolute essences' and 'unbridgeable differences'. Just like food, music, fashion, flu viruses, factories, or films, Taoism should surely be regarded as able to travel.

Can it travel, though? And, if it does travel, will it stay the same? If not, what would any change signify? If Taoism is taken to be a specific example of otherness (or at least a bit of a larger field of otherness), then the question is whether Westerners can really truly 'get' it. Heidegger thought not. He thought it was all just too different.

I'm dwelling on this for a moment because it points to a wider problem. To paraphrase a question once posed by Stuart Hall, if we are dealing with difference, if we are interested in difference, in respecting difference, trading in difference, and so on, then the question is: What do we think difference *'is'*? Does difference refer to something *actually* different, or are differences merely garnish to something essentially similar? Do we think cultural or ethnic others are actually significantly different from us, or do we think that we are all actually the same 'deep down'? Does difference mean different, or does difference mean same? What does difference mean? What does difference do?

Many – including many in cultural studies – solve this by imputing a universal value to 'being human', whilst adding that what produces cultural difference is *different cultural contexts*. But, whether difference is essential or entirely contextual, what does it imply for any 'encounter', 'crossover' and 'relation'?

Heidegger thought that there were absolute and unbridgeable differences between what he called the East Asian lifeworld and the Euro-American one. As mentioned, this may sound very bad to our contemporary anti-essentialist ears. In this case, it seems all the worse since many people know that Heidegger was notoriously a fully paid up member of the Nazi party and that he never renounced or even really reflected on this matter publicly after the war.

But, if we bracket off everything we don't like about Heidegger for the moment, it is possible to reformulate his position in apparently much more palatable ways. For instance, in cultural theory it is not uncommon to hear the idea that all translations from one context to another ought to be regarded as *mistranslations,* or at best partial and biased and *incomplete* translations; that all crossovers should be regarded as transformations and that all encounters are in some sense asymptotic. And so on.

To poststructuralist ears, formulations like this don't sound at all essentialist or fundamentalist. Rather, they sound quite subtle and complex – thoroughly deconstructive, even. It is a tenet of deconstruction that all translation is mistranslation. Similarly, Walter Benjamin argued that the best translations are transformations. And the influential psychoanalyst Jacques Lacan often seemed to regard all of the main kinds of encounters in life as being asymptotic.

Derrida himself was always careful to distance himself from any kind of Heideggerian position vis-à-vis difference as absolute or essential. Indeed, for Derrida, the obligation of the critical thinker was precisely to avoid collapsing difference into opposition. All differences are contextual, contingent effects or institutions. There is no opposition between East and West because these terms and clusters of concepts, notions and ideas are principally the effects of particular ways of thinking more than anything else. So, rather than any kind of retreat from difference, one can find in the work of this father of poststructuralism a principled openness to alterity, difference, encounter and change.

Nonetheless, in one of his earliest and arguably most important works, *Of Grammatology* (Derrida 1976), Derrida effectively inaugurates deconstruction by drawing a line. This is a line between the kinds of languages that he will deal with and speak about (European languages), on the one hand, and, on the other hand, the kinds of language that he will not (surprise, surprise: Chinese). Derrida draws this line because, he proposes, the written Chinese language is just too different to be dealt with in the same kind of way that he is going to deal with European speech and writing.

Much has been written about this undeconstructive inauguration of deconstruction, in which Derrida smoothly slices out a distinction between Europe and China, and in which 'China' stands for that which he cannot and will not try to think, as the outside of the limits of Europe. I mention it here merely to illustrate the ways that even an avowed openness to the ideas of alterity, difference, encounter, crossover, translation, relation, and so on, can be premised on or can flip over into their supposed opposite.

We will soon turn more directly to Taoism. But first I want to emphasise that I have started from such philosophers not out of ignorance or contempt for other kinds of Western engagements – or non-engagements – with either 'Chinese thought' in general or 'Taoism' specifically, but rather, to indicate the complexity of the question of a Western interest in Taoism. Put bluntly: If this kind of thing messes with the heads of both the daddy and the granddaddy of poststructuralism, then what other kinds of mess might we expect?

I'll mention some of these messes. But before we leave Heidegger I want to note the mess as he perceived it. Although he believed in an essential Europe (the pinnacle being, of course, German language philosophy), and although be believed in an 'East Asian lifeworld' that was essentially inaccessible to Westerners, he also believed that Westernisation was ultimately destroying East Asian alterity.

The effect of Western technology – Heidegger singles out the film camera – was to draw the world into what he called a Europeanised or Americanised 'objectness'. With this, he refers to the growth and spread and effects of Western conceptuality, ways of thinking, ways of relating technically to the world, ways of capturing and manipulating the world, and so on.

Again, this might sound deeply problematic and Eurocentric. It may romanticise the other, as something essentially vanishing. But this kind of argument is not a world away from some of the strongest impulses in postcolonial theory, which regard Euro-American cultural and ideological hegemony as being carried not just by gunboats and unequal trade deals but by everything from film and media to language itself and even – or especially – the most subtle and subterranean aspects of the spread of an originally European educational structure and syllabus. (Along with the obvious examples of the effects of the spread of Western medicine and Western science, Dipesh Chakrabarty famously points to the matter of the teaching of history. Along with the nation, history is a Euro-American concept, Chakrabarty argues. The idea that every nation must be a nation with a history ultimately means that Europe is always shown to be the origin and the destination. History always becomes the history of Europe. Emerging nations follow Europe (Chakrabarty 1992).)

In this kind of perspective, the West arguably always obliterates or transforms that which it encounters. So, in any encounter with Taoism, Taoism is obliterated, or transformed, and hence lost. This is because it must be *translated* into an alien conceptual universe.

Thus, in the West, Taoism has been regarded as *alternative* or even subtly *oppositional* to Judeo-Christian and even Islamic traditions, in that it is not a 'religion of the book'. It has been interpreted as a kind of pantheism, or as a kind of stoic atheism – a kind of religion without religion. It has been regarded as a kind of environmentalism, a kind of green ethos or ideology. It has been regarded as the quintessence of ancient Chinese wisdom. It has also been regarded as a kind of anti-Confucian and hence anti-establishment Chinese philosophy. It has been regarded as involving mystical mumbo-jumbo and bizarre rituals. It has also been regarded as an entirely rational and reasonable laissez-faire individualism, organised by the idea of following the path of least resistance.

There is a lot more that could be said about all of this. Even these many words barely scratch the surface of some of the matters that arise here. But, for now, suffice it to say that the idea that we may be barred access to 'the truth' or 'the reality' of something is very familiar in contemporary cultural theory. And, most importantly, it is not an idea that is reserved for application to texts and phenomena from 'other cultures'. It is an idea that has been applied to texts and phenomena from all cultures, including – especially perhaps – those of our own.

Getting it, a Bit

I tend to accept the idea that there is no simple or unmediated access to the supposed truth of a text and that interpretations of texts and phenomena are contextual, conditional, changeable, and revisable. But this does not mean that anything can just be anything. Interpretations are fought over, fought for, and often strongly policed. Just think about the violence that has ensued when different sects have emerged within and around Christianity by interpreting key texts, like the Gospels, differently. So, I tend to accept the notion that no one has direct or unmediated access to the truth of anything. But the question is whether certain Western interpretations of Taoism are obliterations of it, or a transformation or warping away from some kind of essence. Is the true essence of Taoism simply foreclosed or barred from access by Westerners?

I can accept the idea that I have been raised in a culture in which I have not on a daily basis been exposed to Taoist figures, rituals, sensibilities, words, phrases, legends, allusions, quotations, architectures, objects, practices and practitioners. So, in this sense of context, habitus, texture of life, structure of feeling, history and cultural literacy, the claim that I'm 'never going to get it' is fine.

But what about the supposed *messages* of Taoism – the lessons to be learned of or from Taoism? (In semiotic terms, the signified content or the final signifiers of Taoism.) Can these not be 'got'?

If the lessons of Taoism are simply or entirely *conceptual* or communicated in language, and if they are only to be accessed via the texts of Taoism, then arguably all of the complications and caveats and problems and aporias of cross-cultural translation that some call the 'hermeneutic circle' will arise here. So, we will definitely face some serious obstacles. Cross-cultural translation across vast distances of place and time is fraught with hurdles, barriers, mirages, dead ends, wrong trees, halls of mirrors and red herrings. This is because we always interpret from where we are and from what we know – which means that a Western discourse about Eastern things may always boil down to an internal Western monologue about a totally invented non-entity (Said 1978; Sandford 2003).

But the *Tao te Ching* seems absolutely clear on one or two key points. The first is that 'the Tao that can be spoken is not the Tao'. The second (possibly related point) is that spoken or written language is *neither* the medium of transmission *nor* of knowing either the Tao or Taoism. Perhaps the most famous words in the *Tao te Ching* are 'he who knows does not speak; he who speaks does not know'.

As Alan Watts himself once noted at the start of one of his early books on the subject, many people have taken these words to mean that the effort of communication is pointless, or ultimately doomed to failure. Watts disagreed with this interpretation and thought that it was worth the effort to try (Watts 1990).

This is not least because it is possible to talk *about* something without falling into the trap of believing that you are thereby doing it, living it, experiencing it, or conjuring it up, in reality. Indeed, perhaps discussing, listening, or even just 'thinking about' may be a precondition of experiencing or doing. Or at least a supplement. It certainly *seems* that Taoism involves a communicable philosophy or a principled stance in relation to the matter of *doing*. Western authors have tried to express it through all manner of poetic renderings of different topics, subjects and themes, from archery to fighting to flower arranging to motorcycle maintenance and so on.

My own encounter with a practice that conveyed some kind of understanding (through both doing and feeling) of Taoist principles was taijiquan. My own sense over time came to be that the inevitable and necessary lessons to be learned in taiji practice – especially via the interactive partner-work of push-hands practice – offered me a crystal-clear kind of education in Taoism. This is not to say that taijiquan offered me everything. It did not make me an expert on Taoism. But the interaction of hard and soft, positive and negative, fullness and emptiness, the logic of non-clinging, non-ego, non-striving, yielding, and the constant apperception of change and transition all led me to think that after years of taiji practice I really did 'get' the principles of Taoism – at least a bit. At least *that* bit.

But further reflection reminds me that I have also rejected other bits. For instance, supplementary parts of the practice of taijiquan involve various standing, breathing, concentration, relaxation and awareness practices, referred to as a number of things, such as qigong, nei-gong, zhang zhuang, and so on. Some of these I have always accepted fully – the stretching-and-relaxing breathing and postural exercises called *ba duan jin* [*pa tuan chin*], for example. I have never had any problem with these. Standing post qigong [zhang zhuang] too – I am fine with that. But the exercises that allegedly circulate qi internally through meridians in the body…I have always found within myself a profound resistance to these. Whenever I do them, I do them somewhat cynically. And, to be honest, I have all but abandoned even thinking about doing them. They seem to rely on a kind of belief that is just too much like religious faith for my liking.

But, like someone who has renounced their religion, I still often worry and wonder: If I have rejected this bit, what does it do to the rest? I know that I only dabble in bits of the entire possible taiji world – I do the solo form, partner-work, any kind of sparring, some stretching exercises and some standing qigong – but I also know that I have abandoned another huge bit.

So, even within the confines of my own limited experience of one syllabus of a more or less Taoist and more or less (once) Chinese practice, I know I don't have it all. And, what is more, I also know that, besides the 'all' that I am aware I do not know, there is a whole lot more out there – many more 'alls' and 'everythings' – much more than I have ever even imagined. I console myself by telling myself (sometimes in the manner of an old Chinese sage) that this is true of all things. For, could we really ever have it all, or know it all, or get it all? Is the 'all', the totality, even a real thing? Or is it not, in fact, just an effect, either of language or of our experience of a certain state of play? The state of play as we perceive it is always determined by the circulation of ideas and practices, which themselves derive from different kinds of institutions and investments.

Institutions and interpretations are variable and contingent, and they produce different effects.

Just as I began with reference to such vague and shifting supposed entities as 'East' and 'West', so we should be aware of what I characterized in Chapter Two as the shifting and drifting apparent referents of our focus, their different meanings in different times and places, the genetic mutations and quantum leaps that occur in 'cultural translation' from one time to another, one place to another, one language to another, even one utterance or instance to the next, and the rather frustrating fact that, despite our eternal desire to see unity and simplicity, cultures and practices are always 'in bits', always in process, incomplete, disputed and contested. As I read it, the one always gives birth to the ten thousand things and you can never therefore pin down the one.

So, this means both that no one's ever going to get it but also that anyone can get it – but really only a bit.

The next chapter will consider some of the consequences of this.

CHAPTER 6

Mindfulness and Madness in Martial Arts Philosophy

The previous chapters have argued for the inevitability of divergent inter-pretations both of theory (or 'philosophy') and propriety in practice, in and around martial arts. This chapter enquires into what some of the consequences may be as a result of the inevitability of different interpretations – or selective ('partial') constructions – of 'philosophy' in and around martial arts. In line with the de- and reconstructive argument about interpretations and cultures always emerging out of 'incomplete' contingent encounters between chance, contingent or select partial elements, the chapter first seeks to relate the theme of 'Chinese philosophy' to the Dutch word 'rust'.

To readers unfamiliar with this Dutch word, such a combination may seem odd or eccentric. However, it should be remembered that what may seem bizarre in one context may feel natural, obvious, inevitable or even necessary in another. In other words, just because the attempt to express ideas of Chinese philosophy or Chinese martial arts in terms of a specifically Dutch term may seem gratuitous or inexplicable in many contexts, in the Netherlands, such an act could be regarded as anything from totally apt to effectively inescapable.

Of course, full disclosure of my reasons for doing this would have to include mentioning the fact that I was invited to speak about martial arts and Eastern philosophy at a festival of philosophy in Leuven, a festival whose overarching theme was precisely this Dutch word, 'rust'. Leuven was a city that I had long wanted to visit – not least because it is the place in which the wonder-fully subversive educator Joseph Jacotot (1770-1840) famously came up with his conviction that people can teach what they don't actually know and that learners do not really need teachers (see Rancière 1991). This was helpful for me because I am not a philosopher, my knowledge of Eastern philosophy is woefully general, and I don't speak Dutch. In fact, the first time I heard about the Dutch word 'rust' was when I was invited to Leuven to speak about it.

How to cite this book chapter:
Bowman, P. 2019. *Deconstructing Martial Arts*. Pp. 107–123. Cardiff: Cardiff University Press. DOI: https://doi.org/10.18573/book1.g. License: CC-BY-NC-ND 4.0

Given my obvious lack of qualifications to speak about any of these things, some may regard my acceptance of the invitation to be the height of arrogance. However, given my arguments so far throughout this book – combined with those of Joseph Jacotot (and latterly his key interlocutor Jacques Rancière) – accepting the invitation qua challenge seemed appropriate. For, if Jacotot was right to argue that teachers can teach things they don't actually know, then all could be well. By the same token, even if not, according to the rest of that same argument, no one really needed me to teach them anything anyway, and they would definitely still learn something.

To begin: As already mentioned, one of the first things relevant here that I didn't know in advance was the Dutch word *rust*. So, I needed to look it up. To do so, I duly turned to the *OED*, which presented me with a phenomenal amount of etymological information,[1] most of which I could do absolutely nothing with. So, next, I just Googled the word, using search terms like 'Dutch word rust' and 'meaning of Dutch word rust'. Some cross-referencing across

---

[1] Brit. /rʌst/
U.S. /rəst/
Forms:
α. OE–15 **rost**, OE– **rust**, ME **roste**, ME–15 **ruste**.
Frequency (in current use):
Origin: A word inherited from Germanic.
Etymology: Cognate with West Frisian *rust, roast*, Middle Dutch *roest, rost* (Dutch *roest*), Old Saxon *rost* (Middle Low German *rost, rust*), Old High German *rost* (Middle High German *rost*, German *Rost*), Faroese *rustur*, Norwegian *rust*, Old Swedish *rost, rust, ruste, roster* (Swedish *rost*), early modern Danish *rost, rust, røst* (Danish *rust*), probably < a suffixed (or perhaps compounded) form of an ablaut variant of the same Indo-European base as RED *adj.* and *n.* (compare RUD *n.*[1] probably showing the same ablaut grade), hence with reference originally to the red colour of rust. Use in sense A. 6 is also widespread among the other Germanic languages.

Different formations also probably ultimately < the same Indo-European base as RED *adj.* and *n.* and also with the meaning 'rust' are shown by Old Icelandic *ryð, ryðr*, Old High German *rosomo*, and, outside the Germanic languages, by Lithuanian *rūdys*, Old Church Slavonic *rūžda* (Old Russian *r''ža, rža*, Russian *rža*), classical Latin *rōbīgō, rūbīgō*.

In Old English a strong masculine or neuter *a* -stem. The Old Saxon and Old High German forms (and likewise Middle Dutch *rost*) show the expected West Germanic lowering of **u* > **o* in an *a* -stem formation **rusta-*, which is probably also shown by the (rare) early Old English form *rost*. The β. forms suggest the existence of a by-form with a long vowel in Old English, although both the date and the mechanism by which such a form arose are unclear. The modern form *rust* with short vowel could then result from this by-form, with shortening in late Old English before a consonant cluster. However, a form with short *u* could also have existed earlier, since exceptions to the West Germanic lowering of **u* > **o* before a back vowel are not uncommon in Old English. The vowel of Middle Dutch, Dutch *roest* is not satisfactorily explained. (The modern West Frisian form *roast* shows the expected development from West Germanic short **u* in this position; the West Frisian form *rust* probably also ultimately reflects a development from **rusta-*, rather than from a form with a long vowel.)

For evidence of currency of forms showing the (diphthongal) reflex of a long vowel in English regional (northern) use in the 20th cent. see H. Orton *Phonology of a South Durham Dialect* (1933) § 133.

different sites reassured me that I was finding reliable information, so I felt I was learning more and more about the word and its usage and meanings. One site told me this:

> English words for the Dutch word rust calmness dead ease half time hush imperturbability intermission let-up lie-off pause peace placidity quiescence quiescency quiet quietness quietude recess reposal repose rest silence tranquility tranquillity wait at ease[2]

Another site concurred with all of this, telling me that 'rust' means: 'Break; calm; ease; half-time; pause; peace; placidity; quiescence; quiescency; quiet; quietness; quietude; recumbency; repose; respite; rest; surcease; tranquillity'.[3] And it also told me how to use the word, in the imperative, as a command – 'Rust!' – which means, 'Stand at ease!'

At that point, I felt I could rest easy (or rust easy), safe in the knowledge that I had just become a bit of an expert on the word, even though I didn't have a teacher and couldn't otherwise speak Dutch. Even better, I could now see an immediate or obvious potential connection between 'rust', 'Eastern philosophy' and martial arts. For, as is commonly believed, there has long been a connection made between East Asian martial arts and supposedly Taoist or Zen Buddhist ideas of calmness and tranquillity. Of course, much of this connection is based on myths (and mainly media myths, at that). Nor does everything covered in the meanings of 'rust' that could apply to martial arts necessarily have to refer to either Taoism, Zen or Buddhism. Anyone who has ever done any wrestling or ground-fighting learns quickly not to panic or tense up when rolling around on the ground with an opponent who is trying to choke or lock or pin or hold or strangle you out. Beginners tense up to high heaven and panic and expend enormous amounts of energy. The more advanced you become, the more you stay calm, relaxed, tranquil, and the more you can (ultimately) flow.

In such martial arts, the ability to flow is the objective, i.e., not to get knotted up wherever the opponent is trying to take control or issue force and instead to flow (or crash) around or through a problem and turn the tables. If we are face-to-face and you push forward into me and I push forward into you then whoever is stronger will prevail. But if you push forward and I flow around that then you end up pushing nothing and I should be able to capitalize on that – to the extent that I can flow. And the extent to which I can flow is the extent to which I am relaxed and calm in a very particular way.

As Bruce Lee famously put it, 'Be water', because water can flow and it can crash, it can push and it can pull, but you can't grab it with your fist and if you try to punch it you won't hurt it; it fills any space and passes through any gap,

---

[2] http://www.wordhippo.com/what-is/the-meaning-of/dutch-word-rust.html
[3] http://www.majstro.com/Web/Majstro/bdict.php?gebrTaal=eng&bronTaal=dut&doelTaal=eng&teVertalen=rust

but try to wrestle it and you end up wrestling nothing. (It's a wonderful image. But I would add that even water can only be like water when it is not too hot and not too cold. If it's too hot, it becomes vapour or steam and loses something; if it's too cold, it becomes frozen, tense, rigid and brittle.) Perhaps in all martial arts relaxation is the thing. Calmness of mind. Acuity of consciousness. Clarity of intent. Fluidity of body. Each martial art has a different way of being relaxed and in flow, a different ideal that practitioners aspire to. The boxer, kickboxer, Thai boxer, karateka, escrimador or kung fu hard stylist have certain kinds of ways of flowing – combining striking techniques fluidly, rolling with the punches, capitalising on the gaps and opportunities provided by the other, smashing their way through. The judoka, wrestler and jujitsuka rely on the same principle, although it is very differently actualised.

But the premise, aim and ideal is always calm relaxation, if not simply tranquillity.

Tranquillity is normally associated with the 'most internal' of what they (problematically) call the 'internal' martial arts. The ultimate example, of course, is taijiquan. But many anecdotes from many different martial arts styles convey a sense that the highest-level practitioners of almost any martial art can convey an air of tranquillity when fighting.

Training Rust

Still, taiji is certainly a notable case insofar as its training is designed to train relaxation, calmness and a great deal of what is conveyed by the Dutch word rust. Advanced-level taiji practitioners spar like they are strolling, not running, charging or dancing. It's like they are simply carrying out a task that they have done countless times and it's simply second nature. So, watching them deal with opponents is like watching someone steering a boat, flying a kite, mowing a lawn, folding laundry, or rolling up a cable; or a fisherman casting and reeling. It's a very simple, very unglamorous, very relaxed, very natural, yet very skilful thing.

I have occasionally had the pleasure of being the one who is folding and felling opponents like a laundry worker folding and flattening out sheets. And when you are in that zone, that state of flow, it is very much like that – just something that you are doing; pleasurable, but natural – no real effort; no real striving, planning, pursuing, just feeling and doing. Of course, I have much more often been on the receiving end, against someone who wants to treat me like some laundry that needs to be straightened and folded and flattened out. A popular martial art saying is 'you either win or you learn'. And I have done a lot of learning.

And not just in taiji. I have been folded and flattened in many different martial arts styles over many years. Occasionally, it has been me doing the folding and flattening, and that is always a very nice treat. But none of the other kinds of sparring that I know involve activities that are as *necessarily* calm and tranquil as taiji. Doubtless, this is connected with the unique and uniquely philosophical way that taiji training is approached. In it, all attention is put on teaching relaxation. But this is not quite as simple as it may sound. It is actually surprisingly hard to teach relaxation in taiji, and the type of relaxation that is the ultimate goal is not simple relaxation. It takes different forms, from mental relaxation, to the hyper-awareness of tension and looseness in the body (to enable higher levels of sensitivity and responsiveness), to the ability to be relaxed in otherwise difficult postures or transitions, and through to the cultivation of what they call 'sung jin', or relaxed force in the application of techniques. There are other dimensions to taiji relaxation or restfulness, too, but the point is: Learning it all is no simple matter. It takes a great deal of patience, commitment, and trust – trust in your teacher, trust in the investment of time and energy, and trust that it will all pay off or yield dividends.

In many respects, rather than being anything like lying down and relaxing, training for this kind of relaxation is actually analogous to weightlifting, strength training, or bodybuilding. In weightlifting for strength or bodybuilding, a key principle is 'progressive resistance': Over time, you put more and more weight on the bar so that the resistance placed on the muscles progressively increases. In response to increasing demands, and in conjunction with adequate rest and nutrition, the muscles, tendons and ligaments, etc., respond – by growing stronger, often larger, denser, and so on.

Despite appearances, training in and around taiji is similar. However, instead of external resistance, there is more a kind of *progressive intensification of 'rust'* – a 'progressive res[t]istance', so to speak. This progressive intensification is centred on awareness of posture and breath. More refined awareness of posture goes hand in hand with more intensified relaxation. More refined and intensified awareness and control of breath leads to all sorts of unexpected health and skill consequences. On this level, I would recommend it to anyone. Taiji and qigong can become quite a remarkable combination for producing a sense of healthiness. But the idea that taiji and qigong are 'simply' all about rest or relaxation is misleading. As with any martial art, taiji requires really *devoted* and focused training. You have to *learn* how to be relaxed. You have to work hard to take control of your mind and relax it. This is not simple. It is not simple or easy to make yourself train every day when a lot of that training involves standing stock still for half an hour or more in a relatively awkward position, focusing on your breathing and posture and sensations – especially when you have jobs to do, the clock is ticking, there is work to do, and so many other demands. You have to *believe* in it and *trust* in it.

So, when it comes to the relaxation required in successfully mastering taiji, or maybe any physically and mentally demanding skill-set, to speak of 'rest' is *kind* of correct, yet also not quite right. I guess *calmness* would be the best term to apply across the board. When you're not in some sense calm, you're probably not going to be functioning at your best. This is so even though some approaches to combat training insist on forcing practitioners into extremes of adrenaline, fear, and beyond sustainable states of exhaustion. But, again, the reason for this is to get used to it so as to learn how to manage panic and terror and exhaustion – in short, once again, so that you become, in a very particular way, calm, even when operating at high levels of stress.

Zen Again

Of course, as mentioned earlier, many East Asian martial arts are associated with lofty philosophical and cultural ideas and ideals, such as those associated with Zen Buddhism or Taoism. However, I always hesitate before accepting associations like these. This is for two reasons. The first is because such associations tend to come from dubious media myths and often have little historical basis. The second is because there is rarely to never any observable Zen (Chan) or Taoist dimension to them – at least no more than there is in anything else.

Despite this caveat, I still also think that it is easy (and justifiable) to see how and why something like taiji could be regarded as Taoist. Even though it is possible to refute most fantasy histories of taiji, it is undoubtedly the case that everything in its logic of training and application can be (and normally is) expressed in terms of yin and yang plus a range of other terms deriving from Taoist cosmology and principles. However, other than for internal Chinese martial arts like taiji – possibly also aikido – I really don't know how far it is possible to claim that other martial arts are 'philosophical' in the same way.

This is so even though the most popular story of the origins of 'all' kung fu states that kung fu originated as a consequence of Zen Buddhist training in the Shaolin Temple in China. Of course, this is a myth – indeed, perhaps it is an almost perfect myth. It has a grain of truth: Self-defence was required at the Temple, as it was everywhere, and over time the temple gained a fearsome reputation. But, as an origin myth, it is easy to refute. However, even though the myth is easy to debunk, it keeps coming back. Like a phoenix, or a Terminator, the myth of Shaolin Temple Zen training as the origin of kung fu keeps coming back, no matter how well you think you have killed it. This is why people seem compelled to associate East Asian martial arts with pacifism in general and Buddhism in particular. But my claim here is that all of this is just a 'bolt-on' to bolster the myth.

The reason I want to make such a claim here is to suggest that mythic narratives and claims about moral or ethical codes are not what we should be looking at or thinking about when we enquire about the 'philosophy' of this or that martial art. All ethics or moralities or mores are optional extras. Rather than looking for philosophy in the 'blah blah blah' that so often surrounds martial arts, what I want to suggest is that the philosophy of a martial art is *embodied*, in particular ways. All martial arts and approaches to fighting are the manifestation of a kind of theory, or philosophy, or ideology, or fantasy.

The moves, the training, the sparring, they all imply either a conscious or an unconscious 'theory' or 'philosophy' of all sorts of things: What violence is, what combat is, what works best, how bodies work and interact, what teaching and learning should be like, what society is like, what the place of the individual is within society, and so on. All martial arts, from the most supposedly ancient to the most avowedly modern, are based on tacit, implicit or explicit premises, hypotheses, arguments, theories, fantasies or philosophies about the world, society, and our place and responsibilities within it.[4]

Philosophize-a-babble

As mentioned in an earlier chapter, a friend of mine once told me that her kung fu instructor would often sit them all down and give them lectures about the philosophy of their kung fu style. Do such lectures make that kung fu style itself philosophical? I would suggest not.

We could sit down and philosophize anything – everything – that we do. But in what way does that mean that *it* 'is' philosophical? As I have said, I think that taiji 'is philosophical' because it actualizes Taoist principles. It is a physical expression of them (among other things). In a similar way, I think that many other martial arts are based on implicit or explicit theories about the particular kind of toughness and calmness that need to be cultivated.

Consider this. In karate they 'kiai'. Taiji has no 'kiai'. This could be said to be an embodied dimension of the 'philosophy' underpinning each practice. In some martial arts training, what is valued and what is trained is speed, or flow, or power, or sensitivity, or athleticism, and so on. I've never made a noise in taiji – apart from maybe a yelp of pain here or there. But almost every punch I have ever thrown at a pad in escrima training has been accompanied by some kind of guttural shout or grunt or hiss – expressing and intensifying the intent to smash the target as hard as possible. So, there's something there – whether you call it a philosophy or a theory or psychological attitude to be trained and developed.

There are also principles that could (some would argue should) be trained across all martial arts, which could be called philosophical. One is 'go weak for technique', as in: When you are training, always train as if you are weaker than your opponent. That way, you *have* to develop superior technique. For, if it's just strength against strength, then the stronger will always win. Maybe this kind of attitude could be called almost Taoist. Or maybe it could just be called

---

[4] Is it philosophical to say that a person has the right to defend themselves? You may say yes or no or maybe. You may even begin to wonder what it is that makes something a philosophical question at all. And that's all good. Jacques Derrida regularly suggested that the question of what is and what is not a philosophical question is actually a question that is always at the heart of philosophy. So Derrida saw everything as philosophical. (And, of course, we may add, therefore nothing is uniquely or specifically or only philosophical.)

universal. Or maybe Taoist principles are universal. Certainly, taiji advocates such an approach to the most refined degree.

Yet, I still see no *necessary* Zen Buddhism in kung fu or karate or judo or jujitsu. And I actually cannot comprehend why something like taekwondo ever even makes any reference to the yin-yang symbol. For, even though many martial arts make connections to the yin-yang, I firmly believe that this is principally because the yin-yang is a cool-looking symbol. It often has next to no functional connection with what they do. In other words, I am suggesting that the connections that are often assumed to exist between supposedly 'Eastern' martial arts and so-called 'Eastern philosophy' are both not essential and often garbled and convoluted. In fact, I will go further and state that these connections often owe more to mass media myths and fantasies than anything specific to the practices themselves.

But does that mean that I am saying that there are some 'truly' philosophical arts like taiji, which are therefore 'good' (because they are philosophical in my apparently preferred sense), while there are other, maybe modern, corporate and profit-focused arts, like MMA or taekwondo, which are somehow therefore 'bad' (because they are *not* philosophical in my apparently preferred sense)? I'm going to say 'No'. I'm not saying that – for lots of reasons. More reasons than there is time or space even to gesture to here and now. Everything can be philosophized. Everything we do is the manifestation of some kind of implicit or explicit theory or outlook or philosophy. But, even if something is strongly connected with a philosophy that you or I may personally prefer, this does not necessarily make such practices 'good'. Calmness does not mean good. Nor does calmness mean moral, safe, sane or superior.

Madfulness Meditation

Consider this. What is it that makes so many people think that things like yoga, taiji and qigong are somehow simply or necessarily good? I would propose that one of the main things that leads to this conclusion relates to the many regular associations made between these kinds of practices and the idea of 'good health': Mental health, mind-body awareness, mindfulness, work/life balance, and so on.

Now, as I've already confessed, as a practitioner of taiji and qigong, on some level I really do believe in the 'positive mental health' narrative that surrounds internal martial arts and yoga. But, as a practitioner of other martial arts, and also as someone who sometimes has a philosophical bent, and certainly as someone who watches YouTube and so on, I also wonder whether sometimes such positive mental health and supposed awareness come at a cost of positive self-delusion and a particular lack of awareness.

For instance, many (perhaps most) taiji practitioners believe in magic. Some martial artists believe you can hit someone without actually making physical contact with them, like some kind of Jedi Knight. The magic conduit for this and many other things is called *chi* (*qi*) – which is an eminently magic proposition. Nonetheless, many people believe in qi. But for what reasons, on what evidence, and to what ends? Much of this may be harmless. But, at the same time, videos abound on YouTube of hapless qi and *ki* masters who have done things like challenge MMA and other full contact martial artists to fights only to be battered black and blue by them. There are also embarrassing videos aplenty in which poor deluded students bounce and leap about in response to their master's touch, or gesture. Similarly, many people spend long hours and days and weeks and months and years and decades engaged in practices ranging from qigong to push-hands to point sparring and so on believing that they are preparing themselves for the reality of combat. In short, there are many kinds of martial arts self-delusion, all of which I'm sure are also accompanied by many kinds of awareness and insight.

In the wider cultural ideological realm, what are we really to make of employers offering their overworked and stressed out employees free taiji or mindfulness meditation classes? Do firms lay on such services out of the goodness of their hearts? Or might there be other agendas? We might ask the same of the state promotion of martial arts in schools across Asia. Is this motivated by philosophical ideals any loftier than nationalism? And how many financial traders, speculators, yuppies and bankers have believed that they are most in touch with their own fundamental truth and reality when they are engaged in their early morning yoga or meditation, and not when they are speculating on futures? Perhaps at the most extreme end of things: How many sociopaths or psychopaths or misanthropes have either prepared for or dealt with their atrocious acts by meditating? (Anders Behring Breivik prepared himself for what has been called one of the most devastating acts of mass murder by an individual in history on July 22, 2011, by undertaking a long period of training in what he called 'Bushido meditation'. I will return to this in the next section.) Or, at another extreme: Consider the fact that many martial artists of the late 19th Century anti-foreigner Boxer Uprising in China believed that their 'iron shirt' kung fu training would make them *impervious to bullets*. In many different kinds of cases, what seems to sustain and nourish people in many martial arts activities are fantasies about tapping into or communing or connecting with something. Very often, this involves fantasies about an ancient mystical truth. The fantasy is a fantasy of something that may well never have existed. Qi and chakras and meridians may well be tenets of faith, and the internal martial arts training which focuses on moving qi through meridians may well be an exemplary exercise in supreme self-delusion.

Or it may not. Maybe you can never know something unless you try it. Or, maybe more than 'trying', maybe you can never truly know something unless you've *mastered* it. But maybe trying to master something like this will be the very thing that pulls you into a world of self-delusion. Maybe this is particularly so because to try to master anything like this will always require having some kind of faith and some kind of belief. You cannot maintain qigong meditation or taiji slowness training without some element of belief, some element of faith, some element of trust in something – whether that be a teacher, or a promise of health or invincibility or longevity.

Philosophers from Kierkegaard to Derrida have reflected on the decision – the decision to do something, to try something, to make a certain move, to reach a certain conclusion – and they have called it 'a moment of madness', a leap of faith, a step into the unknown, the abyss, the void. Take the blue pill or take the red pill; have faith in an idea or an argument or theory or a philosophy. Persuade yourself to stand in static meditation every day for half an hour or more. Practice forms over and over again for the rest of your life. Maybe this is the path. Or maybe you're swimming on dry land, believing it will help you to swim up a strong river; or maybe you're just playing air guitar, believing that you are turning yourself into the new Jimmy Hendrix.

What is sensible and what is not? Listening to someone or walking away? What if they claim to have all the answers, to be the experts, to know the truth? We know we should eye such people with suspicion. But what if someone told you at the outset that they were going to hold forth on something they might actually know nothing about – like how a word from a language they can't speak relates to a world of philosophy they only know in the most woefully general of ways? What would you do in that situation? What did you do in that situation? Did you trust? Or did you rust?

Philosology and Psychosophy

Clearly, 'philosophy' and 'psychology' can shade into each other, and different interpretations of philosophy, or different philosophies, can have psychological impacts. In martial arts, as well as there being different philosophies, there are differing underlying psychological theories or beliefs that inform or even underpin different disciplines (Bowman 2014b). Different styles, systems, regions and periods often manifest different discourses, theories or ideologies of what we might call martial arts psychology. All of this might be referred to as the martial artist's outlook, mindset, psyche, or subjective stance or attitude. Such outlooks or attitudes might be linked to the ethos of the training environment (García and Spencer 2014).

Of course, sometimes – as in many discourses around boxing or MMA – the dominant idea has often been that 'being a fighter' is something innate – something you are 'born with' (Spencer 2011; see also Wacquant 2004). This seems to be a very common claim among competitive fighters and those involved in some way with what we might call street fighting (i.e., people with some kind of connection to non-rule-bound fighting and violence, such as bouncers, for example). But my sense is that, in most martial arts, being – or, more precisely, becoming – a fighter is conceived of in terms of some kind of notion of 'fighting spirit', and that such a 'spirit' is something that is cultivated, through what Foucault would term 'the means of correct training' (Foucault 1978). My sense is also that different martial arts – or even the 'same' martial art at different times – seek to cultivate very different 'kinds' of martial arts subjects.

In my own life, I have experienced very different kinds of training ethos. Some seemed saturated with a vague sense of the inherent value of 'toughening up' (Downey 2007; Green 2011; Spencer 2011). Others focused more on having fun, competition and competitive play. Still others put the importance of a certain psychological attitude front and centre – whether that be cultivating dispassionate calm responsive sensitivity (as in taijiquan, particularly in push-hands training), developing an explicit 'predator awareness' self-defence mindset, or an insistence on a kind of all-out aggression, such as that which is termed 'forward thinking' in escrima concepts (Bowman 2014b, 2015a; see also Miller 2008, 2015). Some were informed by mysticism, others by hierarchy, authority and deference, and still others by camaraderie and a sense of being involved in a shared research project. Informed by this diversity of experience, as well as other forms of research, I have argued before that martial arts can very often be regarded as intimately imbricated within different kinds of ideology. However, what I am proposing here is something slightly different. Unlike virtually all other studies in this realm, I am at this point less focused on the matter of the ideologies that 'go into' the discourse of a martial art and more interested in the question of the types of subjects that 'come out', that are produced in and by martial arts training: The type of subjective attitude, mindset, sense of identity and orientation towards the world.

Obviously, this is a two-way street – or even an incredibly complex junction. But an article by Oleg Benesch highlights what I am interested in here, in very stark terms. Benesch begins 'Reconsidering Zen, Samurai and the Martial Arts' (Benesch 2016) with a consideration of the case of Anders Behring Breivik, who, 'on July 22, 2011 … committed one of the most devastating acts of mass murder by an individual in history'. Benesch writes:

Over the course of one day, he killed 77 people in and around Oslo, Norway, through a combination of a car bomb and shootings. The latter took place on the island of Utøya, where 69 people died, most of them teenagers attending an event sponsored by the Workers' Youth League. During his subsequent trial, Breivik remained outwardly unemotional as he clearly recounted the events of the day, including the dozens of methodical execution-style shootings on the island. His calmness both on the day of the murders and during the trial, shocked many observers. It was also an important factor in an attempt to declare Breivik insane, a move that he successfully resisted. Breivik himself addressed this subject at some length, crediting his supposed ability to suppress anxiety and the fear of death through concentrated practice of what he called 'bushido meditation'. He claimed to have begun this practice in 2006 to 'de-emotionalize' himself in preparation for a suicide attack. According to Breivik, his meditation was based on a combination of 'Christian prayer' and the 'bushido warrior codex'. Bushido, or 'the way of the warrior', is often portrayed as an ancient moral code followed by the Japanese samurai, although the historical evidence shows that it is largely a twentieth-century construct. (Benesch 2016, 1)

Benesch's own interests in this matter relate to addressing the matter of many misunderstandings of the history of notions like 'samurai spirit' and the supposed connection of this spirit with Zen. As the above passage suggests, he is animated by the fact that what is 'largely a twentieth-century construct' has functioned ideologically. Benesch's project, here and elsewhere, is to set out the ways that such factually incorrect discourses have emerged and to clarify the ways that they have functioned ideologically. However, as noted, my own interests at this point are chiefly related to what we might call the various types of psychology or pseudo-psychologies of violence and training for combat that are attendant to different kinds of martial arts pedagogy and philosophy.

Benesch's article is extremely helpful for me here because it sets out clearly the relations between a number of elements that I contend it is important to realise are interconnected. Specifically, this is the connection between a training ethos and its theory of psychology – or, indeed, its theory of the subject – and the extent to which neither of these are 'innate' or 'necessary', but, on the contrary, entirely 'cultural'. This is not 'cultural' in the sense that we often too easily use the term – as when we say 'Eastern' or 'Western', or 'American' or 'European', and so on. Rather, this is cultural in the sense of engendered, cultivated, fostered, stimulated, managed, produced, even policed, through techniques of discipline, and always informed by ideology.[5]

Indeed, the implications of Benesch's opening reflection on the case of Breivik's 'psychology' go further than many studies of the relations between ideology and psychology otherwise tend to go. For instance, in a very rich and suggestive passage, Benesch notes:

The extent to which the methodical nature of Breivik's terror attack could be ascribed to his meditation techniques, 'bushido' or otherwise, has been called into question by those who see it as another manifestation of serious mental disturbance. On the other hand, Breivik's statements regarding 'bushido meditation' have parallels with the 'Warrior Mind

---

[5]   In a study of language, argumentation, the establishment of truth and ideology, Jean Fran-
çois Lyotard once argued that 'to link is necessary, but how to link is contingent' (Lyotard
1988). My contention here is that both training methods and ideological outlooks are contingent, as is the manner of their linkage. The different forms that the various connections,
combinations and relations take will always produce very different things.

Training' program implemented by the US military during the Iraq War. This program claims to have its roots in 'the ancient samurai code of self-discipline', and is described as a meditation method for dealing with a host of mental issues related to combat. Both Anders Breivik and Warrior Mind Training reflect a persistent popular perception of the samurai as fighting machines who were able to suppress any fear of death through the practice of meditation techniques based in Zen Buddhism. Zen has also been linked with the Special Attack Forces (or 'Kamikaze') of the Second World War, who supposedly used meditation methods ascribed to Zen to prepare for their suicide missions. (1)

Here, not only does Benesch reinforce my contentions about the 'cultural' dimensions of all of this, he actually raises the stakes of my own argument by introducing the question not just of mindset but also of sanity and insanity.

Hopefully, none of us are anything like Breivik. But Breivik claims to have believed himself to have trained for his acts of unimaginably callous mass murder by following a self-styled but not entirely alien or unusual type of 'martial art' psychological training. Which raises the question: Are such martial arts ideologies themselves to be regarded as sane or insane?

Such a question, posed outside of any context or any specific case study, will hardly permit a univocal response. Such a question is based on an unacceptable generalisation at both ends. It is, to borrow a phrase from Freud, an equation between two unknowns. What is a martial arts ideology? What is sanity? Clearly, there is a lot more work to be done here before we can even formulate our question adequately. Nonetheless, I am reminded of the time a few years ago when a student of mine walked out of a film screening. The film I was showing was *Ghost Dog: The Way of the Samurai* (1999), in which the eponymous Ghost Dog (Forest Whitaker) is a late 20th Century black urban character who so identifies with the samurai ideology advocated in the putative samurai manual, *Hagakure*, that he has crafted himself as the 'retainer' of an old mafia gangster who once saved his life. Ghost Dog lives alone, trains martial arts, and undertakes assassinations whenever his 'master' requires.

The film has always raised interesting questions for me about identity construction, cross-cultural interests and historical communication (Bowman 2008). But when I asked the student why she walked out of the screening she replied: *Because Ghost Dog was insane*. Until then, I had not actually stepped outside of the fictional world of the film to ask myself the question of Ghost Dog's sanity. The film presents him as an assassin with a fixation on samurai ideology. What does that make him? Eccentric? Mad?

Ghost Dog spends a great deal of time involved in solitary martial arts training, and he regularly reads the *Hagakure* as if to 'de-emotionalize' himself vis-à-vis 'death' (the *Hagakure* regularly reiterates the necessity of 'meditating on inevitable death'). Ghost Dog believes himself to be the 'retainer' of a mafia boss. So, to this extent, he could easily be labelled insane. Similarly, another contemporaneous film, which is more explicitly about insanity, resonates with cognate ideas. In a memorable scene in *Fight Club* (1999), Brad Pitt's Tyler Durden holds down the hand of Edward Norton's 'Narrator' – aka 'Jack' – on a table and gives him a serious chemical burn. All the while, Tyler holds forth on the subject of experiencing the sensation in the moment and giving up on the idea of escaping from the pain, either in the form of physically running away and trying to soothe the pain or in the form of retreating to 'your cave', or – as they used to say – 'using mind over matter' to escape from the pain of the situation by visualising something else, some other situation, elsewhere.

The dialogue in the scene runs as follows:

Tyler: Can I see your hand please?
[Narrator gives him his hand. Tyler grabs it, licks his lips and kisses the back of Narrator's hand]
Narrator: What is this?
[Tyler looks at him, sprinkles lye on Narrator's hand and says]
Tyler: This is a chemical burn.
[Narrator screams in pain, staring at his hand as it begins to burn, reeling while Tyler grasps it tightly.]
Tyler: It will hurt more than you have ever been burned and you will have a scar.
Narrator: What are you doing?! *[Screams]*
Narrator Voice Over: Guided meditation worked for cancer; it could work for this.
[Narrator closes his eyes. Cut to the scene of a green forest in his mind. Cut back to Tyler.]
Tyler: Stay with the pain. Don't shut this out.
Narrator: No, no, no! God! *[Screaming, moving violently, trying to escape Tyler's grasp]*
Tyler: Look at your hand! The first soap was made from the ashes of heroes, like the first monkey shot into space. Without pain, without sacrifice, we would have nothing.
[Narrator closes his eyes again, trying to shut the pain out, trying to be calm]
Narrator Voice Over: I tried not to think of the words 'searing' or 'flesh'.
Tyler: Stop it! This is your pain. This is your burning hand. It's right here.
Narrator: I'm going to my cave, I'm going to my cave, I'm going to find my power animal. *[Sobbing]*
Tyler: No! Don't deal with it the way those dead people do. Come on!
Narrator: I get the point, okay? Please!
Tyler: No, what you're feeling is premature enlightenment.
[Narrator closes his eyes. Cut to his mind's eye in his cave. Cut back to Tyler. Tyler slaps Narrator across his face]
Tyler: This is the greatest moment of your life, man, and you're off somewhere missing it.

Narrator: I am not!

Tyler: [*Narrator sobs and protests in pain but Tyler cuts him off*] Shut up. Our
  fathers were our models for God. If our fathers bailed, what does that
  tell you about God?

Narrator: [*Grunts, eyes closed, still fighting the pain*] No, no, I don't...

[*Tyler slaps narrator across his face again. Narrator, still reeling, moves his
  hand attempting to reach for the sink, for water. Tyler holds fast.*]

Tyler: Listen to me. [...] You can run water over your hand to make it worse,
  or, look at me. [*Their eyes meet*] Or you can use vinegar to neutralize
  the burn.

Narrator: Please let me have it!! Please!! [*Sobbing*]

Tyler: First, you have to give up. First, you have to *know* – not 'fear' – know
  that someday you're gonna die.

Narrator: You don't know how this feels!! [*Narrator stares daggers at Tyler.
  Tyler stares back and defiantly holds up his right hand to reveal a massive
  scar on the back of it.*]

Tyler: It's only after we've lost everything that we're free to do anything.

Narrator: Okay.

[*As his flesh continues to melt, fizzle, smoke, and burn, Tyler slowly lets go
  of Narrator's hand as he appears to calm down and accept the situation.
  Narrator stares intently at his hand, holding it out in front of himself on
  his own – Feeling it, not trying to run from it or trying to minimize the
  pain somehow. Tyler then reaches for a bottle of vinegar and dumps it on
  Narrator's outreached hand. Narrator, with tremendous relief, clutches his
  hand to his chest and drops to the ground. Tyler looks down at him.*]

Tyler: Congratulations: You're one step closer to hitting bottom.

This moment of madness, in a film that is arguably about madness in multiple
ways and on multiple levels, makes an unusual reference to *mindfulness*.
This takes the specific form of the potential connections between this act, its
rationale, and the kind of Zen-Samurai-madness-martial mindset that Benesch
focuses on.

Quite unlike the therapy culture that Jack has become immersed in at the
start of the film, in which people are regularly enjoined to visit their 'caves',
find their 'power animal', let their feelings out, and so on, Tyler insists on the
necessity of facing up to, looking directly at, and surrendering to the intensity
of the physical experience. Tyler will not allow Jack to run away from or try to
change the situation. He demands that Jack 'give up' and stop trying to escape.
He asks him to accept the inevitability of death, and he adds, at the end, that 'it's
only after we've lost everything that we're free to do anything'.

Immediately after this scene, we see Jack in his office being confronted by
his boss, who brandishes an incriminating copy of the rules of Fight Club
retrieved from a photocopier. In response to the rhetorical question of what
Jack thinks his boss should do when presented with a situation like this, Jack

suggests that his boss should be very, very afraid, as the kind of person who writes material like that is highly likely to be the kind of person who might just snap and stalk through the office building with an assault rifle, wreaking havoc and committing mass murder.

Is it significant that these two 1999 films seem to connect explicitly with what Benesch (following the US military) calls the 'warrior mind' with a kind of Zen-informed martial training (the 'meditation on inevitable death' that Ghost Dog reads from the *Hagakure*)? Certainly, these two filmic texts can be read side by side in terms of Benesch's connection of the chilling approach of Breivik to very real mass murder and my former student's damning statement that she could not sit through *Ghost Dog* because the main character was 'insane'. From this position, there is much that could be thought and said about *Fight Club*. Certainly, Jack is technically insane. The film makes clear that he is hallucinating the very existence of Tyler Durden and quite probably the existence of Helena Bonham Carter's Marla too. Maybe he's hallucinating all of it. But I also find the film to be potentially connected with debates in and around martial arts studies and social psychology in numerous ways.

I have written about much of this before. I have written about the ways that the spectre of Bruce Lee informs the imaginary ultimate male, Tyler Durden (Bowman 2010d). I have reflected on the relations between *Fight Club* and what I called the 'fight-club-ization' that took place in and around martial arts after the televisual explosion of the UFC and the emergence of MMA in its wake (Bowman 2013b). And so on. But here, thanks to Benesch's provocative work on the supposed connections between the 'warrior mind' and something akin to 'Zen' bushido training, I want to reflect on the treatment within *Fight Club* of what we might call its 'moment of mindfulness'.

(Some readers may notice in the phrase 'the moment of mindfulness' an allusion to Kierkegaard's famous line about how 'the decision is a moment of madness'. This is fortuitous, or maybe just fertile. Derrida certainly picked up this idea and ran with it into some of his most stimulating and – I think – important work [Derrida 1996, 2001].)

It seems important to note that *Fight Club* makes a clear distinction between what Tyler subjects Jack to and what Jack has hitherto experienced in his earlier addiction to therapy culture. At the start of the film, Jack is suffering from insomnia. He has pleaded with medical practitioners for medication but to no avail. When drugs are not forthcoming, he takes the advice of one doctor and goes to see 'what real pain is': He attends a testicular cancer support group. Being forced to 'let it all out' in the group, Jack gets cajoled into a situation where sobbing is mandatory, and he finds, after the emotional expenditures in the group, that he is able to sleep at night. Nonetheless, his interest in support groups becomes an obsession and he becomes addicted to therapy culture.

The appearance of 'another faker' named Marla impedes his ability to get satisfaction from his groups, and it is only after Tyler Durden appears and drags him away from all mainstream forms of modern social life and culture, especially the creature comforts afforded by consumerism, that Jack moves from therapy culture and towards fighting as therapy.

I have written about 'fighting as therapy' elsewhere (Bowman 2017b), so I will try not to repeat any of that here. What I am interested in at this point is less the fighting in *Fight Club* and more the moment of mindfulness, where Tyler makes Jack focus on the pain of a chemical burn, give in to it, give up the possibility of avoiding or escaping it, and ultimately accept the inevitability of death.

In response to the pain and his inability to escape Tyler's grip, we see Jack trying not to think of the words 'searing' and 'flesh' – the searing of his flesh being that from which he is trying to escape via entrance into his 'cave'. The cave is a place he has learned to go to during therapy sessions. Tyler shouts him back into the present, however. Then an image of beautiful trees in a forest flash up, but Tyler keeps shouting at Jack and drawing him back into the present moment. The images of/from 'his cave' and the very easily recognisable – indeed clichéd – image of 'a peaceful place' (dappled light through trees) – disappear when Tyler shouts at him.

So, in this film, too, at this moment, the 'warrior mind' emerges through 'reflection on inevitable death', 'meditating on inevitable death' and living one's life 'as dead', as if already dead.

It is very shortly after this that the first recruit to Tyler's paramilitary cult turns up and stands on the doorstep of Tyler and Jack's house, waiting for permission to enter and to begin 'training'. The visual representation here is modern and military. But those immersed in the mythology of Eastern martial arts will recognise the scenario as the first test of potential students seeking to be taught by a given master.[6] Shortly after this scene, of course, we see the production of a small militia and the initiation of 'Project Mayhem'.

What is going on in all of this? The film certainly involves both meta and micro critiques of many things: Consumerism, therapy culture, the supposed vacuity of much work and daily life, the men's movement, and, most prominently, masculinity. But what are we to make of the implicit connection between the film's championing of living in the moment, feeling it, accepting it, not retreating from pain, and so on, and several species of insanity? Is this all 'just in the film', or might there indeed be challenging lines of enquiry between mindfulness and madness?

There are many questions that could be asked in light of all of this. Here, I will concern myself with only one: The (ostensibly 'secondary') question of what is 'just in a film' and what exists or circulates 'really' or 'in the real world'. This is a complex question, one which relates to what we might call the relations between filmic representations or constructions of martial arts and wider cultural ideas about them. This is also the focus of the next chapter.

---

6 To American viewers, there is also a strong reference to the behaviour of 'frat boy pledges'. Thanks to Kyle Barrowman for pointing this out to a very British viewer.

CHAPTER 7

Fighting Talk – Martial Arts Discourse in Mainstream Films

Introduction

This chapter examines conversations, dialogues and statements about martial arts in films that can by no stretch of the imagination be regarded as martial arts films. It does this in order to glean insights into the status of martial arts in mainstream popular culture. As such, although it is a study that reads and takes evidence from films, its concerns are not those of the discipline of film studies. Rather, it is interested in the ways that martial arts are understood, positioned, and given value within the wider flows, circuits, networks or discourses of culture. As well as offering a discrete analysis of martial arts discourse as registered in film dialogue, this chapter also serves as a recapitulation and reiteration of the overarching poststructuralist or deconstructive theoretical framework that has organised this book.

The premise here is that mainstream, non-specialist films in which dialogue about martial arts occurs can be regarded as texts that relate to, arise from, register, and feed back into wider understandings of and opinions about martial arts. This is especially the case for films set in the contemporary world and which implicitly make some kind of claim to having some kind of relationship with realism (even if they are comedies).

Of course, there is no simple mapping of or direct relation between representation and reality here. A statement or conversation offered in a fiction film does not simply reflect or recount opinions circulating in face-to-face or online conversations among real people in the 'real world'. However, in all communicative processes, sense can only be made of utterances that employ shared ideas, familiar conventions, and so on, even if a new utterance (e.g., a conversation in a film) brings in unique, new or surprising elements, formulations, or

How to cite this book chapter:
Bowman, P. 2019. *Deconstructing Martial Arts*. Pp. 125–146. Cardiff: Cardiff University Press. DOI: https://doi.org/10.18573/book1.h. License: CC-BY-NC-ND 4.0

combinations of elements. So, the premise of this study is not that film dialogue simply maps, reflects or expresses established cultural values in straightforward ways; rather, the premise is that film dialogue registers, reworks, reiterates and replays familiar cultural values in complex and creative ways – but ways that always seek to 'make sense' by relating to, playing around with and reworking established ideas and values.

It is in this way that this study seeks to explore and cast light on the 'discursive status' of martial arts in Anglophone popular culture. Given the necessarily interdisciplinary approach and orientation of this work, something should be said first about the notion of discourse and the theory of discourse as it functions in this work, before turning our attention to the discussion of martial arts in non-martial arts film.

Popular Cultural Discourse

Michel Foucault argued that the 'regularity in dispersion' of certain types of statement about an object, phenomenon or practice have a structuring effect on what that object, phenomenon or practice is deemed to be. They influence how it is understood, thought about, related to and treated in cultural, political and institutional discourses (Foucault 1972; Deleuze 2006; Widder 2008). Multiple schools of thought have developed in the wake of this, including several species of discourse theory (Akerstrøm Andersen 2003). A key premise of most of these is that the connotations, meanings and values permeating and congregating around (perhaps) *anything* are determined at least in part by wider representational tendencies (Barthes 1972; Stuart Hall and et al 1997; Laclau 2000; Bowman 2007). There are disagreements about the details, but all schools of discourse analysis concur that key instances, contexts, styles and genres of representation at least 'influence' (and sometimes actually 'produce') the way things are thought about, imagined, and related to – and even what they are deemed to 'be' (Derrida 1982; Laclau and Mouffe 1985; Said 2000).

Regardless of whether or not one or another theory of discourse adequately captures how human societies 'really work', it is certainly the case that between the 1970s and 1990s the concept or metaphor of discourse (along with such related concepts as 'representation' and 'textuality') entirely reoriented the paradigms and approaches of numerous academic fields, and even helped to generate new ones (Hall 1992; Mowitt 2003; Bowman 2015a). Indeed, in this sense, the notion of discourse *itself* generated considerable discourse. In Foucault's own terms, the notion of discourse arguably became what he would have termed a 'founder of discursivity' in its own right (Foucault 1991). It is something that generated new thoughts, new words and new practices.

Although developed conceptually in the 1970s and 1980s, it is still not uncommon for academic subjects of all kinds to conceptualise the world as discourses made up of *texts*. Texts are the constructs that come out of and feed back into discourses. The 'textual paradigm' and/or the 'discourse approach' can be regarded as organising and structuring the focus and language of a great deal of academic work in the arts, humanities and social sciences (Mowitt 1992; Bowman 2007).

This present study is to be situated within this tradition, although it proceeds in full awareness of the complexity, uncertainty and problems associated with both textual and discourse approaches (Hall 1992; Mowitt 1992; Bowman 2007, 2008). Some of these problems include disagreement among scholars about where and how discourses are to be pinpointed or demarcated; whether they exist principally at the level of representation (Said 1995; Young 2001) or at the level of institutional policies, laws and legislations (Foucault 1977; Young 2001); whether they principally relate to the realm of public media (Fairclough 1995) or every micro and macro level of modern human life (Arditi and Valentine 1999); in which direction 'causality' runs in discourses – that is, whether representations are the causes of things (from attitudes and beliefs to policies) or whether other things (from attitudes and beliefs to policies) are the causes of representations (Krug 2001; Judkins 2014b; Barrowman 2015b); and so on. There is a great deal of what arch-theorist of textuality Jacques Derrida would call 'undecidability' in these waters (Derrida 1981). But what all scholars of discourse studies can be said to agree upon is the tenet of the significant cultural, political, and even ontological power of representations.

Following the broadly political orientations of many of the founding theorists of discourse studies, the dominant tendency within all schools of discourse analysis has been to maintain an explicitly political focus. Hence discourse analyses tend either to choose explicitly political topics (for example, the media coverage of elections) and to subject them to further political interrogation, or they take 'cultural' topics (like the practices and identities of everyday life) and unearth the political dimensions of these topics (Laclau 1994; Torfing 1998). In this sense, discourse studies tend to produce insights into the 'political' bias or orientation of whatever is examined.

Yet, despite the inescapably 'politicizing' effect that the notion of discourse produces in its focus on the contingency, variability and hence changeability of the human world, there is no *necessary* reason why discourse studies and discourse analysis should have an explicitly, directly or literally political starting point or end point. Indeed, precisely because the notion of discourse *already* presumes the immanently political character of (potentially) *everything* (Arditi and Valentine 1999; Marchart 2007), employing it to reveal ever more political aspects to ever more areas of life is perhaps not the most interesting or challenging thing to do when employing it at this time. Perhaps scholars no longer need to belabour the inevitable conclusions about the political dimensions of things. This is a conclusion that discourse analysis can easily reach (Hall 2002). For, given that discourse theories tend to posit that 'everything' in human social and cultural life is contingent and hence political, maybe to search for the political dimension and reach a political conclusion over and over again is predictable.

But what else is to be done with a paradigm organised by the syllogism that everything is contingent, that contingency involves variation and change, and therefore everything is political?[1] Is the political focus unavoidable?

The obligation for academic work to discover and rediscover the political dimensions of the world is heavy. Robert J.C. Young once argued that the imperative to focus on 'the political' has been the dominant 'architectonic' organising knowledge production in the arts, humanities and social sciences over at least the last half century (Young 1992). Similarly, Gary Hall notes that even though cultural studies has often claimed to be open to the study of any and all aspects of culture it has overwhelmingly tended to choose worthy political objects and refract everything through a 'politicizing' lens (Hall 2002). Rey Chow, too, notes that even the apparently non-political and firmly aesthetic/cultural field of film studies became settled, stabilized, regularized and more firmly established when its dominant questions, concerns and themes became those of identity (and) politics (Chow 2007).

My current concern proceeds with all of this as its backdrop, but it also fights against aspects of it. The aim is not to paint martial arts as a continuation of politics by other means.[2] Nor is it to look into specific, specialist, niche or actual martial arts contexts, fields or 'subcultures'. Indeed, it is resolutely not looking 'into' anything specifically martial arts 'proper' at all. This work does not look at what martial artists say, think or feel about themselves, in their own specialist contexts, such as blogs, vlogs, magazines, books, and so on. Rather, it is interested in establishing what *non*-martial artists feel, think and say about martial arts and about martial artists. The aim is to establish the range of ideas and values that circulate *about* martial arts, *about* martial arts practitioners, and *about* martial arts fans. The wider research project has so far taken in the realms of comedy, popular culture and journalism research (Bowman 2017a, 2017b). Here, my attention is on the discursive status of martial arts in film. Specifically, the focus is on films that could in no way be construed as martial arts films. My question is whether there are any patterns, repetitions, reiterations, or any 'regularity in dispersion' of discursive statements about martial arts outside of proper martial arts contexts.

---

[1] Moreover, as Freud most famously argued, there is a pleasure in repeating. In different ways and in different contexts, repetition produces stability, intelligibility, familiarity, and gives orientation. So, posing the same kinds of questions and rediscovering the same kinds of answers *makes sense* (in more than one way). Yet, must discourse analysis always and only rediscover the political, wherever it looks?

[2] Many excellent studies have already carried out important work that has shown this, across a range of different historical and cultural contexts. I will not give a list of citations pointing to any of these works at this point, because I do not want to give the impression that such works *only* do this one thing. On the contrary, all good works of cultural studies (and martial arts studies) do much more than 'merely' this one thing. My point is simply that 'perceiving the political' continues to function as a reliable way to confer validity and legitimacy upon an academic orientation.

Methodological Matrix

The importance of film to martial arts culture (and also to the status of martial arts within popular culture) cannot be overstated (Bowman 2017b). Filmic representations of martial arts have long been a key force in stimulating interest and participation in martial arts (Bowman 2010d, 2013b). Moreover, stylised martial artsy fights appear regularly in all kinds of films today. In other words, films certainly do not need to be 'martial arts films' to have martial arts within them. Indeed, the frequency of their appearance suggests that martial arts remain as popular and 'bankable' as they have been since the global 'kung fu craze' of the 1970s (Brown 1997). In Foucauldian terms, this proliferation and frequency of their reiteration in a range of different kinds of texts and different discursive contexts could constitute a 'regularity in dispersion'. Certainly, martial arts are a very familiar part of all kinds of films. This is so much so that they might be regarded as a standard feature of popular culture, a standard part of widespread 'normal' cultural literacy. People might be expected to 'know about' martial arts – albeit only at the level of recognition or acknowledgement if not 'knowledge' – in the same way that one might reasonably expect people to 'know about' ballet, say, or farming, witchcraft or drug dealing, for example. 'People' may never have experienced these things directly, but they more or less 'know' what they are. When this does not come from first-hand experience, it often comes from media representations.

Obviously, comparatively few people could be expected to be able to distinguish kung fu from karate or karate from taekwondo. Fewer still could be expected even to have heard of krav maga or escrima. But the majority of people could be expected to recognise 'martial arts' when they see them. If not unequivocally 'popular', then, martial arts are certainly part of 'the popular' (Hall 1994) – stitched into the current 'popular cultural formation' (Morris 2004; Morris, Li, and Chan 2005). So, the question is: Outside of martial arts films and films that can be said to be steeped in martial arts practitioner discourses, how are martial arts thought about and talked about?

Blurred Lines

In posing this question, the problem of how to demarcate and separate an inside from an outside immediately arises. There is a great deal of grey area around the category 'martial arts film'. It is unclear whether there is even a fixed or demarcated genre of martial arts film in the West. Certainly, many action films feature martial arts choreography. But, in trying to separate martial arts films from non-martial arts film, it may not prove possible to establish a stable boundary between, say, martial arts film, action film, action comedy, horror, and others. It is equally difficult to clinch the case of whether a film is mainstream, niche, cult, or some other designation.

So, in attempting to establish anything about what we might conceptualise as the 'wider', 'mainstream', or 'popular' discursive status of martial arts in 'wider' (non-specialist) circuits of culture, we are facing a number of problems. All of these devolve on the problem of where or how to draw the line between specialist and non-specialist, martial arts and non-martial arts, mainstream and subcultural, and so on.

Rather than attempting to resolve such categorical and taxonomical conundra here, another option was chosen. This involved the decision to impose a radically simplifying and drastically clarifying border, one that may initially seem eccentric but that offered the benefits of being clear, stable, meaningful, and not easily problematized, jeopardised, made unclear, or deconstructed. This was the decision to focus on dialogue about martial arts in unequivocally non-martial arts films.

In applying such a principled limitation of focus, the first thing discovered was that, other than in martial arts and action films, martial arts are rarely *discussed*. They are often *shown*. There are often moves, gestures, visual allusions, and visual references. But *conversations* about martial arts are few and far between. Furthermore, in order to find such elements to analyse, there are no methodological shortcuts: One simply *needs to know a lot about lots of films*. There are no databases to dig into and no search terms that an internet search engine can return results for. Google doesn't understand what is being asked when search terms are phrases like 'dialogue about martial arts in non-martial arts films'. Even Americanising it by changing the word 'films' to 'movies' doesn't help. It was not possible to construct a search question with any mention of martial arts films in it that led anywhere other than to pages about martial arts films.

Having no database and unable to establish 'intelligible' search terms, the only recourse was to rely on memory and knowledge of as wide a range of films as possible. This returned a very limited number of results. So, the question was posed online, in several Facebook groups. Reasoning that people with an interest in martial arts would be most likely to remember references to martial arts in films, I focused my attention on the Martial Arts Studies Facebook Group, which had almost 1,000 members at the time (in early May 2017).

Interestingly (and perhaps significantly), it turned out that it is not just inhuman search engines that do not understand questions about 'dialogue about martial arts in films that are not martial arts films'. It was evident that the overwhelming majority of people asked could not quite get their heads around the question either. In fact, from among dozens of respondents, only one or two people actually *understood the question*. Most knowledgeable among them was film scholar Kyle Barrowman, who came up with a number of valuable suggestions, some of which I will discuss below.

However, the majority of people who understood the question suggested action films. Most people suggested *The Matrix* (1999). Unfortunately, it was clear that I had to exclude *The Matrix* because, even though many people don't seem to think of it as a martial arts film, it was choreographed by famous martial arts choreographer Yuen Woo Ping, it is choc-full of stylistically precise martial arts choreography, and (as I had discovered during my ill-fated internet searches) it regularly features in top tens of 'must see' martial arts films. The fact that people don't seem to recognise when a Hollywood action film becomes a martial arts film (or vice versa) perhaps says more about the porousness of these two supposed genre categories and the essential lack of a fixed and stable Hollywood martial arts film genre than anything else. So, *The Matrix* fell within this study's 'exclusion zone'. But some limit cases do deserve some attention and warrant some quick preliminary consideration.

Liminal Cases

In terms of Hollywood action films that feature martial arts, it seems significant to note that relatively few of them actually *discuss* martial arts. In mainstream US action films, *martial arts are shown, not discussed*. Very few action films with martial arts choreography in them even mention martial arts at all in the dialogue. To illustrate this, and the porousness of the borders between 'martial arts film' and 'action film' in the US context, let us briefly consider some well-known examples, even though they are technically outside the parameters of this study.

One notable case is the amnesiac Jason Bourne (*The Bourne Identity* [2002], *The Bourne Supremacy* [2004], *The Bourne Ultimatum* [2007], *Jason Bourne* [2016]) who wonders aloud in *The Bourne Identity* why it is that he knows so much about combat, strategy, situational awareness, and survival despite not remembering who he is. However, other than one brief moment of musing, there is no specific dialogue about his ample fighting abilities.[3] Elsewhere, long before the *Bourne* films, in *Conan the Barbarian* (1982) the titular warrior played by Arnold Schwarzenegger was sent to study with 'Eastern' sword masters, but it was only the extra-diegetic voiceover that told us this. There was some talk in *Batman Begins* (2005), reminiscent of *Highlander* (1986), of training and deception, but very little. And, it deserves to be noted, the 'action' film, *Batman Begins*, is structured by a martial arts (and) oedipal narrative of a once adopted and subsequently renegade (or 'ronin') *ninja*.

Similarly, the sci-fi fantasy *Star Wars* films have many of the hallmarks of Chinese martial arts *wuxia pian*, or swordplay drama (Feichtinger 2014). Some might call this cultural appropriation, or expropriation. From such a perspective, *The Matrix* can either be regarded as a trailblazing Western 'heir' to the Hong Kong style of 'wire-fu' fight choreography that prepared Western audiences for the aesthetics of the subsequently successful *Crouching Tiger, Hidden Dragon* and subsequent transnational *wuxia pian* 'wire-fu' films, or it can be

---

[3] In terms of Jason Bourne's fighting style, *The Bourne Identity* specifically showcases Filipino martial arts (Bowman 2013b).

regarded as a film that is guilty of the 'cultural appropriation' or 'expropriation' of Hong Kong traditions (Hunt 2003; Tierney 2006; Park 2010; Barrowman 2015b).

This list could continue. But already two points can be made. First, that the lines between 'action film' and 'martial arts film' in the Hollywood context are extremely blurred. And second, that within all such films actual dialogue about martial arts is rare, fleeting and scanty. In *The Matrix*, Neo (Keanu Reeves) wakes up from his software installation and breathlessly announces, 'I know kung fu!' Yet other than a few remarks about fighting skill and strategy, this is close to the pinnacle of martial arts dialogue in the film. And the response from Morpheus (Laurence Fishburne) is not, 'Please tell me all about it', but rather, 'Show me'.

Another significant limit case is the classic 1987 cop actioner *Lethal Weapon*. Early in the film, veteran cop Roger Murtaugh (Danny Glover) tries to engage his undesirable new partner Martin Riggs (Mel Gibson) in conversation, saying, in reference to his Los Angeles Police Department personnel file, '[the] file also said you're heavy into martial arts, taiji and all that killer stuff. I suppose we have to register you as a lethal weapon'.[4]

Of course, *Lethal Weapon* definitely has at least one foot too far into our exclusion zone to be classed as a 'non-martial arts film'. But the way it positions taiji as 'killer stuff' is interesting. This is because, as I have discussed at length elsewhere, taiji is also a kind of 'limit case' martial art. By dint of its complex history, by far the majority of taiji practitioners have little inkling of its combat applications and even less ability to apply them in either free or rule bound sparring or combat (Wile 1996; Frank 2006; Bowman 2015a, 2016, 2017b). Overwhelmingly, taiji is predominantly associated in popular consciousness with calm, soft, flowing, meditative solo sequences. But *Lethal Weapon* presents taiji as the very thing that makes its eponymous 'weapon' *lethal*.

Libidinal Cases

Another slightly less limit case film treats taiji very differently. The 1985 'coming of age' teen wrestling film *Vision Quest* (also known as *Crazy for You*) positions taiji as precisely an esoteric, meditative, restful, relaxing endeavour. But in *Vision Quest* this more typical 'feminized' depiction of taiji comes with a twist. In the scene in which taiji appears, Louden Swaine (Matthew Modine) is delivering room service to a travelling salesman, called Kevin (R.H. Thomas).

---

[4] These lines of dialogue are *technically* unforgettable, in that it is from them that the film itself, all of its sequels, and the recent TV serials get their name. Thanks to Kyle Barrowman for pointing this out to me.

The salesman is practicing taiji in the hotel room when Louden arrives, and the two engage in conversation about it:[5]

Louden: What is that stuff?

Kevin: Taiji. National form of exercise in China. *[Signing the room service receipt]* I'll, uh, put your tip on this, ok?

Louden: Can you get a workout that way?

Kevin: 800 million Chinese can't be wrong. It's mainly a matter of getting the mind into the muscles. I use it a lot when I'm on the road. It helps me sleep like a baby.

Louden: Really? I'm on like a 600-calorie-a-day diet and working out like a madman. I'm so wired when I hit the rack, I can't sleep at all. I lie there for about, I don't know, six hours thinking about my life and stuff before I finally drop off.

Kevin: My name is Kevin.

Louden: Louden. Louden Swain.

Kevin: *[Louden turns to leave]* Let me show you how it's done, Louden. *[Louden turns back]* It'll help you sleep.

Louden: All right.

Kevin: Why don't you stand there. Face this way. Just sort of catch me out of the corner of your eyes. *[Louden stands next to Kevin]* Ok, now breathe in. Raise the arms. Keep the movements slow, fluid. Breathe out. Shift your weight to the left. Step onto the right. Sort of stack your hands like that over the knee. Now step back to the left. *[Kevin moves over by Louden to help him with his form]* Move your arms. Step back to the left. Stack your arms the other way. Step out.
[Kevin's hands, which were initially guiding Louden's arms, move lower on his body. Then his right hand slides up Louden's right leg, at which point Louden flinches and moves away]

Louden [Flustered]: I think I got it now. I'll try it on my own when I get a chance.

Kevin: Do you want to come up later when you're off-duty?

Louden: No. *[Louden picks up the bill off of the dresser and backs away towards the door]* I don't think so, I got to get home. I'm in training.

Kevin: Training, huh? What sport?

Louden: Wrestling.

Kevin: Wrestling? You know, I sell sporting goods for a living. As a matter of fact, I carry a good line of wrestling shoes.

Louden: *[Leaving hurriedly]* Just leave the tray by the door when you're finished.

---

[5] The scene from which the following dialogue has been transcribed can be viewed in full here: https://www.youtube.com/watch?v=5f_MzPVuBq0

There is much that is interesting about both the dialogue and the action in this scene. But one thing that leaps out is the association of taiji practice with homosexuality, especially because here it functions as a pretext for and gateway to attempted seduction. This could be because of a perceived narrative need to set up a clear counterpoint or foil for what the film wishes to construct as the more masculine activity of wrestling. In other words, the lead character's adverse reaction to homosexual advances can be taken as a device to clarify his heterosexuality – as if to reassure viewers, once more, that despite his engagement in wrestling he is not homosexual. The perceived necessity of such a scene could relate to a common representational problem with wrestling: As many commentators have noted in different contexts, the *appearance* of wrestling and grappling can often come to seem a little too similar to the *appearance* of amorous lovemaking for (heteronormative or homophobic) comfort (Downey 2014; Bowman 2017b).

So, the semiotic function is that an already 'feminine' (because 'gentle' and 'Eastern' [Said 1978]) taiji becomes a device of homosexual seduction that Louden must reject. This further clarifies the heterosexuality both of himself and of wrestling. Yet, his final reaction after running away from the hotel room is odd. After racing along the corridor and pressing the button for the elevator, Louden throws himself down to the floor and executes a number of rapid push-ups. The peculiarity of this ostensibly comic act seems to undermine the attempt to safely exclude him from the realm of homoerotic investment. His panicked push-ups have an air of *desperation* about them – as if he *has* to do *something – anything* – to channel his intense feelings (whatever they might be) into a kind of sublimated and socially acceptable form.[6]

This sexual dimension takes us smoothly into another interestingly odd and uncomfortable scene. This is a scene in Stanley Kubrick's adaptation of *Lolita* (1962), in which Clare Quilty (Peter Sellers) discusses judo with a hotel manager, called Mr. Swine:[7]

> *Quilty*: Mr. Swine, do you mind if I ask you a sort of personal question?
> *Swine*: Sure, go ahead.
> *Quilty*: What is a guy like you doing in a job like this?
> *Swine*: What do you mean?
> *Quilty*: Well, you just don't seem to be the type.
> *Swine*: [Laughs] Well, as a matter of fact, I was an actor.
> *Quilty*: I knew it, I knew it. [He turns to his female companion] Didn't I say to you? [He turns back to Mr. Swine] When I first saw you, there was something about you, a sort of aura that all actors and actresses have.

---

[6] The counter to this interpretation, however, is to recall that Louden is presently 'working out like a madman', in order to cut weight; so he would have been acting like this while waiting for the elevator no matter what had just happened. Thanks again to Kyle Barrowman here.

[7] The scene from which the following dialogue has been transcribed can be viewed in full here: https://youtu.be/SX6vrnz5tJY.

Swine: Well, since you're a playwright, uh, maybe you could use me some-time, hmm?

Quilty: Yeah, maybe I could – *use* you – sometime. *[He laughs to himself but then gathers himself]* Mr. Swine, what does an actor-manager do with his spare time in a small town like this?

Swine: Well, I don't have much spare time, but...I swim, play tennis, lift weights. Gets rid of the excess energy. *[He looks at Quilty's female companion and then back at Quilty]* What do you do with your excess energy?

Quilty: *[He looks up at his female companion]* Well, we do a lot of things with my excess energy. *[He looks back at Mr. Swine]* I'll tell you one of the things we do a lot of, that's judo. Did you ever hear about that?

Swine: *[Chuckles with a sort of surprise]* Judo? Yes, I've heard about it. You do judo with the lady?

Quilty: Yeah, she's a yellow belt, I'm a green belt; that's the way nature made it. What happens is she throws me all over the place.

Swine: *She* throws *you* all over the place?

Quilty: Yes. What she does, she gets me in a sort of thing called a sweeping-ankle throw. She sweeps my ankles away from under me and I go down with one hell of a bang.

Swine: Doesn't it hurt?

Quilty: Well, I sort of lay there in pain but I love it. I really love it. I lay hovering between consciousness and unconsciousness. It's really the greatest. *[They both chuckle]*

In this scene, we encounter martial arts combat training depicted as both heterosexual and yet somewhat creepy and uncanny – somewhere between violence and sexuality, somewhere most likely connected with sadomasochism. The perversion hinted at here derives from the impropriety, uncanniness, or 'un-homeliness'[8] of transgressing so many cultural lines and norms at once: The publicly-policed borderlines between pleasure and pain, sexuality and violence, exercise, competition, health, sadism and masochism – and, moreover, *talking about it* in this 'double entendre' manner with a complete stranger, of the same sex, quite flirtatiously, while 'the lady' is actually present.

As mentioned, wrestling, grappling and ground-fighting *already* struggle semiotically because they transgress so many visual and spatial norms that police male to male proximity and interactions (Downey 2014; Bowman 2017b).[9] The 'double entendre' insistence of this uncanny proximity to heterosexual sex, but

---

[8] In the original German, Freud's term 'uncanny' is 'unheimlich', which can also be translated as 'unhomely'.

[9] The situation is not helped by the fact that the most popular form of ground-fighting in the world today is known as Brazilian Jiu-Jitsu, a name that is reduced to the acronym 'BJJ'. All of this seems to render it as apparently 'crying out' to become the butt of sexual innuendo and homophobic and misogynistic sleights, affronts and verbal attacks.

here with a male 'witness' (voyeur) present, amplifies and twists (or queers) it further.

As such, our first two legitimate examples of dialogue about martial arts in non-martial arts films have sexualised it, specifically via discussions of dealing with 'excess energy'. The travelling taiji practitioner in *Vision Quest* is gay (and predatory). The two men discussing judo training with a woman in *Lolita* seem to revel in the perverse hetero, bi and homosexual innuendos involved in talking about it.

As a side-note (with reference to films that fall within the exclusion zone), we can note that it has so far only been in the action films mentioned that martial arts are presented as *non-sexually* exciting and *conventionally* cool. In *Lethal Weapon*, Riggs is the crazy, suicidal, 'lethal weapon' martial artist cop and former soldier. In *The Matrix*, Neo gasps with excitement about suddenly knowing kung fu. The crew of *The Nebuchadnezzar* who watch Neo fight with Morpheus show us how to react *properly* – with amazement and excitement and delight at the combatants' skills. So, the spectrum of value emerging here runs from sexual perversion to heteronormative hypermasculinity. Some films try to police the border between these realms. Others regularly traverse it.

From Kinky to Kingly to General

Consider Charlie Rogers (Elvis Presley) in *Roustabout* (1964). Charlie is about start his motorcycle to leave when a group of 'tough guy' college kids accost him, their aim being to 'get him':[10]

> *Student #1*: Is that your 'cycle? [*Pronounced 'sickle'*]
> *Charlie*: You ought to stop reading those hot rod magazines, buddy. 'Cycle is out. It's either bike or motorcycle.
> *Student #2*: 'Made in Japan', huh?
> *Charlie*: That's right. Made in Japan.
> *Student #2*: What's the matter? Aren't American 'cycles good enough for you?
> *Charlie*: You don't dig world trade, college boy, after all the economics they tried to shove into you?
> *Student #3*: Get off, buddy.
> *Charlie*: [*Charlie gets off and readies himself for the inevitable attack. Students #1 and #3 try to assault him, but he fights them off with deft karate blocks and strikes. He then turns his attention to Student #2, the only one still standing*] Come on! Come on!

---

[10] The scene from which the following dialogue has been transcribed can be viewed in full here: https://www.youtube.com/watch?v=8K98R2VWHCM

Student #2: [*He begins to back away with his hands up waving Charlie off*]
No, no! That's karate!
Charlie: That goes with the 'cycle.

Here a young, modern, rebellious, non-traditional, forward-looking Elvis Presley puts paid to the old-thinking 'college boys' by using an unexpected and culturally new style of fighting from Japan called karate. After two attackers have been floored, the third aggressor hesitates. Charlie eggs him on, encouraging him to 'come on', but he says, 'No, no! That's karate!' Here, martial arts skill is unexpected, superlative, foreign, exotic, educated, novel, problem solving – to be feared and avoided. Basically, it is *masculinising*.

It is precisely this hope, fantasy or promise – as depicted in this scene in *Roustabout* – of attaining a kind of 'phallic agency' by way of achieving relative invincibility that has attracted many to martial arts practice. The desire is the desire for potency, agency, confidence, competence, plenitude, and so on. Traditionally, this has been called *masculine*, of course. However, eventually, the girls have been allowed to arrive. After two *Street Fighter* films with Sonny Chiba (*The Street Fighter* [1974] and *Return of the Street Fighter* [1974]), *Sister Street Fighter* (1974) finally arrived. After three *Karate Kid* films (*The Karate Kid* [1984], *The Karate Kid Part II* [1986], *The Karate Kid Part III* [1989]), *The Next Karate Kid* (1994) was a girl. And so on. Unfortunately, this is not the place to engage with gender issues adequately.[11] The point is that the skill of Elvis in *Roustabout* exemplifies precisely the kind of hopes that many people have about martial arts.

This is certainly what drives the 32-year-old layabout Kip (Aaron Ruell) to want to check out the local martial arts club that he has seen advertised on TV in *Napoleon Dynamite* (2004).[12] However, in the scene in *Napoleon Dynamite* in which Napoleon (Jon Heder) and his brother Kip go to the 'Rex Kwon Do' martial arts club in town, we see martial arts and martial artists treated not as calm, cool, collected and hypermasculine, nor as sexually predatory or kinky, but rather, as bundles of neuroses.

The voice of the sensei, Rex (Diedrich Bader), is gravelly in the extreme. He shouts like a drill sergeant. He is arrogant, self-aggrandising and abusive to his potential students. And his martial arts demonstration contains a large number of clichés and classic one-liners. (I am not sure if it was this scene that led people to refer to 'naff' martial arts demonstrations as 'grab my arm demonstrations'. But, certainly, if you were to say to a martial artist that a certain

---

[11] Moreover, while this was the Hollywood cinema 'gender chronology', in Hong Kong cinema, it was reversed, with the girls – specifically, *the girl*, Chang Pei-pei, from King Hu's *Come Drink with Me* (1966) and Chang Cheh's *Golden Swallow* (1968) – arriving first and then the guys – specifically, *Chang Cheh's* guys, like Jimmy Wang Yu and David Chiang, before, ultimately, of course, the arrival of *the guy*, Bruce Lee – taking over later. Thanks to Kyle Barrowman for making this point.

[12] https://www.youtube.com/watch?v=Hzh9koy7b1E

demonstration was a 'grab my arm demonstration', they would most likely understand what you mean. It evokes a kind of old-fashioned, discredited kind of demonstration, involving unrealistic scenarios and ineffective techniques. Unfortunately, such demonstrations still abound. They are still being given, to this day, and are posted in all seriousness online.) Indeed, the martial arts teacher, Rex, is a composite character, made up of stereotypes and clichés that abound in the world.

Rex declares that to be a martial artist you must 'discipline your self-image'. Rex himself wears stars and stripes pantaloons. This means that, contrary to the orientalist imagery and self-orientalising predilections of many Western martial artists, Rex has disciplined his image in a 'non-traditional' but cultur-ally significant way. The gravelly voice and drill sergeant shout are of course comedic affectations within the film, but they also importantly smack of the military. This is significant because the history of the development of 'Asian' martial arts in the US is a narrative in which the US military features very prominently (Krug 2001). In this context, the stars and stripes clown trousers that Rex is so proud to be wearing reinforce the militaristic/patriotic dimen-sion while adding to it an even more widely ridiculed image: That of the body-builder. (There was a long-running fashion for bodybuilders in the 1980s and 1990s to wear incredibly baggy elasticated pantaloons, not too dissimilar to those made famous by MC Hammer in the 1990 music video for his hit song 'U Can't Touch This'.)

In these ways, Rex is a composite of images of American drill sergeants, 1980s Bon Jovi-inspired rock fans, and vain tough guys, all coming together in the character of a gaudy insecure jingoistic redneck thug. Rex is a comedy caricature that nonetheless points to all the features that went into the making of one enduring image of the martial artist in the US.

However, Rex is not the only one to talk about martial arts in *Napoleon Dynamite*. Nor is his way of talking about them the only way. Rex and his hilarious martial art of Rex Kwon Do could easily draw all of our attention, but in actual fact the entirety of *Napoleon Dynamite* can be read as a film that is deeply and thoroughly infused with an awareness of the status of ideas of martial arts in American teen culture. At the start of the film, Napoleon tries to impress the new kid, Pedro (Efren Ramirez), by telling him that there are a lot of gangs in the school and that some of them tried hard to recruit him – because he has 'pretty decent bo-staff skills'. Later on, Napoleon asks Deb (Tina Majorino) to collect some items of hers that he has been looking after, because, he claims, he can no longer fit his 'num-chucks' [sic] in his school locker.

Indeed, as we learn from his regular mentions of them, the 16-year-old Napoleon is quite heavily fixated on the Asian martial arts weapons the 'bo-staff' and 'num-chucks' (nunchaku). His elder brother, Kip, however, is more taken by the call of the cage: He tells Napoleon early on that he is in training to become a cage fighter, and it is he to asks Napoleon to pull him on his roller-skates to Rex's 'Rex Kwon Do' club in town.

Both of these fantasy fixations start to wane as the characters become involved in real relationships with girls. Kip stops discussing cage fighting when he hooks up with his new girlfriend LaFawnduh (Shondrella Avery) and switches instead to focusing on cultivating a 'black' ghetto sartorial style. Napoleon stops fretting about bo-staffs and num-chucks when he discovers dancing and especially as his relationship with Deb grows.

In other words, martial arts in *Napoleon Dynamite* are fantasy resolutions to problems. Napoleon tries to impress Pedro and Deb by claiming bo-staff and nunchaku skills. But, later on, he laments his lack of them. In a memorable scene, Napoleon sets out his answer to the question of what girls want: They want 'skills'. And he feels he doesn't have any. Pedro asks what he means by skills, and Napoleon answers: 'Nunchuck skills…bowhunting skills…computer hacking skills…Girls only want boyfriends who have great skills!' Kip has also given his answer to the same question, having announced early on in the film: 'Napoleon, don't be jealous 'cause I've been chatting online with babes all day. Besides, we both know that I'm training to become a cage fighter'. And, of course, Rex famously challenges everyone with the belligerent rhetorical question, 'You think anybody thinks I'm a failure because I go home to Starla at night?' (Starla being an extremely masculine-looking bodybuilder played by real-life women's bodybuilding champion Carmen Brady).

Martial arts in *Napoleon Dynamite* are refracted through extant cultural imagery derived from film and TV: Napoleon is interested in the 'classic' martial arts filmic idea of being skilled with Japanese weapons (the bo, the nunchaku); Kip is taken by the 'modern' Western idea of cage fighting; and Rex seems to be saturated in imagery derived from the incorporation of Asian martial arts in US military training.

The vocal style of Rex is not a world away from that of Gunnery Sergeant Emil Foley (Louis Gossett Jr.) in *An Officer and a Gentleman* (1982), who trains the officer cadets in hand to hand combat. Similar, too, is Sensei John Kreese (Martin Kove) in *The Karate Kid*, whose dojo is run like a Marine Corps basic training camp and is adorned with images of Sensei Kreese himself when he was actively serving as a Marine.

The Karate Kid is obviously a martial arts film, so we will have to pass over it here. However, *An Officer and a Gentleman* is not. Nor is it an action film. But martial arts do feature within it, and there is dialogue about them within the film. Therefore, we can give it some attention.

Early on in *An Officer and a Gentleman*, Zack Mayo (Richard Gere) despatches a belligerent aggressor in a scenario not dissimilar to the one Elvis' Charlie found himself in in *Roustabout*, although without the cocky sass. To the contrary, Gere's Zack has repeatedly told the aggressor 'I do *not* want to fight you', and afterwards, despite his friends' joy, amazement and delight in his victory ('Did you see that guy's face!?') and sympathy ('He gave you no choice'), Zack is angry at himself: 'There is *always* a choice!'[13]

This idea of the trained fighter who wishes to avoid fighting emphasizes, in this case, his 'gentlemanliness'. We could trace this particular construction of gentlemanliness genealogically back to the 'gentlemanly art' of Bartitsu and the jujitsu craze of Victorian Britain, as exemplified by Sherlock Holmes. It can also be traced back to various ideologies of pacifism that are often imputed (often apocryphally) to 'oriental' martial arts – such as Buddhist and Taoist pacifism or classic Confucian gentlemanly ideals.

Sherlock Holmes turned out to have 'some knowledge ... of *baritsu*, or the Japanese system of wrestling'. What Conan Doyle rendered as 'baritsu' was actually called 'Bartitsu'. It initially appears as a retroactive 'deus ex machina' in *The Return of Sherlock Holmes 1. The Adventure of the Empty House* (1903): Holmes explains upon his return that he used martial arts to save himself during his fight with Moriarty on the Reichenbach Falls (Godfrey 2010). Recent film adaptations have made much of Holmes' martial arts skills, most recently in the form of the rather messy gentlemanly thug Holmes as played by Robert Downey Jr.

With many gentlemen fighters, what led to the development of their skill was an earlier brutalisation. In *An Officer and a Gentleman*, a flashback shows us that the childhood incarnation of Gere's Zack was beaten up by a gang of local kickboxing kids in a crowded Asian city back street. Hence, we learn his need to develop his own kickboxing skills. They derive from what Sylvia Chong would discuss in terms of 'the oriental obscene' infusing and in part constituting the Western gentlemanly identity (Chong 2012).

Full Metal Jacket (1987) gives us a different creation scenario. Two Marines relaxing in town, photographing a prostitute who is trying to solicit them, have their camera snatched by a Vietnamese thief, who, in a parting display of adrenaline fuelled anger and triumph, turns and performs kicks, finger jabs and strikes in their direction before escaping on a motorbike. One Marine turns to the other and says, 'Wow, did you see the moves on that guy?'[14]

It is easy to see why the West fell in love with Eastern martial arts: The 'moves' can be spectacular. However, it is not compulsory to fall in love with or in thrall to them – nor with the 'moves' of the other guy. For instance, when the Houston team are preparing for a daunting match in Tokyo against a Japanese team in *Rollerball* (1975), the management brings in someone to explain that the Japanese players will be using martial arts techniques from karate and (somewhat surprisingly, the Korean art of) hapkido. The reason for the lesson is because 'forewarned is forearmed'. But the team is cynical. Why should they care about Japanese martial arts when they all already know the 'good ol' Houston fist in

---

[13] https://www.youtube.com/watch?v=5er6ufig0uo
[14] https://www.youtube.com/watch?v=Hch3HL8gPTk

the face technique'?[15] Indeed, in *Rollerball*, the martial moves of the other are rejected, in favour of sticking with the simplicity and homeliness of the pugilistic approach that they already practice.

Fighting Talk

Perhaps the rejection of the oriental other that we see in *Rollerball* is something of an exception. Certainly, in many other films, the oriental otherness of martial arts is fetishized, idealised, and desired. Indeed, even when they haven't actually trained in it at all, some people realise that simply talking about martial arts and claiming to 'know' them can constitute a viable form of self-defence. Eddie Murphy's Billy Ray Valentine exemplifies this in *Trading Places* (1983), in a comic scene in a prison cell.[16]

In this scene, Billy claims to have fought dozens of police officers who attempted to arrest him the night before. When questioned about why he appeared to be crying when brought into the cell, he claims the police had used tear gas (a substance normally reserved for riot situations) to subdue him. Throughout this scene, what Murphy's character invests in are the ways in which martial arts both look cool and might make you seem scary and off-putting to any potential aggressor. The verbal claims to be able to 'do' martial arts might both carry some cultural capital and therefore act as a deterrent.

We see the other side of this logic in an early scene in *The Wanderers* (1979). Again, it is a new kid's first day at school (Perry, played by Tony Gianos). Joey (John Friedrich) is introducing the new 'kid' (his new found 19-year-old friend-*cum*-protector) to the gang culture of his school and neighbourhood. Walking along packed school corridors, Joey points to different groups and reels off their names and ethnic characteristics. Irish gangs, black gangs, Italian gangs, etc. Then Joey points out The Wongs. Excitedly, Joey describes them like this: '27 guys all with the last name Wong, all black belts in jujitsu who could kill you with one judo chop!'[17]

I have known this film and this line for most of my life. For many years, I thought little of it, other than what it is on one literal level designed to make the impressionable viewer think: The Wongs are a cool-looking and formidably tough gang of Asian martial artists. Of course, because of scenes like this, which treat ethnic difference less than 'politically correctly', *The Wanderers* is now held up in various online charts and YouTube analyses as an example of 'Hollywood racism'. And, of course, Joey *is* ethnically profiling the gangs. But the gangs are ethnically organised. Indeed, within this framework the Wongs *are* fulfilling their ethnic stereotype destiny – by being Asians who are martial

---

[15] https://www.youtube.com/watch?v=WUSCpZMbPnQ

[16] https://www.youtube.com/watch?v=4WMErc1n6Ks

[17] https://www.youtube.com/watch?v=GzPeYdeG2co

artists. It needs to be noted that racial tension is part of the dramatic tension, story arc and symbolic order of this film. So, denouncing the film's supposed 'racism' is less interesting than thinking about the matter of Joey's palpable excitement at the idea of them all being 'black belts' who 'could kill you' with one technique.

It was only when racking my brains for filmic examples for this study that I realised that I would be able to make a pedantic aficionado point about the differences between jujitsu and judo, and hence say something about Joey's ignorance. And it was only then that I thought, hang on: Wong? Jujitsu? Judo? The name Wong is Chinese, not Japanese. Jujitsu and judo are Japanese. What is going on here? I confess, to try to learn more, I had to turn to the visuals, not the dialogue, to try to clarify the ethnic situation here – in particular, by turning to the final fight of the film – the huge gang fight on the football field. And, to my eyes, it looks like the Wongs are practicing a Chinese martial art, rather than anything Japanese (although I cannot be sure). Of course, now I could be accused of ethnic stereotyping. But I think it is more interesting to think about the ways in which the film – in the form of Joey – cares not a jot about the actual specificities of whether the Wongs and their martial arts are Chinese or Japanese. Indeed, even if the disjunction between the family name and the ethnic attributions are a knowing joke on the part of the filmmakers, the only thing that the film cares about is the fact that true martial arts skill in a teen-world context makes the martial artists seem fearsome and cool to their non-martial artist peers.

But the martial arts experts who are held in awe are *othered*. They are presented as readymade and complete. We may ask about the aspirant martial artist, the subject who desires to become an expert. Films often seem to face a problem when it comes to the matter of a character *aspiring* to become fearsome and cool *themselves*, via self-cultivation and training. In fact, it seems that, unless this occurs within a martial arts film and is depicted via large doses of training montages, the desire to become a martial artist seems always on the verge of becoming ridiculous. One can 'be' an adept fighter. One can 'be' a martial artist. But if there is desire and training and aspiring, it seems that this is most easily depicted as comic, eccentric, perverse, and weird.

Of course, some non-martial arts films do occasionally associate martial arts training with higher cultural values. At the end of *Once Were Warriors* (1994), for instance, the central characters – a mother and two brothers (Beth [Rena Owen], Nig [Julian Arahanga], and Boogie [Taungaroa Emile]) – come together as a family. The film is set in a poverty ravaged Maori community, and all kinds of violence have been horrifically and relentlessly present throughout. The older brother, Nig, has embraced a close-knit gang community and is covered in Maori tattoos. By contrast, by the end of the film, the younger brother, Boogie, has found a kind of salvation in traditional Maori martial arts training. In an affectionate scene, the older of the brothers asks the younger whether he'd like some similar tattoos. 'No thanks', says the boy, 'my tattoos are on the inside'.

However, even 'higher' cultural values can easily be mocked – especially if there is any kind of ethnic, racial or cultural cross-dressing involved (Bowman 2010b). If the last vestiges of all-but-lost Maori arts are presented as a symbol of a tiny glimmer of hope for the ravaged community in *Once Were Warriors*, any kind of cross-ethnic cultural performance of another culture's art is always going to raise eyebrows and questions. Hence, Gaylord Focker's (Ben Stiller) father, Bernie, played by Dustin Hoffman, in *Meet the Fockers* (2004), practices *capoeira*. Capoeira is an afro-Brazilian martial art that has a great deal of cultural and political significance as a postcolonial practice, and its practitioners and the academics who study it invest heavily in its cultural significance (Griffith 2016). But, in *Meet the Fockers*, capoeira is reduced to the term 'dance fighting'.[18] It is not 'proper fighting', it is 'dance fighting'. The white man who invests in it is obviously a certain 'type'. What kind of type? As I have argued about this before, in the words of the 1998 Offspring song 'Pretty Fly For a White Guy', the white cultural cross-dresser or cross-performer is always going to be regarded as a 'wannabe' (Bowman 2010b).

The 'wannabe' is neither one thing nor another, neither this nor that, neither here nor there. The wannabe wants (to be) something they are not. Sometimes, the desired thing itself is impossible (invincibility, for example). Other times, the wannabe cannot be, attain or obtain what they desire because doing so is impossible (changing ethnicities, for example). Such a person is going to find themselves scorned, spurned, ridiculed, reviled, or at best pitied.

Conclusion

This work has set (and transgressed) some artificial/schematic parameters in order to focus on the margins of martial arts discourse and to see what might be gleaned about the discursive status of martial arts. Drawing the line in such an unusual place required us to give some attention to an area of martial arts marginalia that might otherwise remain ignored, with all of the attention of martial arts studies (or cultural studies of martial arts) going to 'proper' contexts of martial arts, such as the visual realm of fight choreography or the discursive construction of martial arts in 'proper' martial arts films. Obviously, these are important areas of enquiry. But this chapter imposed a principled exclusion of all things 'proper' and 'obvious' (and inevitably failed to maintain the border: In setting it, we transgressed it, and in setting out what we would not talk about we regularly had to engage with what we said we weren't going to). In doing so, the films we were able to examine suggested that outside of martial arts discourse proper, martial arts have multiple potential significations, and diverse potential values.

Because of the attempt to exclude visual representation and prioritise verbal representation, not many films could be found that fitted the bill comfortably.

---

[18] https://www.youtube.com/watch?v=srV41k0NWgo

There seem to be very few non-action films that discuss martial arts. This is so even though visual representations of martial arts abound. Nonetheless, what this unconventional foray into the margins of martial arts discourse in film suggests is that discussions of martial arts in non-martial art films tend to relate to fantasies and desires in relation to identities that originate or proliferate in the face of feelings of insecurity, at transitional times, and in transitional contexts. In Lacanian terms, they emerge and circulate as (if) answering a lack or a need.

This explains why those who are believed to 'have it' or 'be it' can be revered as 'real men'. Conversely, those who are seen to be striving or fantasising about becoming 'it' or getting 'it' can so easily be regarded as *lacking*, as *wanting*, as *losers*. As Kaja Silverman argued of the Lacanian understanding of subjectivity: Identity, fantasy and desire are so complexly intertwined and imbricated that, in Lacanian terms, one cannot really discuss one of these dimensions without discussing the others (Silverman 1983, 6). The fact that non-psychoanalytic discourses do discuss identity without discussing fantasy and desire helps to put things like martial arts practice in such an odd position. Taiji and judo are both 'not meant' to be sexual, and yet can so easily be depicted as *uncannily*, *almost*, or *also* so. This internet meme from many years ago encapsulates if not the full constellation of possibilities then at least some key parallax views:

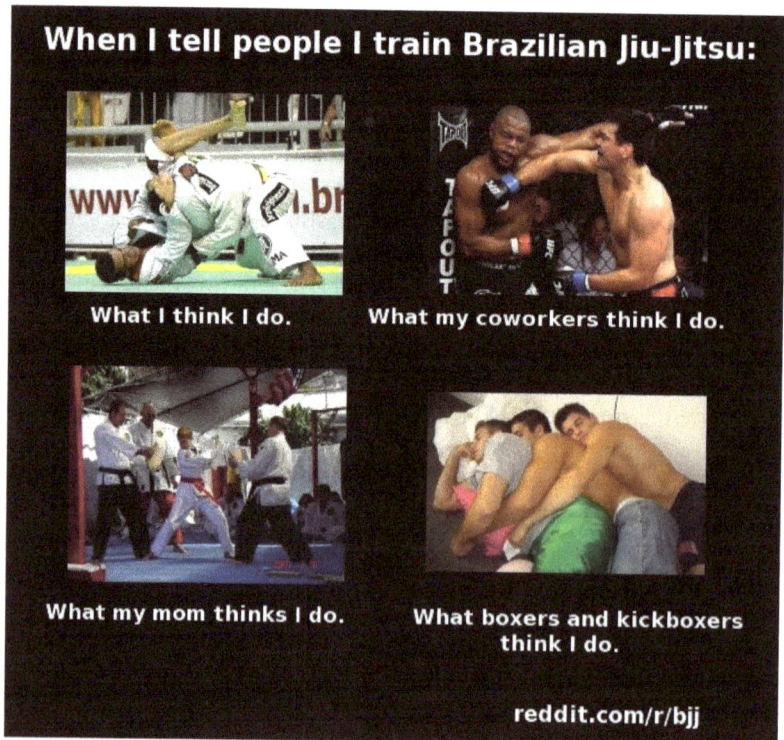

When I tell people I train Brazilian Jiu-Jitsu:

What I think I do.   What my coworkers think I do.

What my mom thinks I do.   What boxers and kickboxers think I do.

reddit.com/r/bjj

There are more potential reasons why, discursively or culturally, martial arts inevitably lie between a rock and a hard place – neither this nor that, both this and that. For instance, they are peculiar structured responses that seek to 'manage' the problem of physical violence in its own terms. However, physical interpersonal violence is itself of a peculiar status: Physical violent responses to the threat or reality of physical violence are rarely regarded as the best or most intelligent possible responses. They are most easily regarded as aberrant responses to aberrant situations. After all, fighting is what children do, what parents enjoin them to grow out of. Attacking others in day to day life is rarely regarded as a mature or balanced thing, even if others attack or threaten to attack you. In (most) 'civilised societies', the state has accrued (almost) all of the rights to the legitimate dispensation and management of violence. Adults should not 'normally' settle differences with a fist fight. To some, such actions signal being 'more' than an average person; to others, it signals being 'less', or abnormal.

Martial arts thrive in liminal spaces, spaces of becoming: Becoming adult, becoming competent, capable, 'strong', and so on. Perhaps 'most properly', martial arts are 'transitional objects' in the psychoanalytic sense, or 'vanishing mediators' in Fredric Jameson's sense of something that enables a new situation to emerge (whether that be adulthood or heteronormative partnering), that must recede and be forgotten once the new condition has been reached. As both one of Wittgenstein's and one of Buddhism's aphorisms puts it in different ways: Once you've used the tool to do the job, you don't lug it along with you; you just put it down and move on.

But martial artists don't move on. To this extent, they fail to become 'normal', or at least defer it. Unless they turn into Rex, this could become socially acceptable. However, unless martial arts training happens in childhood, at the start of the process, the aspirant, desiring martial artist can appear ridiculous – whether 'funny peculiar' or 'funny ha-ha'. This is because martial arts involve effort, process and 'becoming': They have a kind of originary lack inscribed in their heart. The very desire to do martial arts, and practicing martial arts with the aim of becoming different, more, better, other, etc., signals the presence and workings of lack, desire, insecurity, and incompletion. Children can play at martial arts and become more competent. Adults are meant to be complete. The adult who desires martial arts mastery too late in life diverges from the norm.

Martial arts signal liminality, they involve crossing multiple borders at once, the desire to become unproblematically powerful (Elvis' Charlie) or to have hidden depths and untold skills (Richard Gere's Zack), but the entire discourse is haunted by the risk of remaining in the realms of murky conscious or unconscious desires and unclear investments, like those of the predatory Kevin, the insecure Rex, Napoleon and Kip, or the uncannily creepy Quilty. One suspects that such eccentric and idiosyncratic – tragicomic, laughable, weird – characters offer us more insight into what it is to try to become or be something than do the alpha males on screen who perform the supposed ideal and construct the supposed norm. But maybe, 'really', people are 'really' a lot less like Elvis' Charlie or Richard Gere's Zack Mayo, and considerably more like Napoleon Dynamite or Eddie Murphy's Billy Ray Valentine: All talk.

Conclusion: Drawing the Line

This work began by posing the question of what the essence of martial arts might be. It has deconstructed this question and this matter in a variety of ways in a journey around some of the regions associated with martial arts. This has neither been a journey to the heart of the matter (as 'heart' in this sense would be a synonym of centre or essence) nor a cartographic journey around a circumference (as this would involve the circumnavigation of a stable territory). If such a journey were possible, then the essence of martial arts could be defined.

Approaching martial arts as a complex, contingent and variable range of discursive constructs in this way can suggest one of at least two possible relationships to the question of 'definition' with which we began, and which has returned in various ways throughout this book. One relation involves accepting the variability of the construct and defining the object, phenomenon or field of practice anyway. Another relation involves accepting the variability of the construct and declining, on that basis, to offer any firm definition, while nonetheless tacitly accepting that martial arts exist, at least as ideas and notions within various discursive and cultural contexts. Both relations have their benefits and drawbacks, as we have seen.

I have argued for the latter. One symptom of this choice may be said to have taken the form of my repeated assertion that martial arts studies researchers ought to move on from the question of defining martial arts in one breath before I have myself returned again and again to the topic in the next. However, my fixation on encouraging researchers and writers to get 'past' a certain fixation on defining exists because I believe there are more negative consequences to the fixation on definition than there are positives. Consequently, once more, it seems important to reiterate here the argument about why it is that the question of 'how to define martial arts' is not only a pseudo-problem but also regressive and even potentially damaging for martial arts studies.

Consider it this way. The question of definition (in martial arts studies and elsewhere) involves asking and exploring the question of where to draw the line. When we ask 'What is or are martial arts?', we are asking a specifically focused version of 'Where do we draw the line?' Once asked, the question 'What is or are martial arts?' will become a matter that discussion and debate will become stuck on, or stuck in. This is because there is no universally clinching and uncontestably definitive answer.

While there may be no obviously negative intellectual or even ethical or political consequences associated with arguing about definitions, there are some less obvious ones. As such, in order to avoid this quicksand, in what follows, I want to walk around the trap, reflecting less on 'Where do we draw the line?' and more on 'Why draw the line?' and, indeed, 'How – or in what ways – *should* anyone draw the line?'

To do this requires reflection on what the act of defining or drawing a line in the first place is or does. Posed directly: What is the line, anyway? What is a definition? What is the need that is being engaged? While there is a very large amount that could be said in response to such questions, in relation to the definition of martial arts, the line that people believe needs to be drawn is a line between 'martial arts' (on one side – the inside) and 'not martial arts' (on the other side – outside). The line, the definition, is the border between an inside and an outside. On one side of the line (on the inside), there will be martial arts (proper). On the other side of the line is the outside, which is everything else, and which is not proper to martial arts. This is one way to depict the ideal, tidy, well-defined situation: On one side of the line, the inside, the proper object of martial arts studies; on the other side of the line, the outside, all the stuff that is not the object of martial arts studies.

This may seem simple. But it is not. As this book has sought to illustrate in various ways, it does not take too much time to realise that 'martial arts' cannot *actually* be disentangled, disambiguated or extricated from many of the things that any definition will try to say is *not* proper to them. Any such definition will not merely be an *abstraction*, it will also be a *reduction* and indeed therefore a *fiction*. It will share many of the features of a representation of something that does not actually exist anywhere. Rather than this, in the cultural world of martial arts practice and discourse, there are always supplements, images, ideas, practices, products, fantasies, realia, phantasmagoria, simulacra, prosthesis, grafts, add-ons, extras, and 'related', that cannot and will not be removed.

A dawning realisation of this ineradicable proliferation and constitutive multiplicity accounts for why people often attempt to escape from the trap by moving from the singular to the plural. People can often realise that there is no simple unity, but they nonetheless still want to erect a definition. Because of this, realising that the category 'martial arts' is constitutively imprecise, scholars try to return us to precision by *adding* categories. Accordingly, we get *more* categories, we get refinements and differentiations: Martial arts and/or combat sports, self-defence, military combat training, combatives, weapons-based combat systems, religious practices, cultural traditions, calisthenics taught in schools, traditional, non-traditional, deracinated, de- and re-territorialized practices, and so on and so forth. This produces ideas of entities that are called hybrids, and so on. However, each addition, seeking to introduce a level of clarity and precision, nonetheless inexorably introduces even more grey area, imprecision and further grounds for disagreement.

This occurs because the perceived need to introduce more and more terms and concepts in order to try to clarify things is a paradoxical drive that comes in response to a fundamental lack of precision and clarity. This can never fully be eradicated by trying to mop it up by throwing more categories at it. The addition of ever more categories, gradations and combinations does not actually produce clarity or reduce unclarity. Rather, it principally produces metalanguages and ever more intricate language games.

Metalanguages and language games are not somehow simply or necessarily universally true. They are themselves locally-produced cauldrons of terminological soup. When they sound scientific, they may be impressive. But they are, at root, just variable attempts to solve the problem of how to conceptualise and communicate with clarity and precision. But because there is no *necessary* relation between a field and its demarcation, a practice and its conceptualisation, nor indeed between one discourse and another, 'clarity and precision' only exist within a community of language game players. Stated differently, how those steeped in anthropological approaches may have long been inclined to conceptualise and demarcate 'martial arts' may differ hugely from how those working in sociology, cultural studies, philosophy, religious studies, dance or theatre studies may each have done so. Each approach involves a language game, the production of a metalanguage, and each of these is almost certainly going to differ from others.

This is a situation of proliferation, despite all attempts to pin down and wrap up. Producing proliferation, producing more, is what academic (and other) discourses do. They do not simply strip away and reveal bare or naked essentials. They construct and fabricate lenses through which to see differently. They produce alternatives. They challenge each other. They generate *more*.

In the field of martial arts studies, discussions often circulate around different conceptualisations of the object 'martial arts'. It is clear that different people draw the line around their conceptualisation of their object of attention differently. It is my hope that over time it should become more and more clear that the definitional act of drawing a line is *inherently problematic*. Which is not to say that it is not going to be done. Everyone needs to find ways to be able to refer, or to say 'I am talking about this, and not that'. Every academic study needs to draw the line between the inside (what it is about) and the outside (what it is not, cannot or will not be about or even look at). As I regularly say to my PhD students, there are two questions that every examiner will ask you in one way or another. First, why did you draw the line here and not there? And second, why did you approach it in this way and not another?

Both of these questions must be answered. You need to know that you could have drawn your line elsewhere and differently, and that this would inevitably have changed things. You also need to know that you could have approached it differently, and that this would have produced very different kinds of insight, perspective, result, outcome or conclusion. In other words, what academic works need more than some inevitably failed definition is a critical reflection on the necessary act of drawing a line – any and every 'I am talking about *this* (and not *that*) in this way (and not another way)'. Indeed, doing so enables us to see that there are more important matters than where to draw the line. These involve thinking about how and why a line has been drawn.

In conversation with a colleague who works in performance studies, for instance, my colleague voiced reluctance to work under the heading of 'martial arts studies' at all. This is because the act of drawing a line around such practices seemed not only somewhat arbitrary, stifling and artificial, in terms of his own interests, but also *ethically problematic*. As someone interested in performance, he asked why he would separate martial arts from other kinds of physical practice. And anyway, how and why could or would anyone really draw convincing lines between martial arts practices and dance or theatre or ritual or religion, or indeed athletics, somatics, or therapeutics, and so on?

On thinking about this, I became inclined to expand the problem further and wider. Maybe my colleague is actually still too limited – too steeped in thinking about *embodied* practices. For, what about media and technology? Can we separate martial arts, or the study thereof, from practices and studies of film, drama, gaming, literature, or heritage? What about philosophy?

Nonetheless, the ethical dimension of my colleague's reluctance seemed particularly thought-provoking. What does it mean to cast a net that only looks for and at martial, combative, fighting, defensive or offensive practices? What does it mean to insist on identifying all of the practices out there that seem to fit the bill in terms of their 'martial' dimensions? Is this not in and of itself a violent contortion, and a bending of the world to the will or the mind's eye of the observer? Maybe my escrima practice seems fairly obviously martially orientated. But what about my taiji practice? Just because I search in my taiji practice for combative dimensions and applications, must I insist on reducing taiji to this dimension for everyone, and enshrining it in academic discourse in this particular contingent and motivated way?

Inventing and chopping up the conceptual spectrum in such a way as to enable the claim that 'martial arts' is an obvious and necessary field, fit for an academic discipline to congregate around it, may actually seem like a fairly contorted and contorting act, when viewed from a broader perspective. Privileging 'martial' over 'art' may also amount to doing a kind of violence to the very objects that fall within its purview.

How can any such tendentious act be justified? Should perhaps martial arts studies really always be understood as a subset of other fields, such as performance studies, for instance? The answer could be yes. As long as it can also be agreed that it should also be a subset of religious studies, and a subset of film studies, as well as a subset of subcultural studies, ethnic studies, area studies, sports studies, history, and so on. The point is that *none* of these subsets exist on a fixed or immutable map. There is no Venn diagram or flow chart that could adequately depict some real or permanent relation of inclusivity or exclusivity. There is no essential or necessary 'proper place' for this or any other field. Its 'proper place' is always a consequence not of fit but of performative elaboration. This is because 'martial arts', like anything else ('literature', 'religion', 'science') is a contingent discursive establishment (a construct) rather than an essential referential category (a datum).

To evoke a Kantian distinction, 'martial arts' is *synthetic* rather than *analytic*. It is not an object proper to scientific study, and nor does it need to be. The study of something like this is not really scientific because – to borrow an insight that D.N. Rodowick once made about 'film studies' – it is *something we simply know about*, that we experience in different ways at different times and in different places, something that changes, that changes us, that we can change, and so on (Rodowick 2007; see also Rodowick 2014). We can't really 'do' martial arts studies exhaustively or thoroughly, as if it were some kind of science. It doesn't lend itself to that kind of treatment at all. Rather, it presents itself as a range of phenomena for reflection, philosophy, theory, rumination. Martial arts, however conceived or however instantiated, seem or seems to beg questions – questions about 'what it is' and about 'other things': Life, value, health, gender, nation, strength, honour, fun, commerce, ethnicity, culture, identity, and more.

To choose martial arts studies as a category – to attempt to institute it as a field – is to accept or at least trade in an inheritance. We *have* the term 'martial arts'. It is a discursive category, even if it is not properly referential, indeed even if it is barely able to evoke its own content. Nonetheless, history has given it to us. People are likely to 'kind of just know' what you mean when you say it, even if their understandings are hugely different, even utterly incompatible, and even though any attempt to specify the content of the field cannot but produce contradictory objects and practices. This is the most 'obvious' reason I avoided the so-called problem of definition for so long: Because one 'obviously' need not define because 'obviously', 'in the real world', definition is a pseudo-problem – the effect of a certain orientation in the face of what it means to study or do academic work.

Of course, one always has to negotiate competing injunctions. Definitions and categories do emerge. But they often fall down when pressed or pushed. Such definitions need to be pressed or pushed and pulled, because they can come to seem stifling. And they can come to *be* stifling – because of the effects that they can have on our orientations.

This is why I argue that, in martial arts studies as elsewhere, the question should not simply be 'Where do you draw the line?' Rather, the equally – perhaps more – important questions that we should engage with are '*Why* draw a line?' and indeed '*How* can we let ourselves try to draw a line?' If one feels compelled to draw a line around a field or object, and to map it out in a certain way, this is a compulsion one might expect to be matched with an equal compulsion when it comes to policing the territory that has been marked out. In other words, those scholars who seem merely to be exercising an honest and innocent drive to speak clearly and precisely and to define coherently may yet turn out to be the most diligent border guards, hostile to any non-legitimate travellers.

The postcolonial critic Gayatri Spivak once argued that making any distinction, making any discrimination, specifying, erecting or using any conceptual categories, is irreducibly and inescapably political in some sense. This is because producing differentials erects binaries, and binaries are inevitably hierarchical. The inside is the proper, the outside is the improper, the other. The question thus becomes: How hospitable are we to be to difference that presents itself as impropriety, as alterity? How is difference to be treated? This is both the ethico-political and conceptual-orientation problem of all disciplinary discourse. For martial arts studies, it suggests that what needs to be asked is: How do we define the hospitality of martial arts studies to that which requests admittance but seems improper? How do we invent both martial arts and martial arts studies in our discourse? Engaging such important questions relies on deconstruction – the deconstruction both of martial arts and of martial arts studies.

Bibliography

'About the International Hopology Society'. n.d. Available at: http://www.hoplology. com/about.htm#three. Accessed 25 October 2016.

Akerstrøm Andersen, Niels. 2003. *Discursive Analytical Strategies: Understanding Foucault, Koselleck, Laclau, Luhmann*. London: The Policy Press.

Althusser, Louis. 1971. *Lenin and Philosophy, and Other Essays*. Translated by Ben Brewster. London: NLB.

Anderson, Benedict. 1991. *Imagined Communities: Reflections on the Origin and Spread of Nationalism*. Revised edition. London: Verso.

Arditi, Benjamin. 2008. *Politics on the Edges of Liberalism: Difference, Populism, Revolution, Agitation*. Edinburgh: Edinburgh University Press.

Arditi, Benjamin and Jeremy Valentine. 1999. *Polemicization: The Contingency of the Commonplace*. Edinburgh: Edinburgh University Press.

Barrowman, Kyle. 2015a. 'Grappling with History: Martial Arts in Classical Hollywood Cinema'. *Kung Fu Tea*. Available at: https://chinesemartialstudies. com/2015/08/06/guest-post-grappling-with-history-martial-arts-in-classical-hollywood-cinema/.

———. 2015b. 'History in the Making: Martial Arts between Planet Hollywood and Planet Hong Kong'. *Martial Arts Studies* 1, 72–82. https://doi.org/ 10.18573/j.2015.10020.

———. 2019. 'Origins of the Action Film: Types, Tropes, and Techniques in Early Film History'. *A Companion to the Action Film*. Edited by James Kendrick. Hoboken, NJ: Wiley-Blackwell, 11–34.

Barry, Andrew. 2001. *Political Machines: Governing a Technological Society.* London: Continuum.

Barthes, Roland. 1972. *Mythologies.* London: Paladin.

———. 1977. *Image-Music-Text.* Translated and edited by Stephen Heath. London: Fontana.

Bauman, Zygmunt. 2005. *Liquid Life.* Cambridge: Polity Press.

Benesch, Oleg. 2016. 'Reconsidering Zen, Samurai, and the Martial Arts'. *The Asia-Pacific Journal* 14.17, 1–23. http://apjjf.org/2016/17/Benesch.html.

Benjamin, Walter. 1999. *Illuminations.* London: Pimlico.

Bennett, Alexander C. 2015. *Kendo: Culture of the Sword.* Berkeley: University of California Press.

Bennington, Geoffrey, and Jacques Derrida. 2008. *Derrida.* Paris: Editions du Seuil.

Bethell, Tom. n.d. 'Against Sociobiology'. *First Things.* Available at: https://www. firstthings.com/article/2001/01/against-sociobiology. Accessed 9 November 2016.

Bishop, James. 2004. *Bruce Lee: Dynamic Becoming.* New York: Promethean Press.

Bourdieu, Pierre. 1979. *Outline of a Theory of Practice.* Cambridge: Cambridge University Press.

———. 1984. *Distinction: A Social Critique of the Judgement of Taste.* London: Routledge & Kegan Paul.

Bowman, Paul. 2001. 'Proper Impropriety: The Proper-Ties of Cultural Studies'. *Parallax* 7, 50–65. https://doi.org/10.1080/13534640110037813.

——— (ed.). 2003. *Interrogating Cultural Studies: Theory, Politics, and Practice.* Pluto Press.

———. 2007. *Post-Marxism Versus Cultural Studies: Theory, Politics and Intervention.* Edinburgh: Edinburgh University Press.

———. 2008. *Deconstructing Popular Culture.* Basingstoke, Hampshire: Palgrave Macmillan.

———. 2010a. 'Deconstruction is a Martial Art'. *Enduring Resistance: Cultural Theory After Derrida / La résistance persévère : la théorie de la culture (d') aprés Derrida.* Edited by Sjef Houppermans, Rico Sneller, and Peter van Zilfhout. Amsterdam: Rodopi, 37–56.

———. 2010b. 'Rey Chow and Postcolonial Social Semiotics'. *Social Semiotics* 20.4, 329-341. https://doi.org/10.1080/10350330.2010.494386.

———. 2010c. 'Sick Man of Transl-Asia: Bruce Lee and Rey Chow's Queer Cultural Translation'. *Social Semiotics* 20.4, 393–409. https://doi.org/10.10 80/10350330.2010.494393

———. 2010d. *Theorizing Bruce Lee: Film-Fantasy-Fighting-Philosophy.* Amsterdam: Rodopi.

———. 2012. *Culture and the Media.* Basingstoke, Hampshire: Palgrave Macmillan.

———. 2013a. *Reading Rey Chow: Visuality, Postcoloniality, Ethnicity, Sexuality.* New York: Peter Lang.

———. 2013b. *Beyond Bruce Lee: Chasing the Dragon through Film, Philosophy, and Popular Culture*. New York: Columbia University Press.

———. 2014a. 'Editorial: Martial Arts Studies'. *JOMEC Journal* 5, 1-4. http://doi.org/10.18573/j.2014.10262.

———. 2014b. 'Instituting Reality in Martial Arts Practice'. *JOMEC Journal* 5, 1–24. http://doi.org/10.18573/j.2014.10266.

———. 2015a. *Martial Arts Studies: Disrupting Disciplinary Boundaries*. London: Rowman & Littlefield International.

———. 2015b. 'Asking the Question: Is Martial Arts Studies an Academic Field?' *Martial Arts Studies* 1, 3–19. https://doi.org/10.18573/j.2015.10015.

———. 2016a. 'Making Martial Arts History Matter'. *The International Journal of the History of Sport* 33.9, 1–19. https://doi.org/10.1080/09523367.2016.1212842.

———. 2016b. 'The Intimate Schoolmaster and the Ignorant Sifu: Poststructuralism, Bruce Lee, and the Ignorance of Everyday Radical Pedagogy'. *Philosophy and Rhetoric* 49.4, 549–570. https://doi.org/10.5325/philrhet.49.4.0549.

———. 2017a. *Martial Artists in the UK Press (CUROP Research Project)*. Cardiff University: CUROP: Cardiff University Research Opportunity Programme.

———. 2017b. *Mythologies of Martial Arts*. London: Rowman & Littlefield International.

———. 2017c. 'The Definition of Martial Arts Studies'. *Martial Arts Studies* 3, 6–23. https://10.18573/j.2017.10092.

———. 2017d. 'What Can a Martial Body Do for Society? Or, Theory before Definition in Martial Arts Studies'. Available at: http://orca.cf.ac.uk/103002/.

Bowman, Paul, and Benjamin N. Judkins. 2017. 'Editorial: Is Martial Arts Studies Trivial?' *Martial Arts Studies* 4, 1–16. https://doi.org/10.18573/j.2017.10183.

Brown, Bill. 1997. 'Global Bodies/Postnationalities: Charles Johnson's Consumer Culture'. *Representations* 58, 24-48.

Butler, Judith. 1990. *Gender Trouble: Feminism and the Subversion of Identity*. London: Routledge.

Butler, Judith, Ernesto Laclau, and Slavoj Žižek. 2000. *Contingency, Hegemony, Universality: Contemporary Dialogues on the Left*. London: Verso.

Chakrabarty, Dipesh. 1992. 'Provincializing Europe: Postcoloniality and the Critique of History'. *Cultural Studies* 6 (3): 337–57.

Chan, Stephen. 2000. 'The Construction and Export of Culture as Artefact: The Case of Japanese Martial Arts'. *Body & Society* 6.1, 69–74. https://doi.org/10.1177/1357034X00006001005.

Channon, Alex. 2012. 'Western Men and Eastern Arts: The Significance of Eastern Martial Arts Disciplines in British Men's Narratives of Masculinity'. *Asia Pacific Journal of Sport and Social Science* 1.2–3, 111–127. https://doi.org/10.1080/21640599.2012.751170.

———. 2016. 'How (Not) to Categorise Martial Arts: A Discussion and Example from Gender Studies'. *Kung Fu Tea*. Available at: https://chinesemartialstudies.

com/2016/09/15/how-not-to-categorise-martial-arts-a-discussion-and-example-from-gender-studies/. Accessed 16 September 2016.

Channon, Alex, and George Jennings. 2014. 'Exploring Embodiment through Martial Arts and Combat Sports: A Review of Empirical Research'. *Sport in Society* 17.6, 773–789. https://doi.org/10.1080/17430437.2014.882906.

Channon, Alex, and Christopher R. Matthews. 2015. *Global Perspectives on Women in Combat Sports: Women Warriors Around the World*. Basingstoke, Hampshire: Palgrave Macmillan.

Chong, Sylvia Shin Huey. 2012. *The Oriental Obscene: Violence and Racial Fantasies in the Vietnam Era*. Durham, NC: Duke University Press.

Chow, Rey. 1995. *Primitive Passions: Visuality, Sexuality, Ethnography, and Contemporary Chinese Cinema*. New York: Columbia University Press.

———. 2007. *Sentimental Fabulations, Contemporary Chinese Films: Attachment in the Age of Global Visibility*. New York: Columbia University Press.

———. 2012. *Entanglements, or: Transmedial Thinking About Capture*. Durham and London: Duke University Press.

Clarke, J. J. 1997. *Oriental Enlightenment: The Encounter Between Asian and Western Thought*. London: Routledge.

Cooling, B. F., Jack B. Hilliard, Sun Tzu, and Samuel B. Griffith. 1972. 'The Art of War'. *Military Affairs* 36.1, 26–26. https://doi.org/10.2307/1983855.

Cynarski, Wojciech J. 2008. 'An Overview of Polish Martial Arts'. *Journal of Asian Martial Arts* 17.2, 8–26.

Cynarski, Wojciech J., Lothar Sieber, and Gabriel Szajna. 2014. 'Martial Arts in Physical Culture'. *Ido Movement for Culture: Journal of Martial Arts Anthropology* 14.4, 31–38. http://www.doi.org/10.14589/ido.14.4.4.

de Man, Paul. 1986. *The Resistance to Theory*. Minneapolis: University of Minnesota Press.

Deleuze, Gilles. 2006. *Foucault*. London: Continuum.

Derrida, Jacques. 1976. *Of Grammatology*. Translated by Gayatri Chakravorty Spivak. Baltimore, MD: Johns Hopkins University Press.

———. 1981. *Dissemination*. Translated by Barbara Johnson. London: Athlone.

———. 1982. *Margins of Philosophy*. Translated by Alan Bass. Brighton: Harvester.

———. 1988. *Limited Inc*. Evanston, IL: Northwestern University Press.

———. 1992. 'Mochlos; or, The Conflict of the Faculties'. *Logomachia: The Conflict of the Faculties*. Edited by Richard Rand. Lincoln: University of Nebraska Press.

———. 1994. *Specters of Marx: The State of the Debt, the Work of Mourning, and the New International*. London: Routledge.

———. 1996. 'Remarks on Deconstruction and Pragmatism'. *Deconstruction and Pragmatism*. Edited by Chantal Mouffe. London: Routledge, 79–90.

———. 1997. *Politics of Friendship*. Translated by George Collins. London: Verso.

———. 1998. *Monolingualism of the Other, or, The Prosthesis of Origin*. TRanslated by Patrick Mensah. Stanford, CA: Stanford University Press.

———. 2001. *Writing and Difference*. Translated by Alan Bass. London: Routledge.

Derrida, Jacques and Maurizio Ferraris. 2003. 'I Have a Taste for the Secret'. *A Taste for the Secret*. Cambridge: Polity Press, 3–18.

Derrida, Jacques and Elisabeth Weber. 1995. *Points…Interviews, 1974–1994*. Stanford, CA: Stanford University Press.

Downey, Greg. 2007. 'Producing Pain: Techniques and Technologies in No-Holds-Barred Fighting'. *Social Studies of Science* 37.2, 201–226. https://doi.org/10.1177/0306312706072174.

———. 2014. '"As Real As It Gets!" Producing Hyperviolence in Mixed Martial Arts'. *JOMEC Journal* 5, 1–28. http://doi.org/10.18573/j.2014.10268.

Fabian, Johannes. 1983. *Time and the Other: How Anthropology Makes Its Object*. New York: Columbia University Press.

Fairclough, Norman. 1995. *Media Discourse*. London: Edward Arnold.

Farrer, D.S. 2015. 'Efficacy and Entertainment in Martial Arts Studies: Anthropological Perspectives'. *Martial Arts Studies* 1, 34–45. https://doi.org/10.18573/j.2015.10017.

Farrer, D.S. and John Whalen-Bridge. 2011. 'Introduction: Martial Arts, Transnationalism, and Embodied Knowledge'. *Martial Arts as Embodied Knowledge: Asian Traditions in a Transnational World*. Edited by D.S. Farrer and John Whalen-Bridge. Albany: State University of New York Press, 1–28.

Feichtinger, Christian. 2014. 'Space Buddhism: The Adoption of Buddhist Motifs in Star Wars'. *Contemporary Buddhism* 15.1, 1–16. https://doi.org/10.1080/14639947.2014.890348.

Foucault, Michel. 1970. *The Order of Things: An Archaeology of the Human Sciences*. London: Tavistock Publications.

Foucault, Michel. 1972. *The Archaeology of Knowledge*. London: Routledge.

———. 1977. *Discipline and Punish: The Birth of the Prison*. New York: Pantheon Books.

———. 1989. *The Birth of the Clinic: An Archaeology of Medical Perception*. London: Routledge.

———. 1991. *The Foucault Reader*. Edited by Paul Rabinow. London: Penguin Books.

Frank, Adam. 2006. *Taijiquan and the Search for the Little Old Chinese Man: Understanding Identity Through Martial Arts*. Basingstoke, Hampshire: Palgrave Macmillan.

Funnell, Lisa. 2014. *Warrior Women: Gender, Race, and the Transnational Chinese Action Star*. Albany: State University of New York Press.

García, Raúl Sánchez and Dale C. Spencer. 2014. *Fighting Scholars: Habitus and Ethnographies of Martial Arts and Combat Sports*. London: Anthem Press.

Gillis, Alex. 2008. *A Killing Art: The Untold History of Tae Kwon Do*. Ontario: ECW Press.

Godfrey, Emelyne. 2010. *Masculinity, Crime and Self-Defence in Victorian Literature: Duelling with Danger*. Basingstoke, Hampshire: Palgrave Macmillan.

Gong, Neil. 2015. 'How to Fight Without Rules: On Civilized Violence in "De-Civilized" Spaces'. *Social Problems* 62.4, 605-622. https://doi.org/10.1093/socpro/spv014.

Goto-Jones, Christopher. 2016. *The Virtual Ninja Manifesto: Fighting Games, Martial Arts and Gamic Orientalism*. London: Rowman & Littlefield International.

Gottschall, Jonathan. 2015. *The Professor in the Cage: Why Men Fight and Why We Like to Watch*. London: Penguin Books.

Gray, Chris Hables. 1997. *Postmodern War: The New Politics of Conflict*. London: Routledge.

Green, Kyle. 2011. 'It Hurts So It Must Be Real: Sensing the Seduction of Mixed Martial Arts'. *Social & Cultural Geography* 12.4, 377–396. https://doi.org/10.1080/14649365.2011.574796.

Griffith, Lauren Miller. 2016. *In Search of Legitimacy: How Outsiders Become Part of the Afro-Brazilian Capoeira Tradition*. New York: Berghahn Books.

Hall, Gary. 2002. *Culture in Bits: The Monstrous Future of Theory*. London: Continuum.

Hall, Stuart. 1992. 'Cultural Studies and Its Theoretical Legacies'. *Cultural Studies*. Edited by Cary Nelson, Paula Treichler, and Lawrence Grossberg. London: Routledge, 277–294.

———. 1994. 'Notes on Deconstructing "the Popular"'. *Cultural Theory and Popular Culture: A Reader*. Edited by John Storey. London: Harvester Wheatsheaf, 477–487.

Hall, Stuart and Bram Gieben. 1991. *Formations of Modernity*. Cambridge: Polity Press.

Hall, Stuart, David Morley, and Kuan-Hsing Chen. 1996. *Stuart Hall: Critical Dialogues in Cultural Studies*. London: Routledge.

Hall, Stuart et al. 1997. *Representation: Cultural Representations and Signifying Practices*. London: Sage.

Heath, Joseph and Andrew Potter. 2006. *The Rebel Sell: How the Counterculture Became Consumer Culture*. Chichester: Capstone.

Hegel, Georg Wilhelm Friedrich. 2005. *Hegel's Preface to the Phenomenology of Spirit*. Translated and with Running Commentary by Yirmiyahu Yovel. Princeton, NJ: Princeton University Press.

Heidegger, Martin. 1971. *On the Way to Language*. Translated by Peter Donald Hertz. New York: Harper & Row.

Henning, Stanley. 1999. 'Academia Encounters the Chinese Martial Arts'. *China Review International* 6.2, 319–332. http://www.doi.org/10.1353/cri.1999.0020.

Highmore, Ben. 2011. *Ordinary Lives: Studies in the Everyday*. London: Routledge.

Humphreys, Christmas. 1947. *Walk On!* London: The Buddhist Society.

Hunt, Leon. 2003. *Kung Fu Cult Masters: From Bruce Lee to Crouching Tiger*. London: Wallflower.

Iwamura, Jane Naomi. 2005. 'The Oriental Monk in American Popular Culture'. *Religion and Popular Culture in America*. Edited by Bruce David Forbes Forbes and Jeffrey Mahan. Berkeley: University of California Press, 25–43.

Jackson-Jacobs, Curtis. 2013. 'Constructing Physical Fights: An Interactionist Analysis of Violence among Affluent, Suburban Youth'. *Qualitative Sociology* 36.1, 23–52. https://doi.org/10.1007/s11133-012-9244-2.

Jones, David E. 2002. *Combat, Ritual, and Performance: Anthropology of the Martial Arts*. Westport, CT: Praeger.

Judkins, Benjamin N. 2014a. 'Inventing Kung Fu'. *JOMEC Journal* 5, 1–23. http://doi.org/10.18573/j.2014.10272.

———. 2014b. 'The Tao of Tom and Jerry: Krug on the Appropriation of the Asian Martial Arts in Western Culture'. *Kung Fu Tea*. Available at: https://chinesemartialstudies.com/2014/12/14/the-tao-of-tom-and-jerry-krug-on-the-appropriation-of-the-asian-martial-arts-in-western-culture/.

———. 2016a. 'The Seven Forms of Lightsaber Combat: Hyper-Reality and the Invention of the Martial Arts'. *Martial Arts Studies* 2, 6–22. http://doi.org/10.18573/j.2016.10067.

———. 2016b. 'What Are "Martial Arts," and Why Does Knowing Matter?' *Kung Fu Tea*. Available at: https://chinesemartialstudies.com/2016/03/06/what-are-martial-arts-and-why-does-knowing-matter/.

———. 2017. 'The Somatic Joys of Kicking'. *Barthes Studies* 3, 128–132. http://sites.cardiff.ac.uk/barthes/article/book-review-the-somatic-joys-of-kicking/.

Judkins, Benjamin N. and Paul Bowman. 2017. 'Editorial'. *Martial Arts Studies* 3, 1–5. https://doi.org/10.18573/j.2017.10112.

Judkins, Benjamin N. and Jon Nielson. 2015. *The Creation of Wing Chun: A Social History of the Southern Chinese Martial Arts*. Albany: State University of New York Press.

Kato, M. T. 2012. *From Kung Fu to Hip Hop: Globalization, Revolution, and Popular Culture*. Albany: State University of New York Press.

Krug, Gary J. 2001. 'At the Feet of the Master: Three Stages in the Appropriation of Okinawan Karate Into Anglo-American Culture'. *Cultural Studies ↔ Critical Methodologies* 1.4, 395–410. https://doi.org/10.1177/153270860100100401.

Kuhn, Thomas. 1962. *The Structure of Scientific Revolutions*. Chicago: University of Chicago Press.

Lacan, Jacques. 2001. *Écrits: A Selection*. Translated by Alan Sheridan. London: Routledge.

Laclau, Ernesto. 1994. *The Making of Political Identities*. London: Verso.

———. 1996. *Emancipation(S)*. London: Verso.

Laclau, Ernesto and Chantal Mouffe. 1985. *Hegemony and Socialist Strategy: Towards a Radical Democratic Politics*. London: Verso.

Laclau, Ernesto, Judith Butler, and Slavoj Žižek. 2000. *Contingency, Hegemony, Universality: Contemporary Dialogues on the Left*. London: Verso.

Law, Mark. 2008. *The Pyjama Game: A Journey into Judo*. London: Aurum Press.

Lefebvre, Augustin. 2016. 'The Pacific Philosophy of Aikido: An Interactional Approach'. *Martial Arts Studies* 2, 91–109. http://doi.org/10.18573/j.2016.10066.

Leigh, Jennifer (ed.). 2018. *Conversations on Embodiment Across Higher Education: Teaching, Practice and Research*. London: Routledge. https://www.routledge.com/Conversations-on-Embodiment-Across-Higher-Education-Teaching-Practice/Leigh/p/book/9781138290044.

Liu, Petrus. 2011. *Stateless Subjects: Chinese Martial Arts Literature and Postcolonial History*. Ithaca, N.Y.: East Asia Program, Cornell University.

Lo, Kwai-Cheung. 2005. *Chinese Face/Off: The Transnational Popular Culture of Hong Kong*. Urbana and Chicago: University of Illinois Press.

Lorge, Peter. 2012. *Chinese Martial Arts: From Antiquity to the Twenty First Century*. Kindle edition. Cambridge: Cambridge University Press.

———. 2016. 'Practising Martial Arts Versus Studying Martial Arts'. *The International Journal of the History of Sport* 33.9, 904–914. https://doi.org/10.1080/09523367.2016.1204296.

Lyotard, Jean-François. 1984. *The Postmodern Condition: A Report on Knowledge*. Minneapolis: University of Minnesota Press.

Marchart, Oliver. 2007. *Post-Foundational Political Thought: Political Difference in Nancy, Lefort, Badiou and Laclau*. Edinburgh: Edinburgh University Press.

May, Reinhard. 1996. *Heidegger's Hidden Sources: East Asian Influences on His Work*. London: Routledge.

Mayer, Ruth. 2013. *Serial Fu Manchu: The Chinese Supervillain and the Spread of Yellow Peril Ideology*. Philadelphia, PA: Temple University Press.

Miller, Davis. 2000. *The Tao of Bruce Lee*. London: Vintage.

Miller, Rory. 2008. *Meditations on Violence: A Comparison of Martial Arts Training & Real World Violence*. Wolfeboro, NH: YMAA.

———. 2015. *Conflict Communication: A New Paradigm in Conscious Communication*. Wolfeboro, NH: YMAA.

Miller, Rory and Barry Eisler. 2011. *Facing Violence: Preparing for the Unexpected*. Wolfeboro, NH: YMAA Publication Center.

Miracle, Jared. 2015. 'Imposing the Terms of the Battle: Donn F. Draeger, Count Dante, and the Struggle for American Martial Arts Identity'. *Martial Arts Studies* 1, 46–59. https://doi.org/10.18573/j.2015.10018.

Moenig, Udo. 2015. *Taekwondo: From a Martial Art to a Martial Sport*. London: Routledge.

Monahan, Michael. 2007. 'The Practice of Self-Overcoming: Nietzschean Reflections on the Martial Arts'. *Journal of the Philosophy of Sport* 34.1, 39–51. https://doi.org/10.1080/00948705.2007.9714708.

Morris, Meaghan. 1990. 'Banality in Cultural Studies'. *Discourse: Journal for Theoretical Studies in Media and Culture* 10.2, 3–29.

———. 2001. 'Learning from Bruce Lee: Pedagogy and Political Correctness in Martial Arts Cinema'. *Keyframes: Popular Cinema and Cultural Studies*. Edited by Matthew Tinkcom and Amy Villarejo. London: Routledge, 171–186.

———. 2004. 'Transnational Imagination in Action Cinema: Hong Kong and the Making of a Global Popular Culture'. *Inter-Asia Cultural Studies* 5.2, 181–199. https://doi.org/10.1080/1464937042000236702.

Morris, Meaghan, Siu Leung Li, and Stephen Ching-kiu Chan. 2005. *Hong Kong Connections: Transnational Imagination in Action Cinema*. Hong Kong: Hong Kong University Press.

Mouffe, Chantal (ed.). 1996. *Deconstruction and Pragmatism*. London: Verso.

Mowitt, John. 1992. *Text: The Genealogy of an Antidisciplinary Object*. Durham, NC: Duke University Press.

———. 2003. 'Cultural Studies, in Theory'. *Interrogating Cultural Studies: Theory, Politics, and Practice*. Edited by Paul Bowman. London: Pluto Press, 175–188.

Mroz, Daniel. 2017. 'Taolu: Credibility and Decipherability in the Practice of Chinese Martial Movement'. *Martial Arts Studies* 3, 38–50. https://doi.org/10.18573/j.2017.10094.

Needham, Joseph. 1956. *Science and Civilisation in China – Volume 2, History of Scientific Thought*. Cambridge: Cambridge University Press.

———. 1959. *Science and Civilisation in China - Volume 3, Mathematics and the Sciences of the Heavens and the Earth*. Cambridge: Cambridge University Press.

Needham, Joseph, and Ling Wang. 1954. *Science and Civilisation in China – Volume 1, Introductory Orientations*. Cambridge: Cambridge University Press.

Needham, Joseph, Ling Wang, and Gwei-Djen Lu. 1971. *Science and Civilisation in China – Volume 4 Part 3, Physics and Physical Technology*. Cambridge: Cambridge University Press.

Needham, Joseph and Francesca Bray. 1984. *Science and Civilization in China – Volume 6: Biology and Biological Technology Part 2, Agriculture*. Cambridge: Cambridge University Press.

Needham, Joseph, Christoph Harbsmeier, and Kenneth Robinson. 1998. *Science and Civilisation in China – Volume 7 Part 1, Language and Logic*. Cambridge: Cambridge University Press.

Needham, Joseph, Kenneth Robinson, and Ray Huang. 2004. *Science and Civilisation in China – Volume 7 Part 2, General Conclusions and Reflections*. Cambridge: Cambridge University Press.

Needham, Joseph, and Tsuen-hsuin Tsien. n.d. *Science and Civilisation in China – Volume 5, Chemistry and Chemical Technology*. Cambridge : Cambridge University Press.

Nicholls, Alex. 2010. 'The Legitimacy of Social Entrepreneurship: Reflexive Isomorphism in a Pre-Paradigmatic Field'. *Entrepreneurship Theory and Practice* 34.4, 611–633. https://doi.org/10.1111/j.1540-6520.2010.00397.x.

Nitta, Keiko. 2010. 'An Equivocal Space for the Protestant Ethnic: US Popular Culture and Martial Arts Fantasia'. *Social Semiotics* 20.4, 377–392. https://doi.org/10.1080/10350330.2010.494392.

Nulty, Timothy J. 2017. 'Gong and Fa in Chinese Martial Arts'. *Martial Arts Studies* 3, 50–63. https://doi.org/10.18573/j.2017.10098.

Palmer, David A. 2007. *Qigong Fever: Body, Science and Utopia in China*. Kindle edition. London and Paris: Hurst & Co. and Centre d'Etudes et de Recherches Internationales.

Park, Jane Chi Hyun. 2010. *Yellow Future: Oriental Style in Hollywood Cinema*. Minneapolis: University of Minnesota Press.

Phillips, Scott Park. 2016. *Possible Origins: A Cultural History of Chinese Martial Arts, Theater and Religion*. Boulder, Co: Angry Baby Books.

Prashad, Vijay. 2002. *Everybody Was Kung Fu Fighting: Afro-Asian Connections and the Myth of Cultural Purity*. Boston, MA: Beacon Press.

———. 2003. 'Bruce Lee and the Anti-Imperialism of Kung Fu: A Polycultural Adventure'. *Positions* 11.1, 51–90. https://doi.org/10.1215/10679847-11-1-51.

Preston, Brian. 2007. *Bruce Lee and Me : Adventures in Martial Arts*. London: Atlantic.

Protevi, John. 2001. *Political Physics: Deleuze, Derrida and the Body Politic*. London: Athlone.

Rancière, Jacques. 1991. *The Ignorant Schoolmaster: Five Lessons in Intellectual Emancipation*. Stanford, CA: Stanford University Press.

———. 1992. 'Politics, Identification, and Subjectivization'. *October* 61, 58–64.

Reid, Howard and Michael Croucher. 1984. *The Way of the Warrior: The Paradox of the Martial Arts*. London: Book Club Associates.

Rodowick, D.N. 2007. 'An Elegy for Theory'. *October* 122, 91–109. https://doi.org/10.1162/octo.2007.122.1.91.

———. 2014. *Elegy for Theory*. Cambridge, MA: Harvard University Press.

Sacks, Sheldon. 1978. *On Metaphor*. Chicago: University of Chicago Press.

Said, Edward W. 1978. *Orientalism: Western Conceptions of the Orient*. London: Penguin Books.

———. 2000. 'Invention, Memory, and Place'. *Critical Inquiry* 26.2, 175–192. http://www.doi.org/10.1086/448963.

Sandford, Stella. 2003. 'Going Back: Heidegger, East Asia and "The West"'. *Radical Philosophy* 120, 11–22.

Schreier, Herb, Miriam Rosenthal, Reed Pyeritz, Larry Miller, Chuck Madansky, Richard C. Lewontin, Anthony Leeds, et al. 1975. 'Against "Sociobiology"'. *The New York Review of Books* 22.18. Available at: http://www.nybooks.com/articles/1975/11/13/against-sociobiology/. Accessed 9 November 2016.

Sedgwick, Eve Kosofsky. 2003. *Touching Feeling: Affect, Pedagogy, Performativity*. Durham, NC: Duke University Press.

Sieler, Roman. 2015. *Lethal Spots, Vital Secrets: Medicine and Martial Arts in South India*. Oxford: Oxford University Press.

Silverman, Kaja. 1983. *The Subject of Semiotics*. Oxford: Oxford University Press.

Singleton, Mark. 2010. *Yoga Body: The Origins of Modern Posture Practice*. Oxford: Oxford University Press.

Spatz, Benjamin. 2015. *What A Body Can Do: Technique As Knowledge, Practice As Research*. London: Routledge.

Spencer, Dale C. 2011. *Ultimate Fighting and Embodiment: Violence, Gender and Mixed Martial Arts*. London: Routledge.

Spivak, Gayatri Chakravorty. 1990. *The Post-Colonial Critic: Interviews, Strategies, Dialogues*. London: Routledge.

Spivak, Gayatri Chakravorty and Sneja Gunew. 1993. 'Questions of Multiculturalism'. *The Cultural Studies Reader*. Edited by Simon During. London: Routledge, 193–202.

Storey, John. 2000. *Cultural Theory and Popular Culture: An Introduction*. New York: Longman.

Tan, Kevin S. Y. 2004. 'Constructing a Martial Tradition: Rethinking a Popular History of Karate-Dou'. *Journal of Sport & Social Issues* 28.2, 169–192. https://doi.org/10.1177/0193723504264772.

Tierney, Sean M. 2006. 'Themes of Whiteness in *Bulletproof Monk*, *Kill Bill*, and *The Last Samurai*'. *Journal of Communication* 56, 607-624. https://doi.org/10.1111/j.1460-2466.2006.00303.x.

Torfing, Jacob. 1998. *New Theories of Discourse: Laclau, Mouffe and Žižek*. Oxford: Blackwell.

Turner, William A. 1997. 'Review - *The Complete Art of War: Sun Tzu Sun Pin* translated by Ralph D. Sawyer'. *Journal of Military History* 61.2, 355–356. https://doi.org/10.2307/2953972.

Wacquant, Löic. 2004. *Body and Soul: Notebooks of an Apprentice Boxer*. Oxford: Oxford University Press.

———. 2005. 'Carnal Connections: On Embodiment, Apprenticeship, and Membership'. *Qualitative Sociology* 28.4, 445–474. https://doi.org/10.1007/s11133-005-8367-0.

———. 2009. 'The Body, the Ghetto and the Penal State'. *Qualitative Sociology* 32.1, 101–129. https://doi.org/10.1007/s11133-008-9112-2.

———. 2013. 'Habitus as Topic and Tool: Reflections on Becoming a Prizefighter'. *Fighting Scholars: Habitus and Ethnographies of Martial Arts and Combat Sports*, edited by Raúl Sánchez García and Dale C. Spencer. London: Anthem Press, 19–32.

Watts, Alan. 1990. *The Way of Zen*. London: Arkana.

Wetzler, Sixt. 2015. 'Martial Arts Studies as Kulturwissenschaft: A Possible Theoretical Framework'. *Martial Arts Studies* 1, 20–33. https://doi.org/10.18573/j.2016.10016.

———. 2017. 'Book Review: *Mythologies of Martial Arts*'. *Martial Arts Studies* 4, 78–81. https://doi.org/10.18573/j.2017.10188.

Widder, Nathan. 2008. 'Foucault and the Event'. *International Political Sociology* 2.3, 276–277. https://doi.org/10.1111/j.1749-5687.2008.00049_7.x.

Wile, Douglas. 1996. *Lost T'ai Chi Classics of the Late Ch'ing Dynasty*. Albany: State University of New York Press.

———. 1999. *T'ai-Chi's Ancestors: The Making of an Internal Martial Art*. Sweet Ch'i Press.

Williams, Raymond. 1977. *Marxism and Literature*. Oxford: Oxford University Press.

Wilson, Edward O. 1975. *Sociobiology: The New Synthesis*. Cambridge, MA: Harvard University Press.

Young, Lola. 1999. 'Why Cultural Studies?' *Parallax* 5.2, 3–16. https://doi.org/10.1080/135346499249669.

Young, Robert J.C. 2001. *Postcolonialism: An Historical Introduction*. Malden, MA: Blackwell.

———. 1992. 'The Idea of a Chrestomathic University'. *Logomachia: The Conflict of the Faculties*. Edited by Richard Rand. Lincoln: University of Nebraska Press, 98–126.

Žižek, Slavoj. 2001a. *Did Somebody Say Totalitarianism?: Five Interventions in the (Mis)Use of a Notion*. London: Verso.

———. 2001b. *On Belief*. London: Routledge.

Index

,

www.ingramcontent.com/pod-product-compliance
Lightning Source LLC
Chambersburg PA
CBHW071027280326
41935CB00011B/1481